France after 2012

France after 2012

Edited by
Gabriel Goodliffe and Riccardo Brizzi

berghahn
NEW YORK · OXFORD
www.berghahnbooks.com

Published by
Berghahn Books
www.berghahnbooks.com

in collaboration with The Johns Hopkins University SAIS Europe

ALMA MATER STUDIORUM
UNIVERSITA DI BOLOGNA
DIPARTIMENTO DI SCIENZE POLITICHE E SOCIALI

JOHNS HOPKINS
SCHOOL of ADVANCED
INTERNATIONAL STUDIES

ITaM

Istituto Cattaneo

© 2015 Gabriel Goodliffe and Riccardo Brizzi

All rights reserved. Except for the quotation of short passages
for the purposes of criticism and review, no part of this book
may be reproduced in any form or by any means, electronic or
mechanical, including photocopying, recording, or any information
storage and retrieval system now known or to be invented,
without written permission of the publisher.

Library of Congress Cataloging-in-Publication Data

France after 2012 / edited by Gabriel Goodliffe and Riccardo Brizzi.
   pages cm
   Published in collaboration with the Johns Hopkins University SAIS Europe.
   Includes bibliographical references and index.
   ISBN 978-1-78238-548-6 (hardback) — ISBN 978-1-78238-549-3 (ebook)
   1. France—Politics and government—2012– 2. Presidents—France—
Election—History—21st century. 3. Sarkozy, Nicolas, 1955– 4. Hollande, François. 5. Political leadership—France—History—21st century. 6. Political parties—France—History—21st century. 7. France. Parlement (1946–)—
Elections—2012. I. Brizzi, Riccardo, 1978– II. Goodliffe, Gabriel, 1971–
III. Johns Hopkins University. School of Advanced International Studies.
   DC430.F725 2015
   944.084'12—dc23

2014019711

British Library Cataloguing in Publication Data

A catalogue record for this book is available from the British Library

Printed on acid-free paper

ISBN: 978-1-78238-548-6 hardback
ISBN: 978-1-78238-549-3 ebook

Contents

List of Illustrations — vii

Acknowledgments — ix

Introduction — 1
Gabriel Goodliffe

Part I. The Presidency

Chapter 1. The Fifth Republic and Its Presidents — 11
Jean-François Sirinelli

Chapter 2. Socialists in the Elysée Palace: From Mitterrand to Hollande — 27
Marco Gervasoni

Chapter 3. The TV-Presidency: From de Gaulle's "Télécratie" to Hollande's "Normal Presidency" — 42
Riccardo Brizzi

Part II. The Political Parties

Chapter 4. The Union for a Popular Movement after Sarkozy — 61
Florence Haegel

Chapter 5. The Year of the Rose: The Socialist Victory of 2012 — 74
Gérard Grunberg

Chapter 6. The Pyrrhic Victory of the Radical Left — 88
Philippe Buton

Chapter 7. In Search of the Center — 100
Gilles Le Béguec

Chapter 8. The Resurgence of the Front National — 112
Gabriel Goodliffe

Part III. The Electoral Campaign and Hollande's Challenges

Chapter 9. Hollande's Economic Agenda — 133
Jacques Fayette

Chapter 10. Europe in the 2012 French Presidential Election — 152
Renaud Dehousse and Angela Tacea

Chapter 11. Hollande and Sarkozy's Foreign Policy Legacy — 167
Frédéric Charillon

Chapter 12. Immigration and the 2012 Elections in France — 181
Ariane Chebel d'Apollonia

Conclusion. Assessing the Hollande Presidency One Year into Office — 195
Riccardo Brizzi

Bibliography — 203

Notes on Contributors — 208

Index — 210

Illustrations

Figures

   3.1. Presidential Polling in the Fifth Republic   44
   3.2. Popularity of the Executive   47
   3.3. Sources of Voter Information during the 2012 Presidential Campaign   48
   3.4. Audience Rating of Television Debates Prior to the Second-Round Runoff   49
   9.1. French Growth Compared to Select European Countries   137
   10.1. Public Opinion toward Europe at the Start of the Campaign   159
   10.2. Sovereignist Sentiment among the Candidates' Electorates   160
   10.3. Progression of Sovereignism   162

Tables

   4.1. Right-wing Candidate Performance in the 2007 and 2012 Presidential Elections   66
   5.1. 2012 Presidential and Parliamentary Election Results   81
   5.2. First-Round Presidential Election Results (2002–12)   83
   5.3. Second-Round Parliamentary Election Results (2002–12)   84
   5.4. Parliamentary Groups in the National Assembly (June 27, 2012)   84
   5.5. Cumulative Results of the 2012 Parliamentary Elections   85
   6.1. The Radical Left Vote in Presidential Elections (1969–2012)   89
   6.2. The Weight of the French Communist Party in the Radical Left Vote in French Presidential Elections   90
   9.1. French Taxation Structure   137
   10.1. Principal Themes of the 2012 Presidential Campaign   154
   10.2. Sovereignist Sentiment among the Candidates' Electorates   161
   12.1. The French Categorization System   184

Maps

8.1. Marine Le Pen's Performance in the First Round of the 2012 Presidential Elections (parliamentary constituencies in which her score exceeded 12.5 percent of registered voters)   113

8.2. Marine Le Pen's Performance in the First Round of the 2012 Presidential Elections (her final ranking within each parliamentary constituency)   114

Acknowledgments

A book such as this one would not have been possible without the invaluable support of key individuals and institutions. We wish to thank the Istituto Carlo Cattaneo, its president Elisabetta Gualmini and director Stefania Profeti for the generous support they extended to this project. We are also indebted to Gianfranco Baldini who, as director of the book series Elections, Governments, and Democracy, proposed this project to us and has followed it from the beginning; as well as to Marc Lazar, whose advice proved invaluable during the initial phase. Thirdly, we should like to thank the Department of International Studies at the Instituto Tecnológico Autónomo de México and its director Rafael Fernández de Castro and interim chief Stéphan Sberro, who provided funding to see through the final indexing stage. Fourthly, we express our gratitude to our editors at Berghahn Books, Adam Capitanio and Elizabeth Berg, whose steadfast patience and careful assistance undoubtedly improved the final product. Finally, we also wish to thank the book's contributors, who bore with us over all this time, as well as the chapter translators for their efforts.

Last but not least, this book would not have seen the day without the conference that was held on October 13, 2012 at the Bologna Center of the Johns Hopkins University School of Advanced International Studies (SAIS), at which the individual chapters that comprise it were presented and discussed. This conference was made possible thanks to the generous contributions of the following institutions: the Department of Political and Social Science at the University of Bologna, and its director, Fabio Giusberti, as well as administrative staff, especially Simona Nardini and Francesco Lopriore; the Johns Hopkins SAIS Bologna Center and, in particular, Erik Jones, Kathryn Knowles, Alessandra Nacamù and Dea Di Furia; the Centro Studi Progetto Europeo and its director, Paolo Pombeni; the Fondazione Carisbo and its president, Fabio Alberto Roversi Monaco; the Alliance Française of Bologna and its director, Martine Pagan; and the Consulate General of France at Milan and in particular Consul General Joël Meyer and his assistant, Pascal Gay.

Introduction

Gabriel Goodliffe

On May 6, 2012 the Socialist Party (PS) candidate François Hollande defeated incumbent president Nicolas Sarkozy in the second round of the French presidential election to become the Fifth Republic's seventh president. Claiming just over 18 million ballots compared to the 16.86 million won by his opponent, he garnered 51.64 percent of the vote versus 48.36 percent for the latter. In turn, in the parliamentary elections that followed, the PS and its allies won an absolute majority of 314 seats (out of a total of 577) with parties of the left and center left winning 59 percent of the vote and over 340 seats in the second round. Thus, the 2012 national elections marked the first time that the Socialist candidate had won the presidency since 1988, as well as the advent of the first Socialist-led parliamentary majority and government since 1997.

A closer analysis of the results of the 2012 elections and of the campaign that preceded them suggests a number of continuities with and departures from previous presidential and parliamentary elections and campaigns. For obvious reasons, the lines of disjuncture are starkest in relation to the experience of the immediately preceding electoral cycle and presidential term, in this case the 2007 campaign and Nicolas Sarkozy's *quinquennat* (five year term). If we go farther back, however, we find that developments that appeared as departures over the relatively circumscribed span of five years in fact reveal themselves to belong to broader patterns of continuity that evolved over a longer period. For this reason it is necessary to compare the dynamics of the 2012 campaign and its outcomes not just to 2007, but also to 2002, 1995, 1988, and 1981, the year that marked the election of the first Socialist president and first Socialist-led parliamentary majority in the Fifth Republic's history.

In terms of identifying these departures and continuities over both the shorter and longer term, it is helpful to distinguish between two types of factors and trends. The first have to do with the contexts—political and

---

Notes for this chapter begin on page 8.

economic—in which electoral campaigns are conducted, and that thus invariably shape the respective fortunes of incumbents and challengers and the parties to which they belong, thereby giving their immediate significance to the results. Alongside these objective contextual variables that lie beyond the immediate capacity of electoral actors to shape events emerge subjective personal ones that can be resumed by the specific style, method, tone, and so on they adopt—particularly but not only in the presidential race—in order to bend the outcome in their favor. In 2012 as in preceding elections, these objective and subjective factors converged and interacted in particular ways, and it is instructive to see how the patterns of interaction that evolved over this latest election cycle can be compared to those that developed in 2007 and before.

The present volume identifies some of these patterns of interaction as they manifested themselves in the 2012 national campaign and election and illustrates how these resembled as well as distinguished themselves from preceding election cycles. It is divided into three parts. The first traces these patterns of interaction in light of the conduct of the 2012 presidential and parliamentary campaigns, the second illuminates them in the light of the election results themselves (i.e., the performance of the principal parties and candidates), and the third discusses them in terms of the principal policy challenges and choices confronting the incoming administration and government. Four broad themes run through the book and underpin the short-term disjunctures and longer-term continuities revealed by the 2012 campaign and its outcomes.

At a first, political level, beyond marking the first time a Socialist president had been elected since 1988 (on the parallels between François Hollande and François Mitterrand both as candidates and presidential figures, see chapter 2 by Gervasoni), the 2012 elections, in contrast to 2007 in which the candidates from the principal parties of government—the PS; Union for a Popular Movement (UMP); Democratic Movement(MoDem) / Union pour la Démocratie Française (Union for French Democracy, UDF); and the Greens—received 75.6 percent of the vote, marked a notable electoral erosion of the governing party candidates—67.3 percent—and a correlative resurgence of the antiestablishment vote. In particular, the record score of 17.9 percent (vs. 10.44 percent in 2007) garnered by Marine Le Pen, the Front National (FN) candidate, and of 11.1 percent by Jean-Luc Mélenchon, the Front de Gauche (Left Front) candidate, meant that, when combined with the votes won by candidates from the small antisystem parties, nearly one in three French voters cast ballots in favor of candidates opposed to the policy courses enshrined by the governing parties. (For analyses of the respective campaigns run by these candidates and of their electoral performance, see chapter 6 by Buton and chapter 8 by

Goodliffe.) This was in stark contrast to the electoral performance of the centrist MoDem candidate François Bayrou who, after coming third in the first round of the 2007 election with 18.57 percent, was relegated to fifth place behind Le Pen and Mélenchon with only 9.13 percent in 2012. (On the campaign run by the centrist parties and Bayrou's failure to replicate his performance from 2007, see chapter 7 by Le Béguec.) Contrary, then, to the claim advanced in the wake of the 2007 elections that France was moving toward a consolidated bipartisan system of electoral competition and alternation,[1] the 2012 presidential elections suggest that fragmentation continues to be a significant trait of the French party system and partisan polarization to have an especial influence on electoral outcomes in the country.

Indeed, if we consider this phenomenon over the longer run, we find that the incidence of partisan polarization and fragmentation as a function of the proportion of the vote won by the parties of government has substantially increased since the 1980s. It fell from 92.7 percent and 81.2 percent in the 1981 and 1988 presidential elections, respectively,[2] compared to 67.3 percent today, thereby testifying to the growing influence of anti-system or protest parties in French politics. Accordingly, whereas the 2012 elections may have marked a departure from 2007 in terms of the degree of fragmentation and polarization of the French political landscape, they seem to confirm the longer-term advance of these tendencies over the previous three decades.

Second, at the level of the economy, it could be argued that the 2012 election campaign was informed by a much direr economic context than its predecessor. By the end of April 2012 (i.e., between the two rounds of the presidential election), unemployment had just reached the symbolic threshold of 10 percent, the highest level recorded since 1999 and hitting certain groups like immigrants and the young hardest, while economic growth was stagnant at 0 percent. (For the role played by the immigration issue in the campaign, see chapter 12 by Chebel d'Appollonia.) By contrast, in April 2007 unemployment had been at 8.4 percent and the growth rate positive at 0.5 percent. By the same token, the challenger and eventual election winner promised to break with the economic program of his predecessor. In lieu of the deflationary austerity and supply-side policies pursued by Nicolas Sarkozy in the hope of cutting government spending, suppressing wages, and stimulating private investment as a way of enhancing French competitiveness—policies approved by Germany not just to reduce France's budgetary and structural deficits, but also to address the European sovereign debt crisis—François Hollande has instead called for progrowth countercyclical policies designed to stimulate growth and employment by boosting consumer demand through state spending and intervention. (On the economic challenges confronting François Hollande as well as the policy legacy left by his predecessor in this area, see chapter 9 by Fayette.) Not only does such a reflationary policy break with his predecessor's economic program, but it is also at loggerheads with German prescriptions for resolving the eurozone crisis, thereby portending conflict at the level of European economic management.

However, as in the case of the political developments informing the 2012 campaign, one can also point to more fundamental continuities with regard to the economic context that tend to attenuate the differences between 2012 and 2007. In the first place, if the dire economic and employment situation that followed the 2008 global financial crash and, starting in 2010, the European debt crisis, are certainly exceptional, it is worth noting that every French election since 1981 has been fought on the backdrop of economic and social crisis. Likewise, the issues foremost in voters' minds in successive national elections have been how to halt the rise of unemployment and, correlatively, increase their purchasing power. By the same token, policy shifts between candidates and governments, notably their choosing between supply- and demand-side policies as a solution to economic stagnation, is nothing new, with Socialist governments tending to favor the latter and governments of the right the former. Similarly, since the introduction of the single European market and the launch of the process of European Monetary Union (EMU), successive French governments have sought to counteract Germany's deflationary monetarist orthodoxy by calling for some form of European economic government that involves the following elements: greater political control of the central bank, loosening of the deflationary terms of the European Monetary System (EMS) / EMU), and some degree of statist intervention or industrial policy. Seen in this light, Hollande's call during the campaign to renegotiate the European fiscal compact agreed by German chancellor Angela Merkel and Nicolas Sarkozy in December 2011 in a reflationary direction is redolent of Lionel Jospin's attempt to modify the deflationary terms of the Stability Pact at the 1997 Amsterdam Summit, Jacques Chirac's pledge to renegotiate the conditions of EMU during the 1995 presidential election campaign, or the inclusion at French insistence of the provision that alongside the single market and monetary union, the European Union's (EU's) future economic prosperity also be based on the principles of social cohesion and social solidarity in a 1993 European Commission White Paper on "Growth, Competitiveness, and Employment," intended to complement the Maastricht Treaty.[3]

This last consideration points to a third contextual factor informing the 2012 campaign: the influence of Europe on French national elections. (On the direct and indirect intrusion of this issue in the campaign, see chapter

10 by Dehousse and Tacea.) Here, again, we see a contrast between the disjunction regarding the weight of Europe in the 2012 versus 2007 election campaigns on the one hand, and its growing longer-term salience as an issue in French national elections on the other. Indeed, whereas in 2007 European integration figured minimally as an issue in the presidential and parliamentary election campaigns, in 2012, no doubt reflecting the intractability of the European sovereign debt crisis, it attained unprecedented prominence. Accordingly, both governing party candidates made Europe a key theme in their respective campaigns while it served as a fundamental foil structuring the discourses of the fringe party candidates. Thus, Europe had gone from being invisible but omnipresent in previous national contests to occupying front and center stage in the 2012 campaign.[4]

Yet, as the first analogy implicitly suggests, Europe has assumed an increasingly salient role in French national elections and politics in general. Indeed, since the latest round of European economic integration began in the late 1980s and early 1990s with the establishment of the single market and the launch of the process of monetary unification, Europe has become the object of increasingly contentious political debate in France. As the narrow victory by referendum of the Maastricht Treaty in September 1992 and the heavy referendum defeat of the draft European Consitutional Treaty in May 2005 attest, European integration has morphed into an increasingly fraught and risky subject for the pro-European governing parties, while emerging as a potent source of mobilization for Eurosceptic antisystem parties. As disquiet over the European debt crisis and its economic impact broadens into a more general rejection of the current trajectory of European integration,[5] the latter is bound to grow even more significant in structuring voters' choices over the coming years.

Last but not least, and perhaps most overtly, the 2012 campaign introduced a sharp contrast in leadership styles between the two governing party candidates. Defining himself against the impulsive, micro-managing and self-promoting "hyper-president" that was incarnated by Nicolas Sarkozy, François Hollande tried hard to present himself as a thoughtful, deliberate, and modest future president—traits that his campaign staff adroitly packaged under the rubric of *"monsieur normal."* Not only would such a strategy, his advisers believed, make it possible for him to connect with French voters while restoring the traditional solemnity associated by the latter with the presidential office, but it also heralded a restoration of the traditional division of executive power called for under the Fifth Republic's semipresidential constitution. (On the evolution of the presidential role over the course of the Fifth Republic, see chapter 1 by Sirinelli.) In contrast to his predecessor, once elected Hollande would allow his prime minister to attend to the day-to-day tasks of government, setting out only the broad lines of domestic policy while immediately concerning himself with the conduct of foreign policy. (On the continuities and departures staked out in this area by the new administration with respect to its predecessor, see chapter 11 by Charillon.)

Yet this preoccupation with style and with projecting a certain image of leadership—of political decisiveness and voluntarism on the part of Sarkozy to break with the indolence of the Chirac years in 2007, or with normality and calm on the part of Hollande to break with Sarkozy's so-called hyper-presidency in 2012—testifies to a growing personalization of French electoral politics over the long run that was obfuscated by the contrasting styles presented by the governing party candidates in 2012. Of course, this personalization of electoral competition in France, particularly for the office of the presidency, is to some extent inevitable given the considerable powers afforded the president under the Fifth Republic, as well as the regal example set by Charles de Gaulle, the founding figure of the latter (not to mention François Mitterrand, who sought to emulate de Gaulle's example as the Fifth Republic's first Socialist president).

However, deeper institutional factors underlying the evolution of party politics under the Fifth Republic have also contributed to this greater personalization of elections. At one level, the growing professionalization of the political (particularly governing) parties, whereby candidates come to see politics less as a vocation and more as a career and in which institutional procedures have been instituted for selecting their candidates—i.e., the primary systems introduced within the PS in 2007 and since the last election, the UMP—served to paradoxically underscore the importance of the personal style and temperaments attributable to the latter. (On the phenomenon of professionalization that has overtaken the PS and the UMP over the previous election cycle, and specifically the internal procedures they have introduced to select their leaders and candidates, see chapters 4 by Haegel and 5 by Grunberg.) Hence, Mr. Hollande's "normal" allure ended up serving him well not only in contrast to the hyperactive Sarkozy in the presidential race, but also in contrast to the personal pathologies that were brought into the open by the Strauss-Kahn scandal and that constituted the backdrop against which the Socialist primary was held. In turn, at a second level, the growing political role played by protest parties in the French political debate and—at least in the case of the FN—their entrenchment on the fringes of the party system, has also placed a greater onus on the populist appeal of their respective leaders and candidates. Hence the intrinsic importance—previously highlighted by FN founder and president Jean-Marie Le Pen and now illustrated by his daughter and, on the far left, by Jean-Luc Mélenchon—of the oratorical skills and tribunary charisma displayed by these candidates to their parties' electoral fortunes and their capacity to influence the national policy debate. Thus, though François Hollande represented a stark contrast from Nicolas Sarkozy in terms of his personal style and temperament—not to mention the communication techniques and platforms by which he brought these differences across—his campaign and subsequent victory very much reflected and testified to the growing personalization of French politics among both governing and antisystem parties. (On the role played by traditional and new media during the 2012 presidential campaign, see chapter 3 by Brizzi.)

In short, the specific differences and disjunctures that can be seen between the 2012 and 2007 election campaigns and results are subsumed by broader similarities and continuities that have come to characterize French national elections over the past three decades. Reflecting both the respective economic and political contexts in which these elections unfolded and the programs and styles evinced by the respective candidates, these similarities and differences are explored more fully in the chapters that follow. In turn, the latter consider the social, economic, and political trends as well as the policy successes and failures that are likely to mark Hollande's *quinquennat* based on an appraisal of his first year in power (see the conclusion by Brizzi). As such, the book not only seeks to explain the circumstances of his victory, but also assesses the significance of his presidency and the effectiveness of the government he has commissioned to sustain it.

* * * * *

A final note on the timing of the publication of the U.S. edition of this volume and its implications for the discussion of the developments and arguments contained herein. The chapters were originally drafted in March/April 2013 in preparation for the Italian version of the book. The authors were asked to update their chapters for the present edition, but in some cases, particularly in respect to constantly evolving policy areas—the economy, foreign policy, immigration etc.—the shifts undergone in the intervening year and a half would have involved a major rewrite of their contributions and indeed, changed the volume's original orientation. Likewise, a number of significant political events—the replacement of the Ayrault cabinet by that of Manuel Valls in March 2014, and the subsequent collapse and reconstitution of the latter the following August, the victory of the Front National in the European elections in May 2014, and the resignation of Jean-François Copé as head of the UMP in the wake of the Bygmalion scandal in June 2014, for example—have unfolded and the partisan and policy contexts that informed them have changed over the past year, leaving time and space for their mention only in passing.

However, we believe that the fundamental debates and trends that are laid out in the following pages—and which directly shaped and led to the aforementioned developments—continue to be relevant and that they will remain so over the months and years ahead. Hence our decision to publish the book in its present form, despite these temporal lacunae.

Notes

1. See, for example, Gérard Grunberg and Florence Haegel, *La France vers le bipartisme? La présidentialisation du PS et de l'UMP* (Paris: Presses de Sciences Po, 2007).
2. These figures include, on the mainstream right, the vote for splinter Gaullist candidates, and on the left, for the candidate from the PCF, a party of government under the terms of the common program contracted with the PS in 1972, of the left-wing radicals, and (in 1988) of the Greens.
3. See George Ross, "Monetary Integration and the French Model," in *Euros and Europeans: Monetary Integration and the European Model of Society,* ed. A. Martin and G. Ross (New York: Cambridge University Press, 2004), 80–88.
4. Céline Bélot and Bruno Cautrès, "L'Europe, invisible mais omniprésente," in *Le nouveau désordre électoral. Les leçons du 21 avril 2002,* ed. N. Mayer and B. Cautrès (Paris: Presses de Sciences Po, 2004), 119–41.
5. See Pew Research Center, *The New Sick Man of Europe: The European Union—French Dispirited; Attitudes Diverge Sharply from Germans,* May 13, 2013, http://www.pewglobal.org/files/2013/05/Pew-Research-Center-Global-Attitudes-Project-European-Union-Report-FINAL-FOR-PRINT-May-13-2013.pdf

Part I

The Presidency

Chapter 1

The Fifth Republic and Its Presidents

Jean-François Sirinelli

When examining contemporary history, the political historian is bound to be confronted with certain methodological issues. Some are related to heuristic considerations: if the history of the present in France has acquired full scientific legitimacy, its practice has not yet become so despite the fact that it shares a number of subjects with the other social sciences, in particular political science. Other epistemological questions also arise. Compared to the other social sciences, it is in the nature of the historical discipline to place subjects in a temporal frame. Its first function is to situate the analysis within a specific timeframe, taking into consideration that a given situation is always the result of a context, itself the product of a historical evolution. Historical contextualization therefore necessarily exceeds what it semantically ponders, namely contemporaneousness. And putting events into a chronological perspective mechanically facilitates comparison—in other words, a contextualization of various preceding layers of interpretation and analysis.

In analyzing and assessing a presidential term, a comparative approach is therefore called for, because it allows one to go beyond a cursory listing of achievements and aborted reforms so as to reflect on a topic that history shares with political science, namely the study of decision-making, and more broadly, of governance. Such co-ownership also exists with certain branches of sociology or public law, which consider questions related to the implementation of public policy.

However, in adopting a comparative approach the historian is confronted with another major problem which is neither methodological nor epistemological, but ethical in nature. Namely, is the historian entitled to

---

Notes for this chapter begin on page 26.

compare and prioritize the supposed virtues in question? A second question also arises, which though more conventional is no less important. In their relationship with contemporary history, up to what period can historians go while upholding the rules of evidence specific to their discipline? Moreover—and we will come back to this, whatever the answer to this question—it in turn gives rise to a second question, namely that of the collaboration of history with political science, or more broadly, with any of the social sciences that relate to politics.

How to Compare

This desired proximity with other disciplines varies across national historiographic traditions—and even, at their core, with the diversity of intellectual and scientific sensibilities. We assume here not only that this collaboration should exist, but also that there should be communication between the disciplines on these particular subjects. At the same time, taking this position entails summoning the entire production of these disciplines, notably of political science, which is technically impossible within the allotted space limitations and in any case intellectually unfeasible because of the diversity—and this is a euphemism—of the political science field. We therefore consider that the ensuing text, while noting that its object is also claimed by other social sciences, aims to maintain the intellectual specificity of the historical discipline.

That said, if such an approach is conventional, it is also experimental since, resituated within a properly historiographic dimension, it gives rise to a number of questions that are specific to the political history of the present. Indeed, several elements complicate a comparison of the administration of President Sarkozy with those of his predecessors—as well as his successor's early term of office—just as they impede the enumeration of the achievements imputable to the latter. If these intrinsic difficulties are not entirely prohibitive, they must nonetheless be recalled here, precisely since the historian must ponder them so that the comparative approach may retain its raison d'être. The first step of the comparative analysis will therefore be to enumerate these elements.

The first of these is so banal that we would almost hesitate to mention it, if it did not constitute a key parameter of the historical discipline. This is of course the time factor, which structurally differentiates our subject. Nicolas Sarkozy exercised the presidential function within the strictures of a five-year term, only the second such term in the history of the Fifth Republic, after that of Jacques Chirac's second term.[1] Following the constitutional reform of 2000, the time in which subsequent presidents could accomplish their aims would no longer be the same.

The time parameter is also an element of differentiation between heads of state for another, more situational reason. Certain presidents governed for a second term, either fully (Mitterrand, Chirac) or partially (de Gaulle), and thus had access to a longer segment of time. Conversely, the presidential mandate could be hampered by disease (Pompidou) and, here again, situational factors reshaped structural ones. General de Gaulle's second term illustrates, in this regard, the significance of situational factors that alternated over successive terms, first as a result of de Gaulle's reelection and then by a sudden shortening of his term as a result of his voluntary departure following his defeat in the referendum of April 27, 1969.

However, this relationship to time is not analyzed solely across the duration of different presidencies. Some of the presidents of the Fifth Republic occupied influential positions prior to their accession to the presidency, making it difficult to perfectly isolate the accomplishments that derived from the sole period of their presidency.

In this regard, the case of General de Gaulle is both significant and singular, as his presence on the historical scene prior to 1958 was considerable. Even if we disregard the leader of the Free French until his departure in January 1946, as president of the provisional government of the French republic he played a key role in implementing the most important reforms of the Liberation. Should we deduct them from his track record simply because they took place prior to the establishment of the Fifth Republic? The same question applies to François Mitterrand, who was eleven times minister or secretary of state during the Fourth Republic. We can answer these two questions in the affirmative, due to the long interval between each of their successive passages of power—for the first, twelve years, and for the second, twenty-four years—and also by taking into account the historical differences between these passages of time. More complex is the case of Pompidou, who was prime minister for six years (1962–68) and scarcely eleven months later became president of the republic. For other reasons, the case of Chirac, who was twice prime minister in complex conditions—a cohabitation that was ahead of its time with the non-Gaullist Valéry Giscard d'Estaing between 1974 and 1976, and the first cohabitation with a president of an opposing camp between 1986 and 1988—is also worth examining.

Given the preceding analysis, we can measure the singularity of the prepresidential career of the new head of state, François Hollande, who acceded to the presidency without ever having held a ministerial position.

However, the nature of the institutions of the Fifth Republic and the preeminence of presidents ensure that, regardless of each president's past, the counter is reset at zero following his election. Certainly, politics under the Fifth Republic cannot be reduced to a gallery of presidential portraits, but they do form a hall of mirrors in which one can decipher important features of recent French political history.

This is provided, of course, that these mirrors are not too distorting. We must therefore continue to add to the list of factors that may taint the historians' perspective and that they must therefore take into consideration. In fact, in such a comparative perspective a third element of differentiation is required by the analysis: successive presidents did not develop their respective platforms in equivalent historical contexts. In other words, the national situations with which they were confronted and that de facto constrained and defined their administrations were neither permanent nor stable throughout the fifty-four years under study.

By definition, homogeneous contexts—that would be truly comparable—do not exist, which limits the historian's ability to place these subjects in comparison with one another. But such a finding, far from discouraging them, should stimulate researchers. Indeed, they can reverse the argument, their intellectual and scientific role being to highlight such variations by situating them in their proper context.

It is obvious, then, that conducting a term-by-term comparison without considering the underlying French context would have little historical significance. Indeed, the primary role of the historian is to contextualize the actions both undertaken and planned by successive presidents. In this perspective, a distinct line can be drawn through the mid–1970s: after 1973–74, with the ending of the Thirty Glorious Years of the post–World War II era, nothing would be as before. In this regard, Valéry Giscard d'Estaing's seven-year term was unique in that it witnessed the emergence of a fault line in its midst.

The acknowledgment of this fault line not only altered the general historical context, but also transformed the priorities driving political action. On the one hand, the struggle against the crisis must, from this period on, be taken into account by the historian. On the other hand, and especially if we consider that the need for reform is one of the fundamental drivers of political action, the flexibility to actually carry out such reform is not uniform. Even within a given presidential term, it is possible for the margin of action to be condensed as well as strengthened. The first case certainly applies to the five-year term of Nicolas Sarkozy. Every objective study of the actions taken at the time report the sudden occurrence of a change of circumstances in 2008, which was even further impacted by the fact that the change to a five-year term structurally left the president an even smaller margin to absorb, digest, and, if possible, recover from the crisis. In contrast, the first three years of Mitterrand's second term were a time of economic upturn. Could the political crisis gripping the Mitterrand-Rocard diarchy not have been the main obstacle to reform?

These effects of crisis bring up a fourth factor, which is perhaps less obvious but has grown increasingly important over the evolution of the Fifth Republic. The above analysis, though important in attempting to contextualize the actions of successive heads of state under the Fifth Republic, would be ignoring an essential element if it did not consider the global historical context constraining presidential action. Although each head of state was confronted with global issues—the first of them coming to power after the crisis of May 13, 1958—as a result of the dislocations linked to decolonization, their administrations could still be seen as part and parcel of national history. Decolonization was certainly impacted by forces coming from elsewhere, but its processes remained unique to France, since it was France's empire that was confronted with the dynamics of decolonization. It was not until the following decades that France's history became intertwined with that of the rest of the world, as the phenomenon of globalization grew in importance. In the context of our comparative approach, the margin for action of successive presidents has not been the same, and each has been increasingly forced to deal with issues that, although national in origin, cannot be separated from the global context. The reforms of Valéry Giscard d'Estaing could be carried forward despite the effects of the first oil shock, which occurred just a few months before, but the last years of his seven-year term would be hampered by the shock waves of the second oil shock. Similarly, Jacques Chirac's two terms unfolded against the backdrop of growing concerns regarding European integration: the presence of Jean-Marie Le Pen in the second round of the presidential election of 2002 was in part a reflection of these concerns, with the failure of the May 2005 referendum on the draft European constitution being the most obvious symptom of the latter. Continuing deindustrialization under the pressures of globalization during Nicolas Sarkozy's five-year term as well as the worsening economic and financial situation in the eurozone are also indications that the latitude of French presidents vis-à-vis the rest of the world has greatly declined over the previous decades.

The growing global influence on national history has impacted both the margin for action of presidents and the nature of the issues they faced. We define "issue" here as a situation or problem that is at stake during a given period in French society and that it is the duty of governments to manage and resolve. Ultimately, this brings us to the heart of the question posed in the introduction: Is it possible to conduct a term-by-term comparison of presidents? We can answer this question affirmatively provided we refocus the analysis on the issues that have successively impacted French society over the course of the Fifth Republic.

It is ultimately with respect to these issues that politics evolves and that the actions of leaders should be analyzed. And, in this context, one should substitute for a mere accounting of accomplishments what was possible, an assessment that itself derives from the preceding conditions—context and margin for action—as well as the intentions of the actors concerned. Within identical contexts and concerning equivalent issues, the response varies with the political cultures on which presidents draw, as well as their temperaments that can either induce caution or, conversely, encourage movement. These intentions, though complex, can be organized around two long-documented pillars: the intrinsic character and complexity of a state leader as well as the deep multifaceted forces that interact with and inform his decisions.

A President of a Third Type?

The leader of the state engages with such forces in a dialectical relationship. His raison d'être and the worthiness of his action consist in attempting to overcome these forces. However, since the latter shape and circumscribe the range of possibilities open to the state leader, part of a president's action will perforce consist in trying to influence them. Historians, in their comparative approach, would thus be making an analytical misstep if they were to underestimate these forces. They would become demiurgic and be essentially creating or projecting the portrait of state leaders as they *should* be rather than as they really are, with their constraints and limitations.

This brings us to Nicolas Sarkozy: in the gallery of portraits of the heads of state of the Fifth Republic, he is the first of the presidents of the third type. Before him, there was first the stratum limited to the sole General de Gaulle, the founding father, who was anointed as much by history as by the popular vote. The president followed a tumultuous period in the country's history, and, once the Algerian drama ended, he had to steer France through the Thirty Glorious Years. The technocratic Gaullism of this period, however, was shaped by his prime minister of six years, Georges Pompidou. For the head of state, it was national greatness (*grandeur*) and international rank (*rang*) that was paramount. In the spirit of the Fifth Republic's founder, the idea was to straighten and strengthen the country by pursuing the formula "management will follow" (*l'intendance suivra*)—a slogan that summarizes both the voluntarism that underlay the eleven years he spent as head of state as well as his general indifference to economic matters. These qualities either augmented the power of France or were susceptible of socially dividing it.

In any event, these times set a precedent; the man to navigate the country through its storms eventually fell victim to the growing gap between his aging persona and the image of an increasingly prosperous France that had undergone significant socioeconomic changes. To return to the aforementioned parameters, the time was granted to him, and the situation was favorable, yet he eventually stumbled, victim of his growing separation from a country that was changing while he grew old.

Georges Pompidou, in the typology that we have outlined here, was president during a time of transition. First, he did not have sufficient time and second, his health faltered at a time when cracks were emerging in the structure of postwar French society. It is therefore in a context of uncertainty that a second category of presidents emerged. Seven-year terms, even if Valéry Giscard d'Estaing failed in his bid for reelection, gave the latter time to pursue their aims, even though the flexibility that came with these terms remained limited as the economic crisis worsened and globalization intensified. That said, apart from Giscard, who saw his seven-year term disrupted by the rapid reversal of socioeconomic conditions, the next two presidents, François Mitterrand and Jacques Chirac, no longer faced an acute socioeconomic crisis but rather a crisis of social and political immobilism. Despite or perhaps because of this, they were both reelected for second terms.

In this regard, Nicolas Sarkozy is, for now, the only member of a third category: he is the first president to hold a term for five years. Chirac's second term was in this regard simply an outgrowth of a his first seven-year term, even if five of those years were spent under conditions of cohabitation, and moreover, characterized by severe economic crisis. In many ways these five years remind us of the seven-year term of Valéry Giscard d'Estaing: a time for reform that was abruptly suspended due to the acuity of a crisis. We even find a number of striking similarities between Nicolas Sarkozy's five-year term and the last five years of Giscard's mandate. First, the prime minister remained the same during these five years: Raymond Barre from 1976 to 1981 and François Fillon since 2007. Second, in both cases the crisis returned: In 1979, the second oil shock erased any progress that had been made since 1976, while the eurozone crisis of 2010 comprised the sequel of the global financial crisis that had occurred in 2008. More importantly, in both cases the will of both presidents to reform was constrained by outside events beyond their control.

The above analysis certainly is not intended to justify the policies undertaken between 2007 and 2012 and its possible errors, and even less to present the outgoing president as a reformer who had been advised that the misfortunes of the times required inaction. But any contextual approach—and this is, ultimately, the social function of the historian—as well as comparative approach must proceed from the following observation: the length of time granted to the outgoing president was insufficient to implement the policies he had announced or bounce back from the crises that confronted him.

The Challenges and Problems of Political Voluntarism

The terms "denial" or "betrayal" are partisan by nature, and the historian must first evaluate a president's actions not only in light of his or her proclaimed intentions, but also ultimately assess the changes these intentions produced. These successive presidents led the country as it was undergoing profound transition and each of them more or less influenced the course of the latter. However, should we situate their respective actions at the heart of the historical process or on its margins?

This is difficult to answer because, as was previously mentioned, other factors may intervene, such as political ideology or, more prosaically, temperament. Should one promote change or simply channel it? And, moreover, is such change effective? President Pompidou, in his final years, and Jacques Chirac, during his second term, seemed to think otherwise. The second term of the latter was, in this respect, significant. The boldest initiative generally credited to Chirac during his second term is the opposition to the U.S. intervention in Iraq. However, this opposition was supported by public opinion and was driven by a latent anti-Americanism that was further reinforced by his hostility to George W. Bush. On the domestic front, Chirac's three "major projects," to use the president's expression, touches on areas that were necessarily consensual: the fight against cancer; measures against disability; and, difficult to overtly dispute, road insecurity.

The first characteristic feature of Nicholas Sarkozy's term is therefore that he succeeded at least five years—possibly twelve—of relative presidential inaction, years that were entrenched by a further state of cohabitation between 1997 and 2002 that transferred a large part of executive initiative to the government of Lionel Jospin. The rupture proclaimed during the electoral campaign of 2007 therefore also, at least implicitly, signified the return to presidential voluntarism.

In this sense, was Nicholas Sarkozy's term also to be placed under the sign of consistency, these two concepts being, in theory at least, substantially related? For the historian, the answer is complex: each time a president becomes a candidate for reelection his supporters engage in a kind of storytelling, the incumbent having necessarily pursued a linear course of action. Conversely, it is easy for his opponents to condemn the incumbent for pursuing a sinuous, even incoherent, route, replete with omissions and denials, thereby making of the outgoing president an apostate. Between this black legend and the sanitized version of their respective terms, historians find themselves in the position of an arbiter summoned to give a judgment, which in any case is not their role.

In the case of Nicolas Sarkozy, his opponents have often pointed to contradictory statements he has made, often several years apart from one another. Thus, he deemed granting the right of foreigners to vote in local elections "not unusual" in October 2005—although he was not yet president at that time but minister of the Interior—but qualified it as a "risky proposition" in November 2011. Or again, this time at only a few months interval, on December 5, 2011, Sarkozy qualified euro bonds as a "strange idea" after he had initially defended them, and perhaps had been the first to conceptualize them. And, indeed, the *bouclier fiscal* (tax shield), which he had introduced at the start of his five-year term—symbolically, his opponents would say—was then programmed to be almost completely removed by the end of his term.

Certainly, other presidents also witnessed setbacks during their terms whereby their political action was inflected by analytical errors or by the resistance and inertia of the society. But in the case of Sarkozy one cannot but notice that these contradictory statements or decisions were the inevitable byproducts of his advocacy of pragmatism and adoption of voluntarism as a political method. There is, thus, a quasistructural ambivalence between a Doctor Jekyll working toward reform and a Mister Hyde struggling to manage setbacks that necessarily lead to measures that are misunderstood or ideas that are not well thought out, or in any case adequately explained. The ambivalence must be seen in the context of the aforementioned, and it also draws on the classic dilemma of governmental action: to govern is to choose, but provided one can explain and eventually convince voters of one's choices.

At the same time, it is true that political pedagogy may not be sufficient to generate consensus. This fact was apparent for the main reform that took place during Sarkozy's five-year term, namely that of the pension system. Sarkozy was confronted with a problem that was so great that its treatment was delayed by his predecessors. Let us recall the facts and the complexity of the issue, whereby political considerations were overtaken by demography. The postwar population explosion—8 million births between 1945 and 1954—have marked different key moments in recent French history: the baby boomers were the sixteen- to twenty-four-year olds of May 1968, but also the young adults installed in their first jobs just before the first adverse effects of the crisis could be felt. Then, a few decades on, the baby boom cohorts began to retire, which expanded a group that had already been large during the previous generation and became even denser due to increasing life expectancy. The situation grew complicated precisely when the baby boomers entered into retirement; from being contributors, and thus providers, they became beneficiaries, and therefore debtors. This spilled over into the next generation, which was burdened by higher unemployment and lower wages, and thus could not finance pensions under the same conditions. Correlatively, pensions had also become more numerous, particularly due to the growth of female employment, which really took off under the baby boom generation. The resulting situation was even more complex because it entailed a psychological, if not existential element: for the older baby boomers retirement seemed like the El Dorado, reached at a young age and for a long period. In other words, the grandpa boom had to be a happy boom.

Since political action consists of both anticipating and predicting future trends, the pension issue has been on the political agenda for around twenty years now and at least three presidents have had to confront it: Mitterrand in his second term, Chirac, and Sarkozy. Moreover, Jacques Chirac's second term was directly affected by this issue at the end of 2006, when the first cohort of baby boomers turned sixty. The measures taken during his mandate demonstrate that the issue was no longer a prospective one, but had effectively settled at the heart of the public debate. However, most people believed these measures were inadequate and provided no real solution to the problem.

The pension reforms undertaken since the beginning of Sarkozy's five-year term reflected a sharp inflection and form of political voluntarism from what had gone before. Only by guessing at what might have been—which historians are not in the habit of doing—might we be able to say that, pressed by inescapable realities, the candidate of the left, once elected, would have also launched such reforms. Suffice it to say that the opposition parties opposed one another and that the major unions challenged these reforms. We can observe in this episode the manifestation of one of the principal difficulties of governing that is evident in public opinion–driven democracies, particularly in the midst of a decades-long crisis. Likewise, these difficulties also reflected the issues confronting Sarkozy at the start of his term of office. Public opinion remained just as fickle, the crisis was still as present, and the implementation of structural reforms was ever more urgent.

In the background the world had changed, and with it the main issues of political debate. The opening presidents of the Fifth Republic inherited major questions that had divided the national consciousness. This was no longer the seminal issue that had haunted nineteenth-century France, namely what regime to establish following the collapse of the Ancien Régime. It was rather the socioeconomic question of property and the possible role of the state in regulating it that was at the heart of twentieth-century politics in France and that was inherited by the Fifth Republic. The year 1981 both reactivated and closed this political cycle. In turn, subsequent presidents were confronted with a third question, which entailed the sociocultural question of which norms and codes were to underpin the collective morality and behavior of the French.

In this regard, Nicolas Sarkozy is the first president of the Fifth Republic to have been exclusively confronted—in any case, from the 1960s onward, or from his adolescence—to this shifting national-cultural landscape. This was certainly an asset: unlike his predecessors, who were familiar with a France that had preceded the great postwar metamorphosis and therefore had to undergo a period of acclimatization, Sarkozy grew up with this new France from the beginning. That said, with this fact came a paradox and weakness over the medium term. The paradox has often been noted: for a long period he was contemptuous of the so-called effects of 1968 when, without having acted in the May events, he was nevertheless in many ways a product of them. The weakness is more complex to analyze, but it is no less telling for its apparent incongruousness: Sarkozy's electorate as defined by the opinion polls and studies conducted both at the beginning and the end of his term, was generally older than the median French population and, therefore, not necessarily always in line with the social diagnoses and governing style of a head of state who had himself been the product of France's great postwar change.

We should explore further the nature of this change. Since the 1960s the nation-state found itself torn between increasingly constraining external forces—European integration, globalization—and challenged by the development of an increasingly globalized mass culture that saturated French society with new images and sounds. More broadly, the anthropological base of French society, which had been inherited from centuries of history, experienced the combined impact of the acceleration of time and expansion of cultural space. For these reasons, France prior to 1965–85 represented a world of the past. But at the same time, due to the rapidity of such changes, this world remained very close and familiar—to paraphrase Stefan Zweig, it was "the world of yesterday." These moments of sudden and rapid change are ultimately quite rare in the history of any national community and can generally be classified into two typical cases that have historically been the principal accelerators of history: a revolutionary fracture, or the shock of war.

For successive heads of state, confronting this great change whose effects first became apparent in the late 1960s yielded a recurring problem:

How was it possible to avoid the growing gap between a France that would hardly change and an international environment that had been reshaped by the ongoing transformation? In other words, how was it possible to reform and even re-form—as in reconstitute—the country? The rapport of different presidents to reform has varied. General de Gaulle deeply reformed the country but ultimately failed with his project of political decentralization and senate reform. Georges Pompidou at first handed over the reins to his prime minister in the hope of implementing a new society in a country that had been deeply shaken by the shock of May 1968, but grew increasingly reticent about this project as he began to see the country as skidding increasingly out of control. Valéry Giscard d'Estaing, who began his seven-year term under the motto of "Change," ended it mired in a profound economic crisis. François Mitterrand went from announcing a "rupture with capitalism" to embracing a creeping Bad-Godesberg spread out through the span of a decade and that presided over the conversion of French socialism to the market economy. As for Jacques Chirac, his proclaimed willingness to resolve *la fracture sociale* (social division) soon collided with the inertia of a country mired in a crisis of both inaction and duration.

The Fifth Republic's Diarchy

The study of the exercise of presidential power must also take into consideration multiple exogenous factors. These constitute essential constraints that interact with the personal traits of each head of state. But the endogenous aspect cannot be reduced to the purely individual dimension of decision-making. Heads of state are also dependent, first and foremost, on rules that define the scope within which they operate—in other words, institutional arrangements. In the remainder of this brief analysis we therefore focus on the relationship between the president and the prime minister. This leads to two important insights. On the one hand, of course, it is intrinsically important, but the advent of the five-year term also makes this relationship all the more essential. Any analysis of the exercise of presidential power in the present-day Fifth Republic inevitably and logically leads to this question. On the other hand, study of this issue provides a rich basis of comparison between successive presidential terms.

At the beginning of Nicolas Sarkozy's mandate, an institutional diagnosis intersected with a psycho-political one: the five-year term, it was said, automatically reinforced the powers of the president, reducing the role of the prime minister to a mere "collaborator," to use the new president's term. Moreover, the impetuous and impulsive character of the new president would reinforce this hierarchy of roles. These issues persisted throughout his term and intersected with a broader theme: president–prime minister relations are a structural problem that has been inscribed from the start in the institutions of the Fifth Republic and that was reactivated on two occasions by the direct election of the president of the republic through universal suffrage in 1962, and by the introduction of the five-year term in 2000. This problem has engendered all sorts of different situations over fifty years, including the configuration of the past five years, which has crystallized certain traits of the latter.

In fact, if this is a recurring problem it is because it is genetically inscribed in the republican model of 1958, which was revised in 1962 and 2000. From the first government of the Fifth Republic, even though the president was not elected by universal suffrage, the tension was at times palpable in the first executive team, which lasted until the spring of 1962. Michel Debré, torn on the Algerian question, loyally assumed the president's choices, but this first case was not typical: in this case the prime minister was pushed to sacrifice himself, which is not the most common attitude in politics, and moreover the historically crushing weight of de Gaulle has never been equaled up to the present day. Scene 1 of Act I of the Fifth Republic thus set the stage, but the first couple that acted on it remains atypical. In fact everything would be conditioned by the following pair: General de Gaulle, once again, and Georges Pompidou. At its heart, the relations between them went through three successive stages that became templates for successive president–prime minister tandems. First, 1965: The incumbent president does not reveal his intentions until the last moment, but without a competitor having arisen within his own camp. The prime minister, however, from that moment emerges as his likely successor. Then, 1968: The same prime minister appears to be the man to pull the country out of crisis and, from then on, the likely successor becomes a potential rival. The verdict is then immediate: in early July, Georges Pompidou is replaced by Maurice Couve de Murville, in the aftermath of a significant electoral victory for de Gaulle whose principal architect had been the former. Finally, 1969: The call from Rome in January sees Pompidou propose himself as a last resort. In truth, he was only able to do this because he was no longer prime minister.

A precedent was thus created: the prime minister's presidential ambition can only be declared from the outside, and only in such a case does it become historically feasible. It was thus Scene 2 of Act I that was played out in January 1969 and that led several months later to Pompidou's victory following the hasty departure of General de Gaulle, who had been swept from office by his defeat in the referendum of April 27, 1969. However, President Pompidou would soon face, as mentioned above, a novel scenario: a prime minister, Jacques Chaban-Delmas, embodying a political project—the New Society—that remained popular in the polls and that enjoyed the sympathy of a large proportion of the ruling party, of which he was one of the leaders. But this case was less original in terms of its outcome: the head of state remained the master on board, forcing the prime minister to resign.

In essence, this first act in several parts constitutes the primordial scene of the Fifth Republic. From the outset, beyond the changes in institutional roles it entailed, the main parts had all been attributed and the possible variations did not alter the fundamental balance of power favoring the president. Two other acts would follow that altered the situation without resetting the initial scene.

The first of these two acts is the period of cohabitation. The first instance in which the teams at the head of the state were no longer monochromatic was in 1974. The election that year of the candidate of the free market right, Valéry Giscard d'Estaing, and his choice of a Gaullist prime minister, Jacques Chirac, introduced the first form of cohabitation. Twelve years later the failure of the Socialists during the parliamentary elections of 1986 and 1993 resulted in a constitutively pure form of cohabitation, which imposed on the sitting president a prime minister from the opposing camp. The reverse situation occurred following the failed dissolution of the National Assembly in 1997, leading to the Jacques Chirac-Jospin tandem. Although this sequence of cohabitations is not directly relevant to our analysis, since the situation of conflict is explicit in the latter and visible in the balance of power, this second stage in the historical relationship between the president and prime minister is essential for at least two reasons. First, these cohabitations strengthened the power of the latter relative to the former and therefore changed the nature of the executive diarchy. Second, the Fifth Republic has in the meantime become a democracy of opinion and any confrontation between the president and the prime minister is now also governed by popularity ratings; neither of these actors can ignore this. Of course, the president retains the right to remove his prime minister and, therefore, appears to control the situation at all times; the case of Michel Rocard, whose wings were brutally clipped by François Mitterrand in 1991, serves as a reminder of this. It is still necessary to place this episode in its broader context, however. The self-mutilation practiced within the Socialist camp resulted in the worst electoral debacle for any party in the history of the Fifth Republic in the parliamentary elections of 1993. This verified a principle of political physics: one cannot shake a coalition with impunity without weakening it. Moreover, other players in the political game, particularly those elected locally, regionally, or nationally within this coalition, are well aware of this fact.

Yet the country's political representatives were gradually strengthened over the decades, some by the decentralization laws from 1982 onwards, and others, mainly deputies and senators, by the five-year term reform that restored the essential role of parliamentary groups. This reform inaugurated the third act in the history of the Fifth Republic. The scenes that punctuate it are all the more complex because they represent the sum of the historical precedents set since 1958, but they are also the result of a system that, initially bipolar, now entails the interaction of at least four actors. The president and his prime minister, of course, but also public opinion and the binding tissue, heterogeneous and budding, of the custodians of an elective office. Yet, as of May–June 2012, the new majority party, the PS, is primarily a party made up of locally elected officials.

Ultimately, each camp, with a bit of experience, is well aware that if there is one decision-maker, the head of state, that person cannot completely give in to mood swings or to the demons of elective affinities without triggering chain reactions that are difficult to control. Any situation of conflict, therefore, is rendered more complex and can never be reduced only to clashes of personality. The actors here are rational, even in their Shakespearean dimension.

Conclusion

The foregoing analysis leads to a number of different conclusions, both historical and historiographic, that refer back to the original comments. The first of these is quite evident and extends beyond the French case: the analysis of the powers of a French president cannot be dissociated from the broader context, namely that of the possibilities of governmental action in representative regimes submitted to two new types of constraints. On the one hand, these regimes have in many ways become poll-driven democracies, undermined by the emotional and volatile nature of the relationship between political power and public opinion in which voters' political cultures, if not yet fully disintegrated, have at the very least entered into an advanced state of decline. On the other hand, these regimes, which were first consolidated by the unprecedented growth of the Thirty Glorious Years, were inevitably undermined by several decades of various forms of crisis that neither turnovers of power nor political voluntarism have been able to resolve.

Likewise, from a historical perspective, the comparative observation of successive presidents demonstrates once again that historical analysis is inseparable from the study of the relationship to time of these various actors, in particular of these presidents and the public opinion that interacted with them. For a public increasingly weary of crisis, today is unsustainable, tomorrow is consternating, and yesterday is irrelevant, since it refers to the world from before the great transformation. How, in these conditions, do we situate a president's course of action over the long term? Here we return to the time factor, which not only refers to the duration of one or more terms, but also on a larger scale, to the essence of a historical pattern: it is always at the crossroads of several temporalities. Moreover, such a finding reminds us, if this were still necessary, that political action consists of changing the present in order to have as much leverage over the future as possible, without losing sight of the fact that the past cannot be dissolved by decree.

Notes

Translated from the French by Pauline Hovy.
1. We will number in this way the presidencies that exceeded one term, such as those of General de Gaulle, François Mitterrand, and Jacques Chirac.

Chapter 2

Socialists in the Elysée Palace
From Mitterrand to Hollande

Marco Gervasoni

The connection between François Hollande and the figure of François Mitterrand is less simple than would appear at first sight. The relationship has traversed a number of stages: from the young Hollande's more or less direct link to the Elysée in the 1980s, to defense of the departed president's memory, above all against attacks from within the PS. To French socialism, however, up until Lionel Jospin's defeat in 2002, Mitterrand was what was once called a "dead dog." He only began to be exhumed after the shock of 2002, with Hollande being one of the most zealous supporters of his rehabilitation. For all that, Hollande strikes one as being closer to the Mitterrand myth than to the first Socialist president's actual programs, especially during his first *septennat* (seven-year term). With his close ties to Jacques Delors and what was called in the 1980s the Deuxième Gauche (Second Left), Hollande was instrumental in reconciling the Mitterrand and Rocard factions that had split French socialism from the 1970s, at least, down to the Jospin years.

Mitterrand Follows Mitterrand

The two "François": the refrain was struck up the moment Hollande won the PS primaries and the press, discreetly encouraged by the candidate's spin doctors, began comparing the former PS secretary to the Fifth Republic's only Socialist president to date. It might have been yet another fatuous gag in an increasingly brainless and characterless political scene, based merely on their having the same first names. But it wasn't. The com-

Notes for this chapter begin on page 40.

parison between Hollande and Mitterrand deserves deeper investigation because it helps us to grasp how the former mounted a winning campaign and maybe, too, suggests how he might govern from this point.

Before getting down to enumerating the inevitable similarities and differences, we should pause to review the story of Mitterrand's legacy to French socialism—a mantle that has proven far from obvious or banal. The last years of his presidency were actually something of a nightmare for the left-wing electorate. In 1993 the PS touched its historical low in the National Assembly, Mitterrand was forced into an uneasy alliance with the most substantial right-wing majority in the history of the Fifth Republic, while his and the PS's reputations were ably dragged in the mud by journalists who painted them as "Ali Baba and the Forty Thieves." It was an auto-da-fé that claimed its share of suicides: sensational ones like that of ex–prime minister Pierre Bérégovoy, and mysterious ones like that of the president's long-standing friend and coworker, François de Grossouvre. The magistrates were whipped up by the neo-Gaullist and Giscardian right to put on a French-style rendition of the *les mains propres* (who's got clean hands parade), though it got out of hand and backfired on Chirac and the Balladur government. On top of this came Mitterrand's decision to address his Vichy past and, above all, his ties to the former head of police of the collaborationist regime, René Bousquet. To many, Mitterrand appeared to have betrayed left-wing values; some even raked up Michel Rocard's judgment from the 1970s: that Mitterrand was ever a moderate, even a right-winger, who wangled his way to leadership of the left through political opportunism, sharing none of its basic values.[1]

That was the time when Lionel Jospin began to express his doubts about the president. Jospin had been a staunch supporter of Mitterrand's since the 1971 Epinay Conference, but as the second term of the latter got under way he turned more critical, to the point that the president himself banned Jospin from the Bérégovoy government—a major disavowal for a leader of the party who had served as no less than education minister for former executives. Mitterrand initially seemed to have won the battle with his erstwhile supporter, Jospin even failing to be returned to the National Assembly in 1993. However, out of that defeat Jospin managed to work his way to the Socialist candidacy in the 1995 presidential elections, where his best card to play was to distance himself from Mitterrand, so low had the sitting president's reputation sunk with the left-wing electorate. That critical analysis irked the president, though he icily backed the Socialist candidate. Jospin lost to Chirac in the second round, but his was a good result that showed that the French left was ready to move beyond the Mitterrand years. La Mitterrandie (Mitterrandia) thereafter played a dwindling role within the PS, as was seen a mere two years later in Jospin's government in which the sabra (as the by now late president's faithful band were called) gained no major office.

His silence regarding Mitterrand only further cramped Jospin's unfortunate presidential campaign in 2002. He simply deputized a coworker to place flowers on the late president's grave when the anniversary of his death came around on January 9. Though he would not acknowledge it, Jospin actually did take something from Mitterrand's 1988 campaign: he wrote a *lettre aux français* (letter to the French people) and changed the term *socialisme* (socialism) in his own vocabulary to *progrès social* (social progress). But unlike Mitterrand in 1988, Jospin was not an incumbent president. As prime minister, he forgot that *he* was the challenger. That *lettre aux français* was another blunder in a technically disastrous campaign.

It was the post-2002 shock that seemed to obliterate everything, including the memory of Mitterrand. Only the Socialist left under Jean-Luc Mélenchon acknowledged the mantle, Mélenchon having been one of the declining president's bright-eyed boys. This was a paradox within a paradox. Three years later, the so-called *non* (no) faction of the left that fought against adoption of the European Constitutional Treaty was led by a historical Mitterrandiste like Laurent Fabius who led the *"non"* campaign alongside Mélenchon. But history loves paradoxes: here was a Socialist Euroskepticism that was linked to a president who had made Maastricht happen.

To hear more than a sporadic mention of Mitterrand by a Socialist candidate, we would have to wait for the 2007 campaign of Ségolène Royal—another emerging Socialist whom Mitterrand had personally groomed during her political debut back in the 1980s. But the Socialists' first woman candidate did little more than posture and evoke Mitterrandian screenplays on an emotional register that deliberately glossed over certain painful memories of his presidency.[2] She gave no proof of any concrete historical or ideological tie to Mitterrandisme as she faced a right-wing candidate in Nicolas Sarkozy who claimed Jean Jaurès and Léon Blum as his own (but who drew the line at Mitterrand himself). More than ten years had passed since Mitterrand's demise, but in 2007 his name remained controversial to the left.

All this changed with Hollande's candidacy. In fact, the Socialists' rehabilitation of the late president had been in the air for some time. Modernizers like Dominique Strauss-Kahn explicitly mentioned Tonton (Mitterrand's nickname) when his own chances of winning the presidency were high. But by then, the whole party, led by Martine Aubry since 2008, had bought into the Mitterrand cult.[3]

Why the change? Mitterrand's main merit in the Socialists' eyes was that he had shown that the left could stay the course in government and not just fill in gaps, as they had prior to 1981. But there were now fears it might be impossible to win back the Elysée—the plum post in Fifth Republic politics—so that the fourteen years of Mitterrand's two terms might themselves come to be seen as just another such gap. This was the gloom that settled on the Socialists after Ségolène Royal's defeat. Hence the need to resurrect the ghost of the 1980s. When Hollande won his party's primaries, the tie with that other François tightened: Mitterrand became the central reference in the left's historical evolution from Jaurès, via Blum, Mendès-France, and Jacques Delors. Mitterrand became the apotheosis and centerpoint of a Pantheon of the left.

In a sense, Hollande's position resembled that of Bill Clinton's after twelve years of Republican rule in the White House, of Tony Blair's after eighteen years of Conservative prime ministers in Downing Street, or of Gerard Schröder's following the sixteen years of Kohl's chancellorship. The benchmarks left behind by former left-wing leaders had grown too faint and controversial, too, if one thinks of Carter for Clinton and Callaghan for Blair. Clinton, Blair, Schröder, after battling to weed from their parties the conservatives linked to the distant past, had the economic dynamism of the mid-late 1990s to harness, and hence no option but to break with that past, both organizationally and ideologically.

Likewise, Hollande had come to a fork in the road: to go ahead with Jospin and Ségolène Royal's new look, or to build a genealogy of his own. Hollande ruled out the first course as having been three times a loser. Besides, the 2012 campaign unfolded amid a deep economic recession, and it was not the time for taking a risky policy gamble. At any rate, the "third way" had never caught on in France, had lost what little appeal it had, and was accused of being too soft on financial capitalism.

Hollande's only course was to pick up where Mitterrand had left off and present his legacy as the benchmark for anyone on the left trying to govern France. Not omitting to pay his respects to other political epochs and figures, Hollande thus devised his own Mitterrand. Though already a legend, Tonton was still a more concrete figure than Jaurès, Blum, or Mendès. One could take one pragmatic leaf from his playbook in order to run a campaign and a government. Hollande relegated the political memory of the late-1990s Jospin government to the back of his mind, though it was the most recent Socialist mandate and by no means short-lived. After Fillon's last government, Jospin's had been the longest serving in the history of the Fifth Republic and had initiated many reforms, from the legal recognition of homosexual couples to the thirty-five-hour week. Many reasons can be found for that far-from-unintentional memory lapse. The relatively long-lived Jospin's government's agenda may have been progressive, but the left's popularity ratings had flagged at times—witness the high abstention rate and disparate left-wing candidacies that had allowed Jean-Marie Le Pen to accede to the second-round runoff in the 2002 presidential elections. Jospin's had actually been a Jospin-Aubry-Strauss Kahn government from which Hollande as candidate was forced to distance himself: from Jospin whose image was still irremediably tarred as that of a loser even ten years after 2002, from Aubry for her far left connotations, and from Strauss-Kahn for reasons of more recent vintage. It is no accident that the government formed by Jean-Marc Ayrault—as it stood immediately after Hollande's victory or with the slight reshuffles that followed the 2012 parliamentary elections—gave former Jospin ministers precious little scope.

Hollande's Spontaneous Mitterrandisme

Hollande's link to Mitterrand has an undeniable basis of authenticity. Born in 1954, the second Socialist president of the Fifth Republic belongs to a generation to whom the victory of 1981 brought access to the corridors of power after the shortest of apprenticeships. He did not enroll in the PS until the age of twenty-five, after pondering at length whether to join the French Communist Party (PCF). Ségolène Royal, who is only one year his senior, began like him on the Elysée staff (with Jacques Attali), but although Hollande went on to head the cabinet of Max Gallo, spokesperson for the Mauroy government, he was slower than Royal at getting a career footing within the political institutions and for a long time played no managerial role in the PS. He won his first seat in the National Assembly in 1988 and found no place in the final governments of Mitterrand's second seven-year term under Edith Cresson and Bérègovoy, whereas others of his vintage—Royal, Aubry, and Strauss-Kahn—held meaty ministerial appointments.[4] But being removed from the cogs of latter-day Mitterrandie enabled Hollande to develop a more serene relationship with the old patriarch as well as to situate him in proper perspective. A lack of direct dealings with Mitterrand preserved him from the Jospin dilemma of feeling something of a parricide when he gained power and enacted policies that ran counter to those of his former boss. By contrast, Hollande was free to let Mitterrand loom large in his speeches before even setting his sights on the Elysée. As far back as 1998, a matter of months after he took over the PS first secretary post, Hollande crossed swords with Rocard for calling Mitterrand "a dishonest man."[5]

Once he became a presidential candidate, Hollande was bound to step up the references to the patriarch of old. So much transpires from his pamphlet *Changer de destin* (Changing our destiny) that was published early in 2012 after he won the Socialist primaries. It was both autobiographical—with Hollande introducing himself to the French people—and a direct illustration of his program without depending on party activists of his political entourage. That, too, was a Mitterrand-style choice; the former president's books tended to come out on the eve of an election and were always a blend of autobiography and political manifesto.

In his tale, Hollande dates his affinity to socialism back to 1965 when, at eleven years of age, he saw "a nobody called Mitterrand" stand up to de Gaulle with the slogan, "Liberty versus glory." He claims to belong to the Mitterrand generation, of which "I am proud, despite taking my distance in certain respects."[6] The year 1965, date of Mitterrand's first candidature (1971), the Epinay Conference (1981), his historic victory under the slogan *"Changer la vie"* (Changing our lives) represented three stages in Hollande's political *apprentissage* (training). From a candidate who, contrary to Aubry, explicitly favored social democracy, one would expect a connection with the pragmatic Mitterrand of the second term.

But the Mitterrand glimpsed in *Changer de destin* is also the early-style figure immortalized in the famous Epinay speech against "the dominance of money." This was a topical line for Hollande to take, and perhaps especially so in 2012 when "money has taken possession of everything; from a tool it has become master."[7] As for the second Mitterrand who had backed the Maastricht memory, Hollande was bound to stand up for him. As PS secretary in 2005, he had stuck his neck out in support of the "Yes" vote to the European Constitution. But he would claim the right to harbor reservations about Mitterrand and Delors's Europeanism, pointing out "two misunderstandings" at Maastricht. Mitterrand had wanted an "independent central bank," Delors a "strengthened European parliament," the two pillars without which monetary union would be precarious and political union subordinate to financial skullduggery.[8] That neither was achieved was not Mitterrand's fault, however, or even Germany's fault, but was due to tergiversation first by Chirac's France, then Sarkozy's. The third Mitterrand to emerge from the pages of *Changer de destin* is the architect of "a peaceful revolution" through decentralization and a "civilized penal policy," the heart of the reforms of 1981–82 and their liberal guarantees.[9] The fourth Mitterrand is about defense policy. Just as, during the final throes of the Cold War, Mitterrand had "tenaciously refused to back down when the Soviet SS 20s were threatening western democracies from the east," so Hollande argues for a strategy that "must dissuade any would-be aggressor and hence preserve the peace." The booklet closes with a last Mitterrand quotation: "[O]ur duty is to make sure the land around us is at once our home and garden, our refuge and our sustenance." This is a "categorical imperative," adds Hollande, "which he pledges to honor as President."[10]

The Mitterrand from Hollande's autobiography-cum-political manifesto is partly genuine and partly tailored to electoral communication. Which Mitterrand, though? To adapt a famous slogan, the figure Hollande makes of him is one to be taken en bloc. One cannot divide the early Mitterrand of 1981–83—generous and utopian but with an economic policy that just won't work, as Delors and Rocard already knew (and nearly all of today's historians agree)—from the later innovator of a French-style capitalism under the Fabius and Rocard governments. While Mélenchon's campaign harked back to the very early stage including proposals for nationalization, Hollande would indeed revive Mitterrand's ethical anticapitalism from the Epinay speech—but no more than that. Hollande's book hankers after the 1981–83 season more for its decentralization and civil rights implementation than for nationalization, extending pensions, increasing wages, and lowering the retirement age. Only at one point does Hollande pick up Mitterrand's 1981 program: the idea of raising the tax bracket to 75 percent on incomes of over €1 million, which is a faithful rehash of the super-tax applied in 1981. An idea not found in *Changer de destin* or the candidate's program, it would be introduced only in the middle of the electoral campaign, taking aback even his advisers by its timing and form. Which brings us to the question, which Mitterrand did Hollande and company field for the real run-up to the Elysée?

Mitterrandisme for an Electoral Campaign

Such political matches never just depend on the leader, but are the fruit of detailed organization and teamwork. Hollande's team worked scientifically, beginning with a scientific study of the latest presidential campaigns in France. They studied Ségolène Royal's strategy and ruled it out as being too much of a one-man (or one-woman) show, too emotionally charged, too full of promises. It was an intense though lonely campaign, both because the PS chose its candidate only to leave her marooned, and because her opposite number, Sarkozy, was running on a course never tried by his own political camp. Hollande's team naturally rejected the Jospin debacle, too: lack of mobilization, continuity with his long-matured thinking as a minister, and virtually no recollection of his Socialist roots and story. They likewise excluded Mitterrand's 1988 campaign that also lacked in intensity, the incumbent president seeking confirmation not in the name of socialism or the left, but for his own personal showing and performance.

To Hollande's team the only remaining model was Jospin in 1995, which had seen Hollande himself play the role of ringleader. And to begin with, so it was. The Hollande campaign appealed for the pragmatic vote, which worked in 1995 to prevent a second-round between Chirac and Balladur as forecast by all the polls, and in 2012 was designed to stave off the risk of a new shock on the lines of 2002. But after Mélenchon's reaction and the realization that the Green candidate and two Trotskyists would not stand the course, Hollande came to the conclusion that asking for a pragmatic vote might irritate the electorate. Besides, on the left there was no longer much danger of dispersion. This gave him no alternative but to style himself after the Mitterrand of 1981.

On the face of it, the political picture was much the same as thirty years before. The country was gripped by economic crisis (more dramatic now than then, of course), an outgoing president who was still youthful (then Giscard, now Sarkozy) who had been elected on a reform and innovation platform that would later disappoint a sizable swath of his own followers, a rift in the right-wing camp during the first round of voting (Chirac challenging Giscard at the time, and now Marine Le Pen laying traps for Sarkozy), an antiparty protest in full swing (in Mitterrand's day staged by the comedian Coluche's abortive candidature, in Hollande's by abstention and a temptation to vote Le Pen). Finally, those in power were flagging after twenty-three years in Giscard's case and seventeen in Sarkozy's— though one should not forget Jospin's five years at the Hôtel Matignon.

There were similarities, therefore, but there were also some major differences, too. The massed ranks of the Gauche in 1981 were more extensive in terms of voting, more socially compact with a strong working class and a small bourgeoisie, both solidly ranked to the left and with only two candidates to choose from: Mitterrand and PCF secretary Georges Marchais. Hollande in 2012 faced a quite different picture. Since Mitterrand's day the number of French people committed to the left has sharply decreased (abstention being an increasingly frequent option, for one thing). Again, compared with 1981 the right-wing electorate is more compactly structured. Sarkozy pledged to avoid splitting the republican right for whom he became the only candidate. Clearly he could not stop Marine Le Pen from standing, though he underestimated her, thinking that the daughter of Jean-Marie would run a poor electoral campaign and that right-wing supporters would rally to him in the first round, as in 2007. By contrast, 1981 saw the republican right split straight away between two strong candidates, Giscard and Chirac, both of whom were quite legitimate, both of whom were publicly at daggers drawn, while Jean-Marie Le Pen had not even pooled enough signatures to stand. Another major difference from 1981 was in Hollande's favor: the popularity ratings. When Mitterrand launched his candidacy in January 1981, he was tipped to lose against Giscard but the polls all along thought Hollande would win. That is a far from negligible psychological and emotional advantage, for Mitterrand's election was fought with bated breath. Hollande benefited from deep-seated anti-Sarkozy feeling. The latter was demonized not just by the left and Le Pen supporters, but also even by the traditional republican right and what little survived of the center. Giscard may have been discredited in 1981 more than he deserved, but this never amounted to outright anti-Giscardisme, even among Chirac's supporters (who indeed largely swung over to him at the second ballot).

But there are other factors suggesting a comparison with 1981, beginning with the role of the PS. Unlike seven years before and what would happen in 1988, Mitterrand managed in 1981 to keep his party closely involved by overlapping leading roles at Rue Solferino, the PS national headquarters, and on the Mitterrand electoral committee. At the time, with the primaries still only on the horizon, Mitterrand was chosen by the militants at the Créteil Conference. His platform had been largely drafted by the party's left wing, Jean-Pierre Chevènement's Centre d'Etude, de Recherche et d'Éducation Socialiste (CERES) movement, which proved a fundamental ally to Mitterrand in the battle against Rocard when he was seeking to oust him after the PS lost the 1978 parliamentary election.[11]

To an even greater extent than Mitterrand, Hollande was fighting the 2012 campaign with the party rallying round him. Although Mitterrand had been leader of the PS for some ten years, he had never been a classic party man, preferring to delegate such matters to his closest coworkers, from Jospin to Fabius. By contrast, Hollande is a party animal, first secretary of the PS since 1997 when he took over as Jospin moved to Matignon. He was to steer the PS for over a decade through thick and thin, including two losing presidential elections and the risk of a party split (after the 2005 referendum). The party was divided when Hollande left as first secretary, as emerged at the Reims Conference of 2008, which saw Aubry elected to his former post. But it was only *outwardly* a split. In fact, unlike the Mitterrand and Jospin years, the PS had gained strength and a new vigor. Few saw this in 2008, dazzled as they were by the eternal rifts among the "elephants," as the PS leaders are known. Many even prophesied that the PS's days were numbered. Never was a prediction more mistaken. After the debacle of the 2009 European elections, the Socialists began to win all the subsequent municipal and department elections and even gained a majority in the senate, where the left had been in the minority ever since the Third Republic.

The proof of party unity came chiefly during the presidential and general elections. Although it had been run by Aubry who had been narrowly beaten by Hollande in the second-round ballot of the party primaries, the Socialist machine came together solidly behind Hollande. And although there is no love lost between Aubry and his predecessor, as secretary he never wavered from the party choice. In being freed from the job of running the party, Hollande resembles Georges Pompidou, who was the only contender before his day to win without being party secretary (Giscard was secretary in 1974, Mitterrand in 1981, Chirac in 1995 and Sarkozy in 2007). Like Pompidou, Hollande did not need to be running his party to have it solidly with him. Similarly, he could not do without the party's support—not ritual or formal support, but concrete support, given the negative showings by Jospin and Royal who had singularly failed to involve the PS in their campaigns. After the primaries, Hollande marked his insider rivals Manuel Valls and Arnaud Montebourg for important party offices. His challengers in the first round would in fact be promoted to major ministries (the Home Office and Industry). Hollande established a campaign team of party people, and in his electoral journey he sought out local officials for their support. Throughout most of the country they were running town halls, departmental councils, and regional governments.

As in the 1981 campaign, so Hollande in 2012 wooed the provinces: campaign rallies made a comeback compared to media and TV displays. Mitterrand chose the traditional meeting-based approach in 1981, against the advice of campaign chief Jacques Séguela and others who urged him to throw out his previous persona, quit classic left-wing propaganda, and establish a media presence. In 2012 Hollande chose the same course. Had he been able, he would have walked around France, he kept saying. By comparison, Ségolène Royal's campaign had been far more modern; she even used the social networks.

This feature of Hollande's campaign is old-fashioned only in appearance. His advisers took their cue from the grass-roots methods of Obama's supporters in the primaries against Hillary Clinton and again in the presidential campaign against John McCain. Again, the deep economic recession and the decline, or at any rate doldrums, of mass media politics sent Hollande back to the basics: the old-style political rally, albeit dressed up. The same semblance of yesteryear characterized the pacing of the Socialist candidate's campaign. It had a laid-back quality, unlike that of his competitor. Mindful in part of Mitterrand's famous 1981 slogan, the tone was kept moderate. Hollande refused to demonize Sarkozy lest the election be turned into a referendum against the president (which might have proved counterproductive). Unlike Sarkozy in 2007, when every day brought up a new project, Hollande stuck to his program. The only flicker of something not prearranged with his staff was the proposal to impose a 75 percent marginal tax on incomes above €1 million. Even following the capture of an Al-Qaeda sympathizer who had killed three French soldiers of Arab descent and three Jewish schoolchildren and their teacher in Toulouse and Montauban, the management of which was mishandled by the secret services, Hollande opted not to put the boot into Sarkozy, who did in fact catch up the odd point on the strength of that episode. Compared with Sarkozy's typically populist campaign, based on blaming the elites and intermediate bodies, and harping on typical right-wing identity issues, Hollande struck a more presidential note than the incumbent president. He left it to Mélenchon, the Front de Gauche candidate, to stir up left-wing populist issues, which are always popular in France.

Here again, his conduct took Mitterrand 1981 for a model, a kind of division of labor where Mitterrand saw to wooing the center and Marchais looked after classic left-wing voters as well as the Communists. The division of labor was by no means prearranged or calculated, however, and involved a great deal of conflict. Throughout the 1981 campaign, Marchais's barbs were directed more at Mitterrand than at Giscard. Mitterrand was accused of opportunism and playing the moderate on many fronts, above all on international policy.

Hollande also studied the 1981 campaign from a purely communications angle. For one thing, he took with him on tour one recently published anthology of preelectoral Mitterrand speeches as a source-book for quotes: *Politique 2* (Mitterrand the "modernizer," after the Union de la Gauche).[12] His very gestures and tricks of public speaking sought to emulate his model. In this last respect, of course, it is hard to draw the line between Hollande's genuine devotion to his guru and the deliberate building of a personality. The French were used to an ironic and talkative version of Hollande who was more down-to-earth than Mitterrand. In his campaign, the future president learned to don a more presidential style that was both more distant and more charismatic. Hence the Third Republic–style radical-Socialist oratory noted by many in his political rallies. This was the oratory Mitterrand had grown up with politically and that he would never really change even when he became leader of the Socialists and the left. Likewise, Hollande's references to Mitterrand in his campaign were far from accidental or indirect. First, one notes the high number of quotations in his speeches, and then the symbolic assumption of the Mitterrand legacy expressed by Hollande's personal visit to Jarnac on the anniversary of Mitterrand's death, or the far less expected tribute (and tomb visit) to Bérégovoy, symbol of the unhappy last throes of Mitterrandie.[13]

Mitterrand in 1981 again inspired the Hollande campaign for round two of the presidential election. In his day, Mitterrand had been trailing behind Giscard but only marginally changed his tactics. Though he targeted the outgoing president more, he never forced the tone. In the televised debate, rendered famous in history by Mitterrand's dismissal of Giscard as *homme du passif* (a deliberate play on words condemning both the passivity and debt-ridden economic performance of the incumbent president), many noted that Mitterrand bore the manner and conduct of a president-in-office; Giscard did all the drawing out and provocation of his challenger.[14] If Mitterrand kept his cool, Hollande—who was ahead on points after the first round—had no interest in raising the tension. Like Giscard, though for different reasons, Sarkozy appeared the more aggressive, especially by his courting of Le Pen voters. But that ultimately made it easier for Hollande to campaign against the president, down to the TV duel at the close of the campaign.

Mitterrandisme for Government

It is too early to say whether Hollande will take his cue from Mitterrand in government, and if so, which Mitterrand? My own theory is that Mitterrand served the new president as a model more for how to gain power than how to wield it. From the outset, Hollande made this clear. Since 1981 only thirty years have passed but they weigh like centuries. Mitterrand's accession to the Elysée was overstated and ritualized. Hollande's enthronement was sober and prosaic. Nor was it just the killjoy economic downturn. Hollande wanted to underscore the fact of being *normal*, and the adjective bears out this interpretation. Mitterrand's was the first real rise to power by the left, and it was correct to make something of such a momentous occasion. Hollande, by contrast, stands for the normal business of democratic alternation: right and left contend for power without the outcome being hailed by the losers as God's punishment or as a revolutionary breakthrough by the winners. The first steps in government and first proper difficulties have shown the new president to be cautious in asserting policy. The commentator Jacques Julliard—an Hollande stalwart, to boot—thinks Hollande remains locked in the mediator stance of PS secretary and still has to acquire the decision-making manner of a Fifth Republic president (something Mitterrand donned from the very first day). Again, not only is Hollande more prosaic in his 2012 platform compared to Mitterrand's 110 resolutions in 1981, but also, even in the points that most distinguish him from Sarkozy, we find Hollande's approach is Fabianist in its pace. This is nothing like Mitterrand who brought in various key points on his agenda even before the general election—in contrast, therefore, to the token proposal by the first Ayrault government to restore the retirement age to sixty. It is very much as former *Le Monde* editor Jean-Marie Colombani predicted: "[U]nlike Mitterrand, in Hollande's case realism will always prevail over rhapsody."[15]

It would of course be folly for Hollande to ape Mitterrand's 1981 government. As it was, that wrecked the country's finances (as Delors had warned from his post as finance and economy minister), though at the time European economic integration and globalization were in their infancy, nation states and governments still had many levers to intervene economically, and the French budget deficit was minimal compared to today. For all that, Mitterrand's reforms caused such bedlam that he was soon forced to backtrack and set in motion stringent forms of austerity. In the election build-up and for a few months after gaining power, Mitterrand allowed the French to dream; the dream soon turned to a nightmare, however, or, at least, deep disillusionment.

Mindful of all this, Hollande made sure his electoral campaign did not ignite the French collective imagination. Politically, this smacks strongly of Rocard's Deuxième Gauche and above all Delors' plain speaking, not fooling the electorate, not promising more than you can reasonably deliver, taking stock of the harsh reality, especially in terms of the restrictions imposed by the markets and today's European institutions. In this sense, Hollande is far more Delorsian (and Rocardian) than Mitterrandiste. But anyone with a political head on their shoulders would be.

Above all else, the radical difference between 1981 and 2012 on the home front is the French people's consensus. At that time the French social and political center of gravity had swung leftwards. This process had begun in the early 1970s, to the extent that in 1974 Mitterrand was robbed of victory over Giscard by a handful of decimal points, while the Gauche lost only the 1978 parliamentary elections on technical grounds, following the end of the union between the PS and PCF. That explains the *vague rose* (pink wave), the landslide victory in the June 1981 parliamentary election, when the PS polled 49.6 percent in the second round and the left finished with over 2 million votes more than the right. That result can only partly be put down to the Mitterrand effect.[16] Such outcomes are the fruit of gradual and complex social processes. Something of the kind occurred with the French sociological rightwards rebound in the 1980s. This was actually at work in 1988 when Mitterrand was reelected thanks to the split between the Neo-Gaullists and the Giscardians, on top of his competitor's general weakness. Just as "right-wing" president Giscard found himself governing a left-wing France, so our left-wing president Hollande leads a France that is far more right-wing than in the past. Part of the UMP employs the same rallying cries as Le Pen, the two electorates have grown less distinguishable than ever before.

In the 1980s Mitterrand craftily exploited the divisions of the republican right and the rise of Le Pen senior, which objectively penalized Chirac and Giscard. That is no longer the case, as the 2012 parliamentary election showed. With its 40 percent of the vote, the PS may have been given a majority like that of 1981 and even more power, since it now controls all the main cities and regions as well as the senate. But the high rate of abstention, largely on the part of Sarkozy and Le Pen voters, tells us that times have changed since 1981. In the subsequent parliamentary election, France did not rally to Hollande as it did to Mitterrand in his day.

This is not a bad thing. We can do without the tones of 1981 when a prominent Socialist member of parliament (MP) harangued the opposition in parliament, accusing them of being "legally in the wrong" after they had been "politically defeated."[17] Which goes to show once again that the Mitterrand inspiring Hollande is not the Jacobin of 1981, but rather the Girondin of 1988, and is more open-minded and more conscious of the huge effort required. However, the 1988-style Mitterrand did a nosedive—something Hollande, France, and Europe cannot afford today.

Notes

Translated from the Italian by Ralph Nisbet.

1. M. Gervasoni, *François Mitterrand: una biografia politica e intellettuale* (Turin: Einaudi, 2007), 218–21.
2. A. Chemin, "Ségolène Royal: du bon usage de Mitterrand," *Le Monde* [online], January 9, 2007, http://www.lemonde.fr/a-la-une/article/2007/01/08/segolene-royal-du-bon-usage-de-mitterrand_853048_3208.html; I. Mandreau, "Mise en scène mitterrandienne et soutien 'people,'" *Le Monde* [online], February 11, 2007, http://www.lemonde.fr/cgi-bin/ACHATS/acheter.cgi?offre=ARCHIVES&type_item=ART_ARCH_30J&objet_id=976571&xtmc=mise_en_scene_Mitterrandienne_et_soutien_people&xtcr=1.
3. "Strauss-Kahn, 'heritier le plus fidèle' de Mitterrand," *Le Monde* [online], January 9, 2011, http://www.lemonde.fr/politique/article/2011/01/09/strauss-kahn-heritier-le-plus-fidele-de-mitterrand_1463062_823448.html?xtmc=strauss_kahn_heritier_le_plus_fidele_a_mitterrand&xtcr=2; S. Landrin, "A un an de 2012, la 'ton ton mania' règne au PS," *Le Monde*, May 10, 2011, 5.
4. S. Raffy, *Le président: François Hollande, itinéraire secret*, (2nd ed). (Paris: Fayard, 2012).
5. J.M. Aphatie, "Le 'point d'équlibre' de Lionel Jospin," *Le Monde*, November 22, 1998, 6.
6. F. Hollande, *Changer de destin* (Paris: Laffont, 2012), p. 12
7. Ibid., p. 18
8. Ibid., p. 78
9. Ibid., p. 101
10. Ibid., p. 121
11. Gervasoni, *François Mitterrand*, 122–34.

12. F. Mitterrand, *Politique 2* (Paris: Fayard, 1981).
13. T. Wieder, "L'hommage très politique de François Hollande à Pierre Bérègovoy," *Le Monde* [online], May 1, 2012, http://www.lemonde.fr/election-presidentielle-2012/article/2012/05/01/l-hommage-tres-politique-de-francois-hollande-a-pierre-beregovoy_1693850_147.
14. J. Attali, *Verbatim I 1981–1986* (Paris: Fayard, 1993), 26; J.-P. Azéma, "La campagne presidentielle de François Mitterrand," in *François Mitterrand: les années du changement 1981–1984*, ed. S. Berstein, P. Milza, and J-L.Bianco (Paris: Perrin, 2001), 47–51.
15. J.M. Colombani, "Hollande n'est pas Mitterrand," *Challenges* [online], May 13, 2012, http://www.challenges.fr/economie/20120509.CHA6234/hollande-n-est-pas-mitterrand.html.
16. Only at one other time did parliamentary elections held on the heels of a presidential election yield a better result for the president's party: in 2007 in which, following Sarkozy's victory, 54 percent of the second-round vote went to the UMP, bringing off a kind of *vague bleue* (blue wave).
17. M. Gervasoni, *François Mitterrand*, p. 281.

Chapter 3

The TV-Presidency
From de Gaulle's "Télécratie" to
Hollande's "Normal Presidency"

Riccardo Brizzi

Since the 1965 Presidential Elections, No Looking Back

In any major election, the experts harp on the crucial role of communications, emphasize how personalized politics has become, point to the growing media consciousness of the public sphere, and stress how much public opinion is conditioned by the media. The 2012 presidential elections were no exception to this iron law, which has underpinned French history since the dawn of the Fifth Republic.

By the end of a five-year term that was characterized by an extremely mediatized concentration of executive power in the person of Nicolas Sarkozy, the electoral campaign—that played out in a less intense climate of political mobilization compared to 2007—was nevertheless characterized by a massive participation of public opinion due to the growing articulation between old and new media. The victory of the so-called normal candidate, François Hollande, translated a profound break in the style of presidential communication, characterized by a lesser degree of activism of the new chief of state compared to his predecessor. This strategy reflected Hollande's strong desire to break with the hyperpersonalization of the Sarkozy presidency, but it also highlighted the difficulties of the new president in managing a constantly changing media environment.

To give an idea of this growing role of the media, the expression *télécratie* (TV-cracy) entered French political parlance in late autumn 1962 to describe de Gaulle's style of government. He had pushed for direct elec-

---

Notes for this chapter begin on page 56.

tion of the president of the republic by universal suffrage, and a referendum had been held. The outcome disappointed the opposition, as did the general election held a month later. Both tended to confirm the conviction that television was a mighty, if not invincible, means of conditioning public opinion. That de Gaulle had carried the day against the will of the main political formations, the guardians of the republic, the principal news dailies, and trade unions, was because he had television at his beck and call, a one-way channel of persuasion. To account for such a turning of the tables, the small screen clearly had to be accorded an almost absolute power of direct coercion—though no scientific proof of this was ever claimed.[1]

Decisive confirmation of this myth of TV omnipotence would come three years later with the first plebiscite to elect a president. Suddenly, in December 1965, the personalization of power—hitherto confined to General de Gaulle who jealously monopolized the small screen[2]—spread to opposition leaders as well. Thanks to new rules governing the official campaign, de Gaulle's adversaries each got a two-hour slot in the public media. Their participation caused a sensation: until that time they had never had access to the cameras, while the president in office was so confident of winning in the first round that he refused to go on the air or stoop to competing with rivals he deemed beneath him. Opinion polls—the other great novelty of that ballot—dwelled on the broadcasts' success: one in two of the population said they watched the various candidates' performances, with the figures rising to 64 percent in the Paris region where TV sets were thicker on the ground (during the election campaign the TV rental company Locatel recorded a 65 percent increase in television hire in Paris alone).[3] Opposition leaders—beginning with the left-wing candidate François Mitterrand and the centrist representative Jean Lecanuet—rapidly picked up the technique and proved to be talented communicators. Lecanuet in particular, following the advice of his brilliant publicist, Michel Bongrand, was hailed by the press as the most telegenic candidate, and soon earned the nickname of the "French Kennedy." Virtually unknown to the people on the eve of the ballot and expected to poll a mere 2 percent of the vote, he topped 16 percent in the first round, taking a sizable swath of moderates away from the reigning president, who was forced to the indignity of a runoff.

The 1965 presidential elections were a real political earthquake, ushering in television as a political medium once and for all. De Gaulle had scoffed at the media ratings given to his rivals, but decided to return on the air for the second round (using the innovation of an interview, with journalist Michel Droit), and managed to get back into the Elysée. The mediatization of the 1965 elections met with a chorus of criticisms. In a provocative *Le*

Monde article entitled "The Pestilential Candidates," Gilbert Cesbron likened the competition for the Elysée Palace to a "country fair where what counts most is the candidates' faces."[4] The main contenders were accused of cheapening politics; Lecanuet was especially mocked for his marketing techniques; the Gaullists dubbed him "Little Kennedy . . . peddled just like a soap powder."[5] But behind the vituperation there lurked the awareness that from then on even the most authoritative leaders would no longer be able to win if they remained aloof from the electoral arena, as de Gaulle had misguidedly opted to do.

The "Hyperpresidency" and the Media: The Sarkozy Experience

Since 1965, media communication has steadily gained credence and interacted more and more with politics.[6] Those in charge of the so-called holy trinity of political communication—television, polls, and advertising[7]—increasingly muscled in on the public scene. The number of polls published at each election tells the whole story: 12 in 1965, 19 in 1969, 24 in 1974, 111 in 1981, 153 in 1988, 157 in 1995, 193 in 2002, 293 in 2007, and nearly 400 in 2012 (figure 3.1). At the same time, new names made their appearance and began to split the media pie.

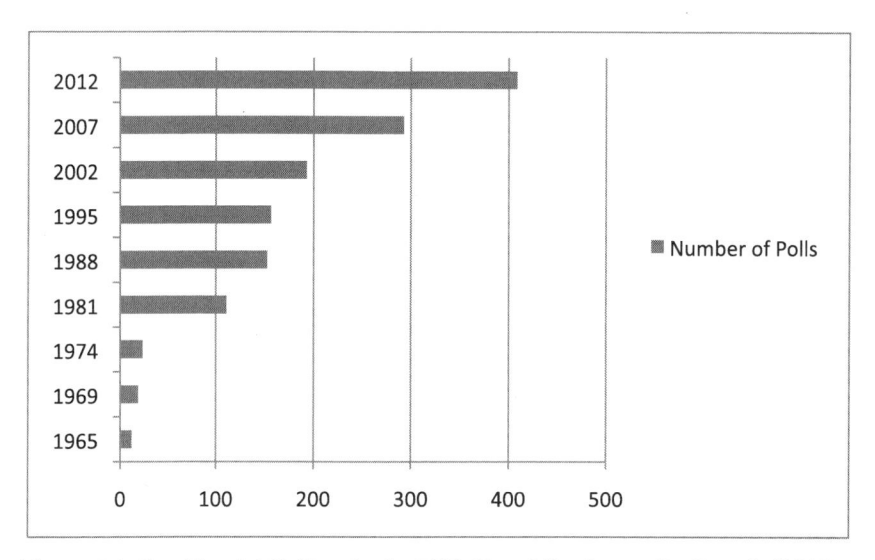

Figure 3.1. Presidential Polling in the Fifth Republic. *Source:* R. Cayrol, "Médias et sondages: le couple maudit des élections présidentielles françaises." In *Médias, opinions et présidentielles,* edited by R. Cayrol and J-M. Charon, 59–68. Bry-sur-Marne: INA Editions, 2012; p. 59.

In the course of the past thirty years, France has successively witnessed the eclipsing of the radio oligopoly, the end of the TV monopoly, the development of cable and satellite television, and the inroads of the Internet. In 1981 a presidential campaign would simultaneously unfold over three television channels, five radio stations, and a dozen quality dailies and weeklies. The president of the republic might easily command one-third of the French audience, even two-thirds, at key political moments. Today the figure is less than a quarter.[8] Five presidential elections on, the media panorama has changed beyond recognition: there has been a proliferation of TV channels (eighteen of them offering free access) and radio stations, nonstop information channels have entered the scene and, above all, the Internet is everywhere, enabling the press to provide instant coverage of events, whatever their degree of frequency. At the same time, smartphones and the social networks have enabled all users to set up personalized information blogs and become channels of communication in their own right.

This development, far from being confined to the communications world, has had political and institutional consequences of major importance. To grasp this, one need only observe the last term of the presidency. Somewhat superficially, analyses seem to have concentrated on Sarkozy's intense *peopleisation* (celebrity seeking)[9] while the most significant political fact is the link between media hype and hyperpresidential activity that emerged during Sarkozy's five-year term.

The omnipresent president was a key feature of that term: the agenda consisted of punctuating the mandate with bursts of television saturation, announcements of impromptu decisions, and watchwords coined by the Elysée communication-tank and insistently repeated by ministers or the head of state's chief collaborators.[10]

Concentrating executive power in a highly media-conscious presidency had a material influence on how the constitution evolved. Sarkozy openly sought to break with the constitutional custom handed down from de Gaulle's and Mitterrand's presidencies with their "sacred" distinction of roles: a president of the republic responsible for the essentials of governing and a prime minister handling ordinary power. Sarkozy's predecessors used to dose their appearances in public. They engaged in grand international strategy and would sketch the main lines of domestic policy, leaving the prime minister to see to the details. By contrast, Sarkozy wanted his finger in every executive pie, not hesitating to replace members of the government and saturating the media space to a degree that was unparalleled in the history of the Fifth Republic. Whereas for half a century the occupant of the Hôtel Matignon had traditionally borne the brunt of political failure—his role carried no time limit and was precisely designed to shield the head of state—Prime Minister François Fillon unexpectedly emerged as a factor of stability amid Sarkozy's wild excesses. Each starting out with a popularity rating of around 57 percent, they peaked in September 2007 at the end of the honeymoon, with Sarkozy at 67 percent and Fillon at 59 percent—before Sarkozy's inability to manage his private life led to a fall in his ratings (he lost thirty points in autumn 2007 alone).

It is rare for a president at the start of his first term to be less popular than his prime minister. In the history of the Fifth Republic, this had only happened twice: in 1981 with the Mitterrand-Mauroy tandem, and in 1995 with Chirac-Juppé. But never before had there been such an inversion of the popularity ratio, and it would remain fairly constant throughout the rest of the five-year term. From early January 2008 Sarkozy was in free fall and Fillon overhauled him, remaining the more popular of the two until the end, with a popularity level oscillating around 50 percent. Sarkozy's ratings were more up and down. His popularity slumped during the "bling-bling" period (34 percent in July 2008). Then the European presidency gave him international standing—historically dear to every French person's heart—and he appeared to invert the trend (48 percent in January 2009). But a new slump set in during the second half of his term (30 percent in January 2012), which was partly redeemed at the end when he announced he was standing again (figure 3.2).

Sarkozy's image became threadbare through overexposure. His unduly personalized approach to the presidency brought weightier consequences than an (albeit significant) fluctuating popularity index. On such a model, the presidency no longer acted as the guarantor of stability that social life and democracy so badly require. On the contrary, it added to the general public bewilderment, undermining the symbolic basis of power. The failure of such a political strategy did more than discredit the *man*, who was perennially in the limelight. It directly implicated his *function* as head of state, betraying the expectations aroused by his election and exposing the country to the siren calls of antipolitics and democratic disillusionment.[11]

The Media and the 2012 Presidential Campaign

Against many experts' expectations, the 2012 presidential elections failed to instate the Internet as the new predominant medium of information. Instead of becoming the decisive tool on which the fate of the campaign would hang, the plethora of sites and networks (Twitter, Facebook, Instagram, etc.) meant that the Web never really caught up with, let alone eclipsed, television, which continued to head the field in at least three evidently correlated respects.

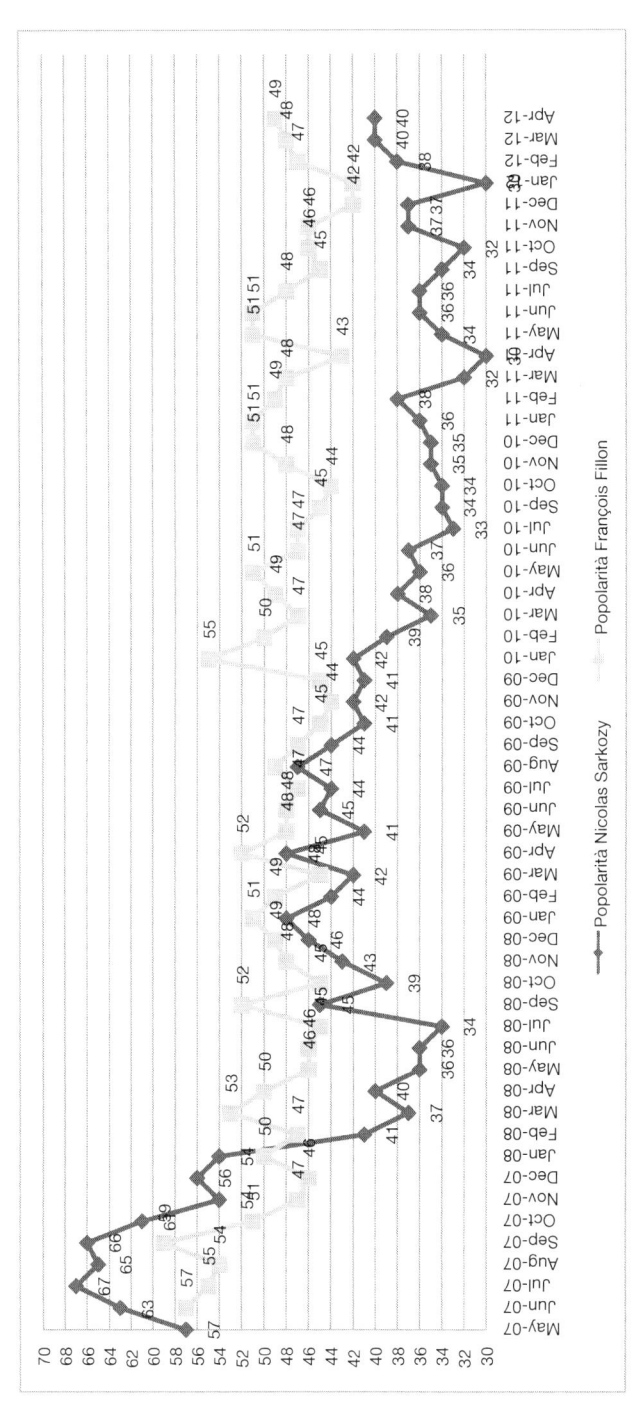

Figure 3.2. Popularity of the Executive. *Source: Le Nouvel Observateur*, April 12, 2012.

First, it proved yet again to be the medium the French prefer for keeping abreast of a presidential campaign (74 percent), with the Internet next (40 percent), then the radio (34 percent), the national dailies (10 percent), the "freebie" press (6 percent), and the regional newspapers (6 percent) (figure 3.3).

Second, television once again proved to be the medium for the big turnout and campaign event. Political broadcasts vied for the biggest audience, especially *Paroles de candidat* on TF1 and *Des paroles et des actes* on France 2. The latter undoubtedly carried the day, attracting 5.6 million viewers on March 6, 2012, when Sarkozy was on, and 5.5 million on January 26, 2012 when it was Hollande's turn. Of course, since 1974 the central event of electoral campaigns has been the TV face-to-face on the eve of the second-round runoff, and this time it also ran true to tradition: the 2 hours 51 minutes-long debate between Hollande and Sarkozy was followed by 17.8 million television viewers.

Third, the politicians chose television as the medium for making important announcements—not just because of numbers, but also because it was the place to be when sending a short and punchy message. Television was the host when candidacies or the flashier measurements in the various programs were announced. Thus, Sarkozy chose to announce his own candidacy on the 8 p.m. evening news on TF1 on February 15, 2012, while Hollande first declared that he was standing for president at Tulle on March 31, 2011, before rushing before the 8 p.m. news cameras of France 2. TF1 again carried Hollande's proposal to set a 75 percent marginal tax

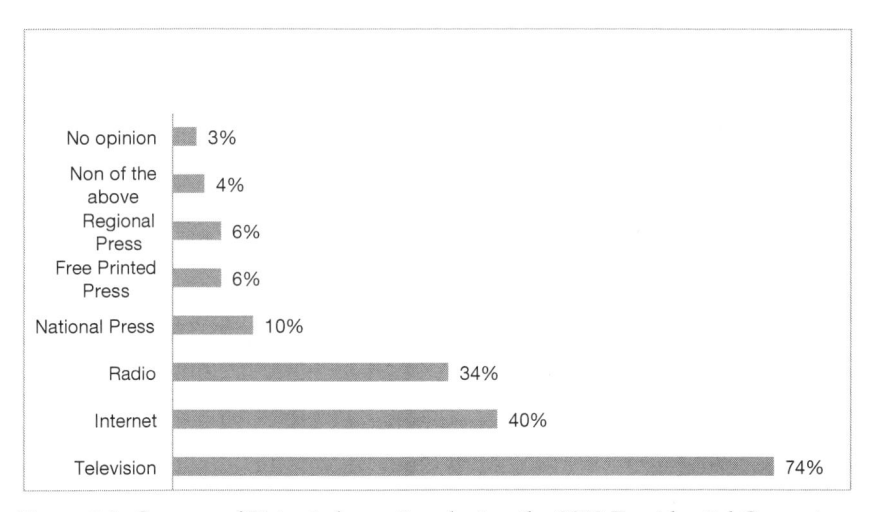

Source	Percentage
No opinion	3%
Non of the above	4%
Regional Press	6%
Free Printed Press	6%
National Press	10%
Radio	34%
Internet	40%
Television	74%

Figure 3.3. Sources of Voter Information during the 2012 Presidential Campaign. *Source:* CSA Poll conducted for *Le Figaro*, March 2012.

on incomes over €1 million, while Sarkozy chose France 2 to propose a minimum tax on the biggest multinational firms.

By contrast, no candidate decided to advertise the salient measures of their platform on their own Web site, Twitter, or Facebook. Sarkozy did launch the idea of a virtual Twitter-meeting, but it didn't come off. In terms of investment, the various candidates' Web campaigns recorded a fairly modest outlay, though there were some surprises. Going by the documentation lodged with the national board for campaign accounts and political funding, Sarkozy spent €1,331,846 on his Web campaign out of a total of €21,339,664 (6.2 percent, therefore), and proved to be the most Web-conscious candidate with the biggest fan-page following on Facebook and a rich timeline (a kind of biography-cum-panegyric). Hollande neglected the Web even more, investing no more than €549,251 of his total €21,769,895 (2.5 percent). This was sharply down from Ségolène Royal's investment five years before, when her project *Désirs d'avenir* cost €866,000.

The two candidates who proportionally invested most on the Web were Front de Gauche leader Jean-Luc Mélenchon (€715,603 or 7.5 percent of his total campaign expenditures) and the MoDem leader François Bayrou (€606,363 or 8.6 percent), while Philippe Poutou, candidate for the Nouveau Parti Anticapitaliste (New Anticapitalist Party, or NPA) brought up the rear, spending €319 (or 0.04 percent of his total).[12]

Though Web spending may not have taken off, the campaign did enable candidates to experiment with a range of online support platforms (Web

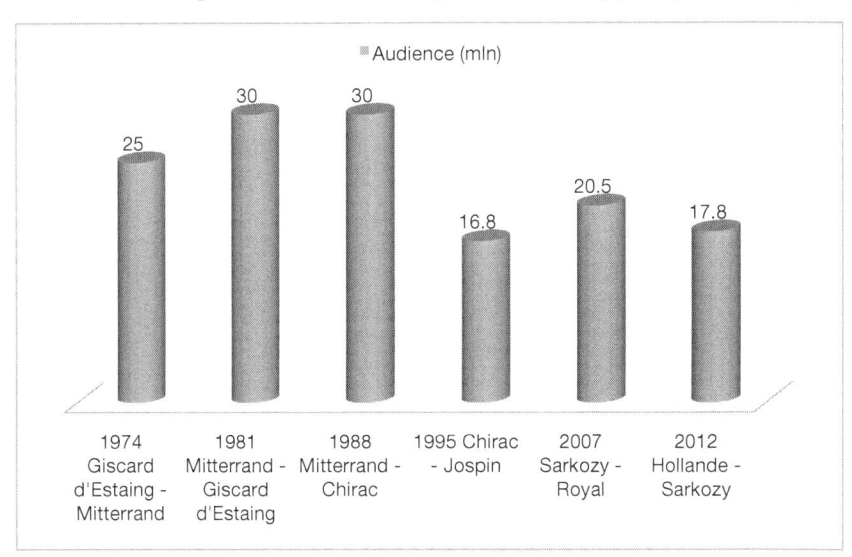

Figure 3.4. Audience Rating of Television Debates Prior to the Second-Round Runoff. *Source:* Médiamétrie.

sites, social networks, photos on Instagram or Flickr, etc.). Here Twitter seemed particularly on the up, though the way this came about surprised many observers.

Most pundits pointed to the role of Twitter as a possible dueling ground for the main contenders, as well as a probable forum for interaction between journalists and politicians. However, with very rare exceptions there was a dearth of tweet-interviews (the only attempt was Bayrou's) and tweet-clashes, if one makes an exception for the tweet-assassination (during the June parliamentary election) of the new *première dame* (first lady) Valérie Trierweiler against Ségolène Royal. This earned Trierweiler the soubriquet of "Tweetweiler." Twitter tended to be seen and used by journalists (direct reporting of events, comments, and behind-the-scenes disclosures) and the public as a source of information and civic mobilization of a kind that sees politics as an object of often derisive judgment, based on fact-checking or archive tweeting regarding politicians' statements, with a view to highlighting their contradictions.

There was significant interaction with the traditional media: especially a burst of Twitter activity around the main televised events of the electoral campaign, culminating in 355,000 tweets posted by 75,500 users during the May 2 debate between Hollande and Sarkozy. On that occasion Twitter appeared to act as an amplifier of the small screen, probing and dissecting the candidates' utterances, checking them point by point, contesting, mocking, and generally debunking—or even discrediting—the language of political debate.

Another novel aspect of the campaign was the vindication of nonstop information channels (headed by Bfm Tv and I-Télé), which drove the traditional generic channels into second place in terms of coverage of the presidential campaign. In the two weeks leading up to the second round, the information channels devoted a total of eighty-four hours to politics versus the fifty hours allotted by the generic channels. Such new vectors of information, which had been totally marginal in 2007, redoubled the candidates' need to release press statements and gain as much news space as possible. They heated up the pace of the campaign, came to the fore in press conference broadcasting, and tended to bring rallies back into fashion, giving them a second youth. It was especially the nonstop information channels and their direct coverage of political meetings that gave the latter a return to relevance as a show of strength, worth investing campaign funds in. (Thus, on the eve of the first round of the vote, April 15, Hollande and Sarkozy staged simultaneous rallies—one in front of the Château de Vincennes, the other on the Place de la Concorde.) Such demonstrations would be far and away the first item in election campaign expenditure for all candidates, showing a marked increase from five years before. Sarkozy spent €13 million, or 61 percent of his total, on campaign rallies, while Hollande invested €9.4 million, or 43 percent of his total expenditures, marking a considerable increase from the €7.1 million (34 percent of his total) spent by Ségolène Royal in 2007.

Such hybridization of old and new means of communication contradicted the prophecies that the TV era was over, and showed that the media are a constantly evolving whole in which various aspects play greater or lesser roles and change means adding and combining, not replacing. It is in this sense that the Internet and the nonstop information channels have forced their way onto the scene, as the 2012 presidential campaign clearly confirms.

Candidate Strategy: A Program and a Style

Inevitably, every election campaign hinges on the hope of change. Throughout the Fifth Republic, that has demonstrably been the case. One never makes it to the Elysée if one is not prepared to raise the banner of change. In 1974 Valéry Giscard d'Estaing said his ambition was to pilot "change without risks." In 1981 François Mitterrand's great bid for alternation was accompanied by the ambitious slogan, "*Changer la vie.*" Even Jacques Chirac in 1995 gambled on the issue of repairing the *fracture sociale*. For his part, in his 2007 campaign, Nicolas Sarkozy, embodied the idea of a clean break with consummate skill, playing on a kind of collective catharsis in a country where crisis was at its height as the election campaign began.

For the hope of change to take root, whoever aspires to supreme office must identify the country's expectations and build communications around a coherent program and style. Whichever candidate's manifesto manages to dictate the central issue of the campaign and impose his or her own reform agenda, inevitably becomes the hot favorite in the running. This is what Chirac achieved both in 1995 through his diagnosis of the *fracture sociale*—which picked up on a real concern of the people and forced his opponents to take a stand on his chosen ground—and in 2002 with the issue of safety, which the media rapidly turned into the fulcrum of the campaign.

The 2007 agenda was a slippery one to begin with. The candidates were casting around for a strong issue when Sarkozy came up with the two questions that would polarize the campaign. The first was the issue of purchasing power, conveyed through the slogan, "Work more to earn more." This combined the proposal to exempt overtime pay from taxes with increasing the fiscal shield to 50 percent, and reviving the attack on the "folly" of the thirty-five-hour work week. The second issue was national identity, addressed through the proposal to create a minister for national identity and immigration. This forced his rivals to take a position, causing Ségolène Royal to intone the *Marseillaise* at meetings and festoon the podium and squares with tricolor flags.

A program or platform is one side of the coin. The other is a candidate's *style*, which expresses and captures a national aspiration. In 2007 the diagnosis of "France at a low ebb" was common, as was the perception that politics had grown autistic, incapable of changing the course of events.[13] All candidates—including members of the parties of government who were vying for the Elysée—rode the antipolitics bandwagon.[14]

If they were to get in tune with the people's aversion to politics, Sarkozy and Royal had to forget their long pasts in politics and government and seek to build a new image, standing for a clean break with the system and even with their own party establishments. Sarkozy's proactive energy tangibly belied the electorate's gloom and fatalism and symbolized a break with Chirac's institutional lethargy. Though president of the UMP (his candidacy was backed by 98.1 percent of the party members), Sarkozy repeatedly remarked on the ill-concealed hostility he received from the outgoing president as well as Prime Minister Dominique de Villepin, hoping thereby not to be a victim of popular discontent with a government in which he himself had figured prominently. (Giscard d'Estaing had performed a similar acrobatic feat in 1974.) Likewise, Ségolène Royal, with four parliamentary mandates and three ministerial appointments under her belt, studiously cultivated the image of an outsider who had been thwarted by her own party. From 2006 on she posed as the "gazelle in the land of elephants," emphasizing the need for participatory democracy while suggesting that voters should exercise greater control over their representatives.

Owing to the deepening recession, the 2012 presidential campaign went decidedly for style rather than a concrete agenda, probably because the French were afraid of hearing what needed to be said: that they were in for five years of austerity and sacrifice. Unlike the previous election, no clear-cut issue dominated the electoral landscape. Issues appeared and melted away, with none of them impacting the competition.

The economic doldrums in which the competition took place produced a paradoxical effect: the crisis and solutions to it, which should have loomed large in all candidates' electoral platforms, was mainly tackled by outsiders (Le Pen, Dupont-Aignan, Philippe Poutou), or by the antisystem candidates (Bayrou and Mélenchon), whereas the two favorites (Hollande and Sarkozy) played down their economic programs for strategic reasons. Sarkozy was determined that the election should not turn into a referendum on his own performance, while Hollande bore in mind the fact that the polls put him in the lead and opted for vagueness on the central issues ranging from education to taxation. However, such a bland program proved dangerous to Hollande: he could not afford to "do a Balladur." (In 1995 the prime minister of the day, Edouard Balladur, was tipped to win by all surveys right up to the last months. He decided that standing on his position rather than rocking the boat would help him keep his lead over his adversaries. In the end, the favorite came in third in the first round.) As a result, it was only toward the end of his campaign that Hollande hit on the winning issue of social justice and a fair division of labor: his proposed tax bracket of 75 percent for incomes over €1 million went on to polarize the debate.

Failing any real battle over the issues, the campaign inevitably came to focus on the candidates' personalities and styles, which struck two very different registers. Sarkozy was forced into a sudden change of tack. The second half of his presidency had been concerned with the need to restyle the presidency: the "people's president" gradually slid toward the "father-figure" image. The shift had entailed a change of organization whereby the head of state formally stood back from his own party's internal affairs. (Thus, Sarkozy stopped his customary Monday meetings with UMP leaders, among other things.)[15] Yet having spent half a term restyling his presidential image, Sarkozy conducted the election campaign on another register altogether, attempting as in 2007 to play the role of the outsider. Burgeoning unemployment, spiraling public debt, and a worsening trade deficit, which were symbolized by France losing its AAA credit rating, gave the impression of the country's ineluctable decline and left no room for any trumpet-blowing over the some 240 laws that had got through parliament during his mandate (reform of the university and pension system, for example, were successful reforms from a government angle). Sarkozy decided not to run on the ticket of his accomplishments over his five-year term but instead to take on the role of challenger, of the "French people's candidate against the elites," primarily in order to recapture the jaundiced FN electorate. From the time he announced he was running for reelection, he attempted to win back the Le Pen vote, egged on by adviser Patrick Buisson who had begun his journalistic career on the extreme right. Thus, he called for a return to traditional values, railing at the media and Parisian elites for their alleged Socialist bias, proposing a recourse to referenda so as to bypass parliament, and giving the people a say, criticizing ritual butchery methods, and so on.

But the strategy soon lost its usefulness. After the first round vote, Sarkozy found that he had to court not just the FN vote, but also the center minus Bayrou, from whom he had diverged too far over the previous months and who would not to be brought around by the promise to adopt the "golden rule" (i.e., making the squaring of the national accounts a constitutional obligation).

In contrast to his rival's hectic pace, Hollande steadily and single-mindedly worked to build up a president's profile, as well as that of a normal candidate designed to ride the wave of anti-Sarko feeling, which had been mounting since 2008. This was a far-from-simple plan: many doubted whether the former Socialist first secretary had the charisma and stature of a president. As late as one year before the election, very few could imagine him entering the Elysée. The first daily to turn the spotlight on him was *Libération,* whose January 12, 2011, headline called him "the outsider" and asked "What if it were him?"[16] This was a rhetorical question, or so it seemed, and the large final question-mark expressed the general skepticism about the MP for Corrèze, as opposed to the obvious and natural PS candidate, Dominique Strauss-Kahn. In the twelve months following the official launch of his candidacy at Tulle, Hollande underwent a personal and political transformation. The nickname of the "normal candidate" (which Hollande himself coined during a visit to Algeria in December 2010) proved useful not just as a means to distinguish himself from Sarkozy, but also as a means to distance himself from the former IMF director, who was embroiled in a tawdry sex scandal, thereby inevitably redounding to Hollande's credit. His striking of this presidential manner saw Hollande through the Socialist primaries, especially the three TV debates in September 2011, in which he stood head and shoulders above the other contenders. While his rivals, like Martine Aubry, detailed their proposed programs, Hollande remained vague and concentrated more on looking like the right candidate to beat Sarkozy than on outlining his own platform. (It was anchored by three leading ideas: truthful accounting, priority to the young, and equitable economic recovery).[17]

The moment the campaign officially kicked off marked another waystage. Right from the January 22, 2012, meeting at Le Bourget, Hollande tried to assume a de facto presidential status. He quickly needed to plant in the French collective unconscious the fact that a former secretary-general of the PS and president of the Corrèze Regional Council possessed the stature, caliber, language, and deportment of a president (hence the restyling of his appearance, the strict diet, etc.). The same need was felt when the first-round results came in, placing him in the lead for the second-round runoff. This translated into the formula, "As president of the republic I...," which he repeated fifteen times during his television debate with Sarkozy on May 2, 2012. Hollande scored a bull's-eye with his self-representation as a "normal president," distancing himself from his forerunner's "omni-presidency" and constant upheaval. If Hollande could not revive the enthusiasm Mitterrand had enjoyed in 1981—the background of crisis hardly permitting him to promise the French a change of lifestyle—after five years of continuous electricity in the air, he could plausibly claim that the country primarily needed serenity. Thus, voters rewarded the Socialist candidate's managerial realism.[18]

President Hollande's Communication Style

Ten months after he acceded to the Elysée, Hollande appears to be in serious difficulty. His popularity rating touched 35 percent in the BVA-Orange survey commissioned by *L'Express* in mid-March 2013—the lowest ever recorded by a Fifth Republic president while still less than a year after his investiture. His government is deemed "very ineffective" by eight French people out of ten. Hollande has not even enjoyed the state of grace accorded to Sarkozy in his first months of office. It is true that right from the start many observers had forecast a short honeymoon, given the intense crisis and the new president's intention to start where the going was toughest, namely by reducing the budget deficit. But nobody had expected such a rapid and deep loss of popularity. The problem has not just been the recession, but also Hollande's personality and manifest inability to feel the pulse of the nation.

In looking askance at their president, the French are not so much denying the crisis as diagnosing a lack of leadership that breeds insecurity. The foundation of the Fifth Republic itself and the presidential style of its founder teach us that times of crisis call for a charismatic leader capable of dialoguing frankly and authoritatively with public opinion. Hollande, by contrast, seems obsessed with dissociating himself from his predecessor's hyperactivism. His low-profile approach is disorienting the French, giving the image of a wishy-washy and ineffectual presidency. If overpersonalization à la Sarko lacerated French society, Hollande's dullness is failing to pacify the nation, instead only causing greater anxiety and distrust.

Communications-wise, the "normal" presidency has meant less presence in the media, faltering communications initiatives, and growing difficulty in imposing his agenda, directing the government, and harnessing the media.[19] In 2012 the Socialists rediscovered presidential communications after nearly twenty years since Mitterrand quit the scene. They seem not to have grasped how much the fragmented media system now detracts from the head of state's traditional advantage, the initiative with communications. While the Fifth Republic's institutions still enable the president to pace his mandate as he pleases (though the five-year term has somewhat cramped his style), public opinion, Internet users, and the media are less patient, dictating a real-time agenda that has little room for silence. The president's utterances in his first months in office have been too rare. Hollande would seem to be the only president of the Fifth Republic who does not like talking to the nation. Under pressure from the media, Gallup polls, the majority, and the opposition, presidential communications must learn to adapt.

At the start of 2013, in an attempt to recapture goodwill, Hollande summoned a new image-adviser to the Elysée, Claude Sérillon, who will be working with a team already made up of three members: Aquilino Morelle political adviser and speechwriter of the head of state, Christian Gravel who handles press relations, and Claudine Ripert, the president's communications adviser. After a few weeks on the presidential staff, Sérillon insisted on two policies for Hollande to regain consensus: to increase his media presence and to step up tours of the country so as to look provincial France in the eye and regenerate the momentum of his campaign—a constant need for political leaders to address nowadays. Hollande's trip to Dijon in mid-March 2013, designed to illustrate what the government was achieving, did nothing but brush up a traditional method of communicating, which was first inaugurated by Napoleon III with his presidential tours of the provinces, and then extensively employed by de Gaulle and Mitterrand. (The first provincial tour of the latter in October 1981 comprised a charge round four departments in Lorraine, consisting of fourteen stops in forty-eight hours). Hollande needs to get out there and talk, physically shake hands in the town squares, as well as virtually on the social networks, meet the French and provide a kind of after-sale service on government reforms. He must keep up his pedagogical role while maintaining the initiative in his communications. These first ten months Hollande has skulked behind the scenes, failing to see that the recession is so bad and complex that it needs to be explained and given a face. The slogan "Change is now" most obviously applies to the president's own communications: he must try to persuade the French that the head of state knows the way out of the present plight. It is nearly a year since he entered the Elysée; he must realize that governing differently means first and foremost communicating differently.

Notes

Translated from the Italian by Ralph Nisbet.
1. R. Rémond and C. Neuschwander, "Télévision et comportement politique," in *Revue française de science politique*, 2 (1963), 325–47.

2. R. Brizzi, *De Gaulle et les médias* (Rennes: Presses Universitaires de Rennes, 2014).
3. F. d'Almeida and C. Delporte, *Histoire des médias en France: De la Grande Guerre à nos jours* (Paris: Flammarion, 2003).
4. G. Cesbron, "Les pestilentielles," *Le Monde,* October 25, 1965, 4.
5. "Les leaders de l'UNR attaquent les candidats de l'opposition, et principalement M. Lecanuet," *Le Monde,* December 2, 1965, 2.
6. For a quick reconstruction of this process, see P.J. Maarek, "La comunicazione politica in Francia sotto la Quinta Repubblica: professionalizzazione, personalizzazione o 'peopolisation?,'" in *Una splendida cinquantenne: la Quinta Repubblica francese,* ed. G. Pasquino and S. Ventura (Bologna: Il Mulino, 2010), 185–218.
7. R. Cayrol, *La nouvelle communication politique* (Paris: Larousse, 1986), 59.
8. Yves Mourousi's interview with François Mitterrand on TF1 in autumn 1985 totalled more than 20 million viewers, while President Sarkozy's two main appearances on the TF1 program *Paroles de Français,* broadcast on January 25, 2010, and February 10, 2011, gained audiences of 8.6 and 8.3 million, respectively. See J.-M. Benoit,, *Communication oblige. Du candidat au Président,* in "Le Débat", 172, n. 5, 2012, p. 14.
9. J. Dakhlia, *Politique people* (Paris: Bréal éditions, 2008); and Dakhlia, *Les politiques sont-ils des people comme les autres?* (Paris: Bréal éditions, 2012). For an even more recent analysis of this issue, see Dakhlia, "La présidentielle de 2012 vue du people: bis repetita ou 'normalization,'" paper presented at the conference Politics, Media and France's Electoral Year 2011/12, Nottingham University, Nottingham, UK, September 13, 2012.
10. P. Guibert, *La téléprésidente* (Paris: Plon, 2007); and F. Jost and D. Muzet, *Le téléprésident. Essai sur un pouvoir médiatique* (Paris: Aube, 2008).
11. P. Perrineau (ed), *Le desénchantement démocratique* (Paris: Aube, 2003); and from a historian's viewpoint, P. Rosanvallon, *La contre-démocratie: la politique à l'âge de la défiance* (Paris: Seuil, 2006).
12. *Journal Officiel de la République Française,* July 31, 2012, http://www.legifrance.gouv.fr/jopdf/common/jo_pdf.jsp?numJO=0&dateJO=20120731&numTexte=1&pageDebut=12415&pageFin=12455.
13. On this point, see N. Baverez, *La France qui tombe: un constat clinique du déclin français* (Paris: Perrin, 2003).
14. For a comparative theoretical and historical approach, see D. Campus, *L'antipolitica al governo. De Gaulle, Reagan, Berlusconi* (Bologna: Il Mulino, 2006). For a look at the French background on the question of the leadership and its image, see D. Campus, "L'immagine della leadership nella presidenza francese," in *Una splendida cinquantenne: la Quinta Repubblica francese,* ed. G. Pasquino and S. Ventura (Bologna: Il Mulino, 2010), 61–90.
15. C. Meeus, "Nicolas Sarkozy à la reconquete de son électorat," in SOFRES, *L'Etat de l'opinion en 2012* (Paris: Tns SOFRES, 2012).
16. L. Joffrin, "Tortues," in *Libération,* January 12, 2011, p. 1.
17. M. Ecoiffier and L. Bretton, "De Tulle à l'Elysée, la longue mue du candidat 'normal,'" *Libération* [online], May 6, 2012, http://www.liberation.fr/politiques/2012/05/06/de-tulle-a-l-elysee-la-longue-mue-du-candidat-normal_816820.
18. R. Cayrol, "Election et communication," in *Commentaire,* 139 (Fall 2012), 845–52.
19. J.-M. Benoit, "Communication oblige: Du candidat au Président," in *Le Débat* 172, no. 5 (2012): 17–18.

Part II

The Political Parties

Chapter 4

The Union for a Popular Movement after Sarkozy

Florence Haegel

Ten years after its creation, France's UMP party can truly be said to have changed the partisan right in French politics. Created in the very special circumstances of Jacques Chirac's victory over Jean-Marie Le Pen in the 2002 presidential election runoff, the UMP spent its first ten years as a party of government and only now, since its 2012 defeat in the presidential and parliamentary elections, has it found itself in opposition. At the same time, and in particularly acrimonious circumstances, the party had to choose a new leader after Nicolas Sarkozy stepped down following his electoral defeat.[1] Now, after a period in government and with a change of leadership, the time is right to take stock of how the UMP has been transformed since its founding and, more specifically, to assess the impact of Nicolas Sarkozy's leadership on the party.

The UMP came into existence in November 2002 as part of a broader overhaul of the right wing of the French political spectrum with the creation of a new party with a new name, a new logo, new members, and new regulations.[2] The resulting political formation was not, however, a radically new party but the result of a highly asymmetric merger in which the former members of the neo-Gaullist Rassemblement pour la République (Rally for the Republic; RPR), created by Jacques Chirac in 1976, not only held on to the leadership, but also formed the bulk of the new Party's middle management, elected membership, and supporters. Compared to the other large parties of the European right, such as the German Christian Democratic Union (CDU) and Spanish Partido Popular, two organizations that were often held up as models at the time of the UMP's creation, the former RPR and French right wing appeared both less professionally

Notes for this chapter begin on page 71.

organized, with few sector professionals in its administration, and less institutionalized, with a much more flexible approach to compliance with its own rules. On the ideological side, the RPR was less to the right on a certain number of issues than its European counterparts. This chapter looks at the organizational and ideological shifts undergone by the French right between 2002 and 2012. It argues that although the party did professionalize, adopting a business organizational model, this was not accompanied by the development of strong institutionalization. Moreover, while the party adopted a more radical ideology, this has occurred against a backdrop of ongoing Europeanization.

Professionalizing with a Business Model

Most European political parties have structured themselves along corporate lines. Business management discourse and methods as well as marketing practices are increasingly essential parts of political party organization. British and Italian parties are typical examples. The British political parties were precursors of the move to corporate governance models while Italy's Forza Italia is an extreme example of how entrepreneurial and political party networks can intermesh. Nor did the French right adopt a business organizational model only in 2002. The 1970s had witnessed a large-scale move to this management model that was evident both during the period of Giscard d'Estaing and when the RPR was created in 1976. Nonetheless, the French right appeared less professionalized and less beholden to the entrepreneurial system than did other right-wing European parties. With the UMP, the move toward the business model became apparent. Management techniques were adopted at all levels of the party, underpinning not only the way party headquarters were run, but also how its federations were managed. Marketing tools were used in all sectors.[3] Political support was galvanized by offering a range of products with a view to facilitating membership. For example, recruitment was promoted with reduced membership fees. Indeed, fees varied over time, and were even lowered during the presidential campaign.[4] Alongside the traditional personal-contact recruitment format, new forms of extending membership were adopted (the Internet, telephone, and even text messaging). The arrival of Nicolas Sarkozy's team at the head of the party at the end of 2004 was marked by an acceleration of its Internet strategy, which was outsourced to a group of specialist agencies. Commercial marketing tools deployed a promotional offensive to push the "partisan product." This was followed up by attempts to attain the tougher marketing goal of electronic participation, failing, however, to create an active Web community.⁵ Fundraising practices were also imported with a certain degree of success.

Party expenditure as recorded in UMP accounts disclosed to the committee charged with controlling party finances shows communication to be a key expense item.⁶ During 2009—not an electoral campaign year—the UMP spent €8,854,498 on communication and propaganda (i.e., 20 percent of its total outlay) while its main competitor, the PS spent only €3, 396,523 on this budget item (i.e., 6 percent of its total expenditure). A plethora of communication professionals, ad men, pollsters, and event management specialists worked for the party either on an outsourced service-provision basis or as part of the organization itself, further professionalizing the party machine. Indeed the embedding of communication specialists within the party appeared to go well beyond the broker or intermediary model generally used to describe the relationship between the two worlds of political parties and professionals.⁷ Within the UMP, career paths intermingled, hierarchies were turned on their heads, and frontiers became porous.⁸

Poor Institutionalization

Although the party underwent a general process of professionalization, this was not accompanied by any real institutionalization. By institutionalization is meant the creation of a set of formal codified rules of governance that ensures an institution's existence as an autonomous entity. In the case of the UMP, although its constituent political groups could be described as only loosely institutionalized organizations, the founding of the new entity could have been an opportunity to put in place a well institutionalized right-wing party underpinned by a set of stable and binding regulations. Attempts to do this were in fact made but nonetheless the UMP is still today a weakly institutionalized organization in the sense that the rules that do exist are readily waived according to the particular situation and whim of the leader, and generally have very limited binding force. The circumvention of the party's written rules goes hand in hand with the habit of changing regulations and practices to suit changing contexts. As a result, the UMP, more than any other party, can be considered the political organization that presents different faces depending on whether it is in campaign mode or not, in government or in opposition.

Two examples illustrate the flexibility of the UMP's statutory regulations. The first is the failure to enforce the articles of the new statutes providing for a faction-based party organization (known within the UMP as movements). The 2002 statutes provided for internal pluralism that would have profoundly changed the genetically charismatic model of the neo–Gaullist political parties.[9] Although officially sanctioned by party rules, recognition of internal groupings or factions within the party was continually postponed right up to 2012, with blithe disregard for the statutes. After the defeat in the 2012 presidential and legislative elections, these statutes, along with voting on motions of principle, were enforced for the first time at the November 2012 congress after being shelved for some ten years (see below).

Under the leadership of Sarkozy, the refusal to acknowledge factions within the party was countered by the creation of myriad fringe clubs and think tanks. The groups structured themselves either around one of the lower-profile party leaders or on the basis of ideological affinities between individual parliamentary members. During Nicolas Sarkozy's presidential mandate, several like-minded groupings came into being within the party's parliamentary group that largely dominated the French National Assembly (314 deputies, of which seven were allied deputies, out of a total of 577), their aim being to bring pressure to bear on parliamentary proceedings and, more generally, to influence the life of the party and public debate. As will be seen later, one of these groups, La Droite Populaire, which was set up after the poor showing in the March 2010 regional election, was to play a key role in the ideological evolution of the party (see below).

A second indication of the failure to institutionalize the UMP is the elimination of the functions of the party chair following Nicolas Sarkozy's election as president of the republic, on the grounds that "the chairman (of the UMP) is morally still Nicolas Sarkozy."[10] In the wake of this, provisions were adopted "in waiver of the applicable provisions in the event of the current UMP chairman becoming President of the Republic."[11] In fact, from 2007 to 2012 the UMP was not headed by a chair elected by party members but by a team (a secretary-general and two deputy secretary-generals) who were selected and could be dismissed by the Political Bureau. This provision confirms the fact that as long as Nicolas Sarkozy was president of the republic, the party's center of gravity was firmly located at the Elysée Palace. Such ad hoc changes of rules adopted five years previously with such fanfare, and such flagrant instrumentalization of the party by its leader, clearly testify to the fact that the UMP was hardly a strong, independent institution. This state of affairs went hand in hand with the rapid turnover of UMP secretary-generals. The function was successively exercised by Patrick Devedjian, Xavier Bertrand, and Jean-François Copé, who although formally elected by the Political Bureau, were in fact appointed by Nicolas Sarkozy.

Strategic and Cultural Radicalization

Radicalization in this context signifies a shift to the right and, in accordance with the etymological sense of the word, the return of right-wing politics to its roots.[12] Nicolas Sarkozy declared as much when he implemented this move after gaining leadership of the party at the end of 2004, and during the presidential campaign of 2007. The question reappeared during the summer of 2010 after the party's slump in the regional elections, and was a cornerstone of the 2012 campaign. After the 2012 electoral defeat the whole question of the party's right-wing positioning became a topic of internal UMP debate. Some questioned the president's strategy; others saw it as the reason for Nicolas Sarkozy's relative comeback after a poor electoral start.

Looking at how the ideological positions of the French right have developed, and considering both the opinions of its voters and what transpired from its legislative programs, it would appear that, compared to the electorate of other European right-wing parties, French right-wing voters were by and large less to the right than their counterparts in Europe for a considerable period, the only exception being on the issue of immigration. In fact, it was the potential for radicalization on the national identity issue that would be tapped to make the shift to the right. What set the candidate Sarkozy apart from the various versions of his predecessor Jacques Chirac (in 1988, 1995, and 2002) was not the economic discourse, but his position on national identity.[13]

The shift to the right has to be understood as motivated by the need to counter competition from the FN. Faced with the rise of the extreme right, the European right tried a number of strategies. Overall, if one excludes the details of flip-flop Chiraquism or its application at the local level, the French right chose not to clinch an alliance with the FN but rather to return to a traditional right-wing agenda.

During the presidential campaign of 2007, Nicolas Sarkozy's strategy was to go further to the right than the moderate right in order to weaken the so-called radical right. The move was successful since a significant portion of former FN voters opted for Nicolas Sarkozy.[14] After 2007 this approach was muddied, however, by other tactical considerations, especially the so-called *stratégie de l'ouverture* (strategy of openness) of co-opting into government well-known, reputedly left-leaning public figures. Subsequently, however, with the approach of new presidential elections, there was a return to more-traditional right-wing positions. This adjustment was first seen during the debate on national identity from November 2009 to January 2010. It was further accentuated after the defeat in the March

2010 regional elections, which endorsed the resurgence of the FN. In the summer of 2010, this radicalized discourse was at the core of the whole debate on wearing full face veils in public that was initiated by Jean-François Copé, who was then UMP parliamentary group leader; it was then taken up by the president in a speech following the August riots in Grenoble. These events gave the president of the republic the opportunity to publicly establish a link between the issues of crime and immigration,[15] and announce repressive measures and provisions impacting families (i.e., stopping benefits to delinquent minors or schoolchildren failing to attend class) and immigration (tightening rules on forfeiture of French nationality) and justifying the implementation of the decisions to dismantle the Roma camps on the ground that two of them had been involved in the Grenoble violence. This radicalization was continued with the April 2011 project to start a "debate on religious worship—namely Islam—in France and its compatibility with the secular laws of the Republic," a move that was contested even within the UMP itself, particularly by Alain Juppé.[16]

Although successful in 2007, the radicalization of Sarkozy's discourse did not avert the 2012 defeat, as was shown by the success of Marine Le Pen (see table 4.1). It is true, however, that in the meanwhile the economic crisis had emerged and the election's outcome could not be viewed as a crushing defeat for the right or exclusively as the result of this strategic approach. In any event, the radicalization approach did not make inroads into the electorate of the FN, which in the meantime had also partly undergone its own transformation. Rather, the stalemate set the scene for an infernal downward spiral on account of the joint and perverse effects of

Table 4.1. Right-wing Candidate Performance in the 2007 and 2012 Presidential Elections

	First Round		Second Round	
	2007	2012	2007	2012
Number of votes				
Sarkozy	11, 448,663	9,753,629	18,983,138	16,860,685
Le Pen	3, 834,530	6,421,426		
Bayrou	6,820,119	3,275,122		
*Droite souverainiste**	818,407	643,907		
% of votes cast				
Sarkozy	31. 18	27.18	53. 06	48. 36
Le Pen	10.44	17.9		
Bayrou	18.57	9.13		
*Droite souverainiste**	2.23	1.79		

* *droite souverainiste* (extreme right) represented by Philippe de Villiers in 2007, and Nicolas Dupont-Aignan in 2012.
Source: Ministère de l'Intérieur

two aspects of the strategy that had been adopted: the refusal of an alliance, which only entrenched extreme right radical positions,[17] and the retrieval, and hence legitimization in the eyes of right-wing voters of the issues raised.[18] So this strategy that risked not achieving its objective clearly contributed to polarizing political debate in France and helped fuel what could be called anti-Sarkozyism. Indeed, the UMP under Sarkozy was instrumental in putting confrontation and polarization back to the center of the political arena.

The ideological radicalization of the UMP is also significant in terms of the other political parties. It casts into question the broadly accepted model first postulated by Kirchheimer whereby ideological differences between the parties have given way to a process of ideological demobilization driven, it is argued, by party professionalization and a greater emphasis on electoral objectives.[19] The case of the UMP contradicts this thesis. While the impact of organizational changes is clearly evident within the party, this has not been accompanied by any ideological weakening. Indeed, two aspects that many political analysts tend to separate here continue to go hand in hand: external and internal pressures, and strategic and cultural dimensions. An analysis of the UMP not only reveals the mechanism by which ideologies were reinforced by relating them to changes in the competitive political arena, but it also shows how this was due to mechanisms at work within the party itself.

In turn, ideological changes take their cue not only from national and local cultural factors, but also from the personalities involved. This suggests not only the strategic, but also social and cultural frames that shape ideology. In short, ideological radicalization cannot be simply reduced to a communications strategy disconnected from the intra-partisan dynamic. A case in point is the creation in summer 2010 of the aforementioned group, La Droite Populaire. On Bastille Day (July 14) 2010, this group published a "Charter of the Popular Right Collective" with the objective of "contributing to the action program of the presidential majority."[20] Inveighing against so-called politically correct taboos, this collective first and foremost declared its support for patriotism and economic liberalism. More specifically, the thirty-five signatories, all members of the House of Deputies, presented a very specific profile. First, geographically, most came from regions where the FN had garnered the most support—the south of France and large urban areas (mainly the Paris and Lyon regions). Northern France was represented, although not on a par with the success enjoyed by the FN in this region. From an ideological point of view, the voting patterns of these deputies, their proposed amendments, and their bills and public statements painted an ideological portrait characterized by calls to limit immigrant rights (in terms of social benefits, e.g.), emphasized issues of security and authority (bringing back the death penalty for certain crimes), resisting changing moral values (curtailing rights granted to homosexuals, e.g.), and reasserted national symbols (respect for the flag) and religious identity (criminalization of blasphemy), and so on. Many deputies who signed up to La Droite Populaire have been personally marked by the impact of the Algerian war, either coming from repatriated families who had supported French Algeria, who had fought in the Algerian War, or whose political commitments had been born of the opposition to decolonization. Some had even started their political career in extreme-right youth movements. Most notably, this group did not occupy a marginal position within the party. With the arrival of J-F Copé at the head of the UMP, there was a reshuffle of its senior management. Of the thirty-five La Droite Populaire deputies, twenty-three received a place on the new management team.

A considerable percentage of these members of La Droite Populaire were candidates in the 2012 legislative election and were beaten by the FN. Nonetheless the acclaim they have received within the party and the public arena testifies to the fact that the UMP's center of gravity significantly shifted to the right during Nicolas Sarkozy's tenure. Ideologically, one symptom of this transformation is the way in which many UMP group leaders now identify themselves with the right. Following the presidential and legislative electoral defeats of 2012 and the follow-up to the November 2012 congress, factions were once again permitted within the party after having been in abeyance since its creation (see above). In fact, the establishment of La Droite Populaire was followed by the birth of La Droite Moderne,[21] La Droite Forte,[22] and La France Droite.[23] Moreover, whereas previously the word "right" has not always been in vogue with right-wing party politics in France, it has now become a central reference, with all these groups claiming to represent it. The November 2012 party congress vote on certain party motions provides further proof of this shift to the right—even if this did not profit La Droite Populaire, which received only 9.2 percent of the vote compared with an opposing motion from La Droite Forte, which was proposed by two young *sarkozystes* who embody the UMP's radicalization during the 2012 presidential campaign.

Sarkozyism was a key driver in revamping ideological identification. Strategically, too, the Sarkozy period led to a change in attitude toward the FN. Since the regional elections of 1998 when local alliances were clinched between the right and the radical right in some regional councils,[24] polls have been taken that measure popular support for this strategy. Forming local electoral alliances with the FN was met with steady approval by one-third of right-wing supporters. In 2012[25] such approval increased enormously, with 52 percent of UMP sympathizers supporting the move. A series of indicators therefore provide proof of a clear-cut ideological shift to the right by the UMP during Nicolas Sarkozy's mandate. This transformation was however accompanied by the party pursuing the process of European integration.

The European Card

What can be called the Europeanization of French right wing is in fact a series of widely different processes. Europeanization can first of all be the adoption by party leaders of a more favorable stance on European integration. The term can, however, also indicate the move to transfer organizational models or the dissemination of symbolic references to Europe as a means to legitimize the party or even a form of long-term convergence that has led the Gaullist right to draw closer to the programmatic positions of European conservative parties—a convergence that has deepened with increased European integration. This adoption of more-favorable positions on Europe by a right-wing party drawing on a Gaullist heritage of ambivalence and even hostility to European integration is part of an incremental process that started well before Sarkozyism and before 2002. It was played out between the Maastricht referendum of 1992 and the ratification of the Treaty of Amsterdam in 1999, and caused tensions and divisions. A decisive moment was when the RPR finally joined the European parliamentary group Parti Populaire Européen (PPE). In the opinion of the major players in the operation, it paved the way for the merger and formation of the UMP. It at least in part bridged the gap between the non-Gaullist faction that had already by and large come around to the European view (with the exception of the faction personified by Philippe de Villiers), and another grouping up to then reluctant and indeed opposed to a process of denationalization. The 1990s publicly revealed the divisions within the party caused by the European question that involved leaders, militants, and voters, so much so that Peter Mair considered the Gaullist right in France, like the British right, an exception in the right-wing political arena on account of the divisive effect the European question had on party cohesion.[26] In the 1992 referendum, two-thirds of RPR sympathizers voted "no," and 63 percent of the elected members of the lower house declared they were opposed to the Maastricht Treaty.[27] This, together with the split of the Rassemblement Pour la France (Rally for France; RPF) in 1999 and the defeat of the pro-European right-wing ticket headed by Sarkozy in the 1999 European election, caused severe disarray within the party. Nonetheless, despite widespread internal opposition, the leadership's pro-European position prevailed. It did so, however, by resorting to devious or ambiguous means: avoiding overt appeals to vote in favor of Europe, or with key party figures simply expressing their pro-European positions. Nicolas Sarkozy was one of the first RPR leaders to come out in favor of a "yes" vote at the Maastricht referendum; Alain Juppé also voiced his pro-European views.

The creation of the UMP in 2002 took on board this progressive yet painful process of Europeanization. Indeed, the issue gained in visibility and emphasis. Greater visibility was afforded by a strategy of legitimization based on references to Europe and the mobilizing of models taken from several European right-wing organizations. There was very little real transfer of practices, however. Contacts between right-wing parties within Europe remained limited and superficial. In addition, the pro-European movement was again reinforced within the party when pro-European players, many formerly belonging to the UDF, were taken into the fold when two clearly pro-European leaders, Alain Juppé then Nicolas Sarkozy, were chosen to head the party, and finally when the anti-European factions defected following their unsuccessful attempts to lead opposition to Europe from within. From 2002 to 2007, some of the most anti-European integration groups that had rallied around the UMP, following the brief RPF interlude, finally left the party. Former RPF leader Nicolas Dupont Aignan's Debout la République (Arise the Republic) movement did initially try to put up some opposition from within, but later split off, with Dupont Aigan making an unsuccessful presidential bid in the 2012 election (see table 4.1). Ideological radicalization was not therefore accompanied by anti-European extremism. Nonetheless this pro-Europe stance was at risk of being undermined by the economic crisis and subsequent calls for renationalization. In any event, the UMP was susceptible to internal tensions on account of the tug-of-war between its support for European integration as the party of government and its radicalism on immigration and national identity issues, which was fueled by the effects of globalization.

The UMP entered a new phase in 2012. Having arisen out of a presidential victory and existed until then within the precinct of governmental power, the party now finds itself in opposition. This is also a new phase because the UMP is forced to broach questions left unresolved since its inception: its presidentialization and the selection process of its presidential candidate; the question of open primaries of the kind successfully conducted by the PS; the question of changing its genetically charismatic model with the introduction of internal pluralism, and creating a movement-based organization; and possibly the question of a more deliberative model based on inter-party debate rather than the disciplined, toe-the-line model adopted thus far. It is a new phase also because Sarkozyism has clearly shifted the UMP's ideological center of gravity to the right, paving the way for closer ties with the extreme right-wing FN, a move that, however, would fly in the face of the party as a European party of government.

The controversial election of the new party leader in November/December 2012 has highlighted how difficult this change is proving to be. The uncertainty and the acrimonious election of Jean-François Copé, which was challenged by the François Fillon camp; the accusations of fraud; the calling into question of the party's supervisory bodies; and the generalized defiance expressed within the party has led to an interim management team being set up comprising representatives of the party's two opposing factions with the aim of organizing new leadership elections by September 2013. This episode testifies to the UMP's weak institutionalization and its summary application of the rules it has set itself. It also reveals the lack of any real democratic tradition within the party. Furthermore, the leadership election clearly showed just how far to the right the party has gone. The UMP has emerged from the Sarkozy period a truly different animal.

Notes

Translated from the French by Stephanie Johnson.
1. The question of Nicolas Sarkozy's possible return to party politics remains open. The majority of UMP sympathizers declare they would be in favor (IFOP: *Le Journal du Dimanche* poll, August 19, 2012).
2. Florence Haegel, "The Transformation of the French Right: Institutional Imperatives and Organizational Changes," *French Politics*, 2 (2004):185–202.
3. Anne-Sophie Petitfils, "L'institution partisane à l'épreuve du management. Rhétorique et pratiques managériales dans le recrutement des 'nouveaux adhérents' au sein de l'Union pour un Mouvement Populaire (UMP)," *Politix* 79, no. 3 (2007):53–76.
4. During the 2007 presidential campaign, the party launched a membership promotion campaign priced at €10 per member. Subsequently, basic membership fees were progressively increased to €20 then to €25, associated with a further optional €15 presented as a specific contribution to the electoral campaigns. There are also membership rebates for couples and people under thirty. During the 2012 campaign, prices were once again lowered.
5. The UMP site "Les créateurs du possible" (creators of the possible), inaugurated in January 2010, was closed after a year for its poor take-up.
6. Commission nationale des comptes de campagne et des financements politiques (CNCCP), France's national committee on campaign accounts and political funding. General publication of the accounts of the political parties and groupings during the 2009 financial year, *Journal Officiel: Lois et décrets*, Wednesday, December 29, 2010.
7. Robin Kolodny, "Electoral Partnership: Political Consultants and Political Parties," in *Campaign Warriors. Political Consultants in Elections*, ed. J. Thurber and C. Nelson (Washington, DC: Brooking Institutions Press, 2000), 110–32.

8. For example, a female professional trained at one of Paris' top business schools is in charge of party finances and administration while the head of communication was head-hunted from one of France's largest advertising agencies.
9. Angelo Panebianco, *Political Parties: Organization and power* (Cambridge, UK: Cambridge University Press, 1988).
10. Statement by Jean-Claude Gaudin, June 25, 2007. Quoted in *L'Express* [online.] "Devidjian-Raffarin: une direction à deux têtes pour l'UMP." June 26, 2007. http://www.lexpress.fr/actualite/politique/devedjian-raffarin-une-direction-a-deux-tetes-pour-l-ump_465179.html.
11. Ibid.
12. Florence Haegel, "Nicolas Sarkozy a-t-il radicalisé la droite française ? Changements idéologiques et étiquetage politique," *French Politics, Culture and Society* 29, no. 3 (2011): 62–77.
13. For a more in-depth overview of these developments, see Haegel, "Nicolas Sarkozy a-t-il radicalisé la droite française ?; and Haegel, *Les droites en fusion* (Paris: Presses de Sciences-Po, 2012).
14. Nonna Mayer, "Comment Nicolas Sarkozy a rétréci l'électorat Le Pen," *Revue Française de Science Politique*, 57, no. 3–4 (2007):429–45.
15. "Finally it must be recognized, and I have to say this, we are suffering the consequences of 50 years of insufficiently regulated immigration that has led to failed integration." Speech given in Grenoble, July 30, 2010, to mark the taking of office of the new prefect, available on official Web site of the French president of the republic. See Richard Mallié, "Nicolas Sarkozy–Discours de Grenoble–30 Juillet 2010," *Daily Motion* [online], July 11, 2010, http://www.dailymotion.com/video/xf0ih7_nicolas-sarkozy-discours-de-grenobl_news.
16. Alain Juppé likewise came out against Islamophobia, viewing the position on Islam as causing a cleavage within the UMP. Statement to France Inter, August 28, 2012. See AFP, "Pour Juppé, 'l'islamophobie' est un point de clivage fondamental à l'UMP," *Libération* [online], August 28, 2012, http://www.liberation.fr/politiques/2012/08/28/pour-juppe-l-islamophobie-est-un-point-de-clivage-fondamental-a-l-ump_842327.
17. Kay Arzheimer, "Contextual Factors and the Extreme Right Vote in Western Europe, 1980–2002," *American Journal of Political Research*, 48 (2009): 335–58.
18. Joost Van Spanje and Wouter van der Burg, "The Party as Pariah: The Exclusion of Anti-Immigration Parties and its Effect on their Ideological Positions," *West European Politics* 30, no. 5 (2007):1022–40.
19. Otto Kirchheimer, "The Transformation of Western European Party System," in *Political Parties and Political Development*, ed. J. La Palombara and W. Myron (Princeton, NJ: Princeton University Press, 1966), 177–200.
20. La Droite Populaire, "La Charte du Collectif de la Droite Populaire." July 14, 2010. http://ladroitepopulaire.com/demo/notre-charte/ or http://archive.wikiwix.com/cache/?url=http://ladroitepopulaire.com/demo/notre-charte/&title=Charte%20du%20collectif.
21. Group created by liberals coming from Démocratie Libérale.
22. Group created by the young *sarkozyste* generation who also adopted the 2012 presidential slogan "La France forte" (strong France). One of its leaders, Guillaume Peltier, a member of Nicolas Sarkozy's campaign team, was a former member of the FB youth movement and was national director of Philippe de Villiers' Movement for France (MPF).
23. Group started by Nathalie Kosciusko-Morizet, former Minister for Ecology, and Nicolas Sarkozy's spokesperson during the presidential campaign.
24. These alliances involved UDF-, not RPR-elected members.
25. See Jérôme Fourquet and Marie Gariazzo, *FN et UMP: électorats en fusion ?* (Paris: Fondation Jean Jaurès, 2013), 38.

26. Peter Mair, "The Limited Impact of Europe on National Party System," *West European Politics* 23, no. 4 (2000), 36.
27. Bernard Denni, "Du référendum du 20 septembre 1992 sur l'Union européenne aux élections législatives de mars 1993," in *Le vote sanction. Les élections législatives des 21 et 28 mars 1993*, ed. P. Habert, P. Perrineau, and C. Ysmal (Paris: Presses de la Fondation nationale des sciences politiques, 1993), 91–109, and survey carried out by l'*Express* that interviewed 285 deputies of the RPR majority and UDF-elected members in 1993. See *L'Express* [online], "Exclusif: Ce que pensent vraiment les deputes UDF et RPR" July 8 1993, http://www.lexpress.fr/informations/exclusif-ce-que-pensent-vraiment-les-deputes-udf-et-rpr_595216.html.

Chapter 5

The Year of the Rose
The Socialist Victory of 2012

Gérard Grunberg

After ten years in opposition, the French Socialists returned to power in the spring 2012 elections. How is this victory to be explained and interpreted? First, it should be noted that the Socialist victory cannot be credited to the party alone. Since François Mitterrand's election in 1981 and his reelection in 1988, no Socialist has won a presidential election. In 2002 the incumbent Socialist prime minister, Lionel Jospin, was eliminated from the first round of elections and in 2007 the Socialist candidate, Ségolène Royal, lost by a large margin to Nicolas Sarkozy, head of the UMP.

The triumph of 2012 was most commonly explained by the incumbent president's unpopular record. It was widely thought that François Hollande would have won by default, the general attitude of "anyone but Sarkozy" driving the incumbent president's defeat. Certainly, the Socialist victory was first of all rooted in the disinclination of a significant majority of the French to see Sarkozy reelected. But the weakening of Nicolas Sarkozy's position was not the sole factor that explains the Socialist victory. In particular, Sarkozy's respectable results during the second round of the latest presidential elections—48.4 percent—illustrated that, even if weakened, he had fought back, confirming that electoral forecasts could not be based with confidence on the opinion polls. Even if the incumbent president was experiencing difficulties in the period leading up to the 2012 elections, an adversary capable of prevailing over him was still necessary.

In addition to the public's disappointment with Sarkozy, the Socialist victory can be attributed to four elements. The first was François Hollande's political career and achievements. The second was the PS's estab-

---

Notes for this chapter begin on page 87.

lishment of an open primary system to designate the Socialist candidate for the presidential elections, a procedure that strongly benefited the party and its candidate. The third factor was the spillover effect of the presidential victory on the parliamentary elections that followed in its wake. The last reason was the territorial reach of the PS, which permitted that party, owing to the advantage of majority voting in two rounds, to represent the left in the second round in a majority of parliamentary districts and thus conquer an absolute majority of seats in the National Assembly.

François Hollande's Political Career

Only the PS could select a candidate capable of defeating the incumbent president. Indeed, since 1981 only the two large parties of government, the Gaullists (RPR, which later became the UMP) and the Socialists, have won these elections. Since the establishment of the five-year presidential term and the inversion of the election calendar in 2002, national elections have been transformed into a contest conducted in four rounds—two each for the presidential and parliamentary elections. Only these two parties have any prospect of winning these four rounds of voting and, thus, of exercising complete power. Since the Fifth Republic is a mixed parliamentary and presidential regime, the president cannot utilize executive power to its full extent unless he holds a majority in the National Assembly.

In short, defeat of the incumbent president would have been impossible unless the PS was able to advance a credible candidate in opposition to him. With Nicolas Sarkozy's popularity eroding since 2010, the party expected that Dominique Strauss-Kahn, former finance minister and IMF managing director, was its ideal candidate. Polls indicated that he had a good chance of beating the incumbent president. But his arrest in New York on May 15, 2011, left the PS dumbfounded and disoriented. The party leadership pressed First Secretary Martine Aubry to run instead. However, this candidacy appeared to be pro forma and victory seemed less than certain. Aubry had been struggling to establish her leadership after her narrow win to become head of the party at the 2008 Reims Congress. As a result, a presidential victory for the PS seemed uncertain. Nevertheless, a year later, François Hollande was elected president of the republic. In order to explain Hollande's victory it is necessary to examine his career track and actions in the run-up to the 2012 presidential elections.

Like other Fifth Republic presidents, François Hollande exhibited his political ambition very early on. In 1974, when he was twenty at the University of HEC Paris (Hautes Études Commerciales de Paris), he was in charge of the committee in support of François Mitterrand's presidential campaign. Five years later he joined the PS. After graduating from ENA (Ecole Nationale d'Administration) and entering the national Court of Auditors (Cour des Comptes), he became special adviser to the president following Mitterrand's election in 1981 and director of the Government Spokesperson's Office under Prime Minister Pierre Mauroy in 1983.

François Hollande's political career has been remarkably multifaceted. Entering the executive branch in 1981 as part of the presidential team, he supplemented that experience with a partisan career within the party and as a locally elected MP. In the meantime, he climbed the partisan hierarchy within the PS. After the Socialists' parliamentary defeat in 1986, he rejoined the team of experts surrounding Lionel Jospin, first secretary of the party since 1981. In 1994, he was named party national secretary for economic issues. After the refusal of Jacques Delors, with whom he had worked in the club "Exchange and Projects," to present his candidacy in 1995, he began associating himself with Lionel Jospin, who named him spokesperson of his 1995 presidential campaign. After his defeat to Chirac in 1995, Jospin appointed him spokesperson of the PS and then as acting first secretary of the party following the Socialists' parliamentary victory in 1997. At the Brest party congress of Brest that same year, François Hollande was elected first secretary by beating Jean-Luc Mélenchon, who represented the left of the party. He remained in this position until the Reims Congress of 2008.

Similar to François Mitterrand, Hollande adds to his career within the party a rich experience in local elections. In 1981 he was elected city councilman for the commune of Ussel in the department of the Corrèze, the fiefdom of Jacques Chirac. Like the radical Henri Queuille and Gaullist Jacques Chirac, Hollande would become political leader of this electorally strategic department. In 2001 he was elected mayor of Tulle; he was reelected in 2008, winning the first round with 72 percent of the vote. At the same time, he was elected to the General Council of the Corrèze of which he accepted the presidency, a post that had been held by the right since 1970. Having predicated his 2012 presidential candidacy on the renewal of his leadership position in the General Council, he officially declared himself a candidate at the Socialist primary in Tulle several hours after his reelection for this position on March 31, 2011.

In turn, on the national level, François Hollande was first elected to the National Assembly in the 1988 parliamentary elections for the first district of the Corrèze. He then became secretary of the Commission of Finance and Planning, followed by a position as reporter of the defense budget at the National Assembly. Having lost his seat in 1993, he recovered it in 2002, holding it until 2007. Hence, Hollande successfully wore two hats as parliamentary representative and leader of one of the two governing parties, a requisite "cursus to follow" for anyone aspiring to the highest political function.

Even if François Hollande has by most measures enjoyed a successful political career, 2005 was to be an annus horribilis that nearly broke him.[1] Indeed, during the previous year he had taken the risk of proclaiming his support for the ratification of the European Constitutional Treaty and of organizing an internal referendum within the PS over this question. While he won this referendum, the initiative fundamentally divided the PS, particularly since it appeared to some of his rivals as a first step toward a presidential candidacy. Party members who voted against the referendum initiated an open national campaign against the leadership's position.

Furthermore, the victory of the "Non" in the national referendum considerably weakened the first secretary's position. Rather than continuing to fight naysayers, he attempted to reunify the party under his leadership. However, the motion he put forward at the Le Mans Congress of 2005 was criticized for lacking any real political content and qualified as weak by observers, and so instead brought serious harm to his leadership. Lacking sufficient public support and criticized within the party, he decided to not run in the 2007 presidential elections and even withdrew from his position as first secretary in the wake of the Reims Congress in 2008. The position was then filled by Martine Aubry, with whom he did not get along. This opened a new period for him: he found himself isolated and lacking public support. In the eyes of the French, he was a man lacking in charisma and leadership qualities. No one at the time would have guessed his political future.

Looking back, however, François Hollande was not entirely unprepared when he embarked on his journey through the desert in 2008. He had acquired important experience as a political leader and inside knowledge of the party, which he had led for eleven years and where he had established a number of personal connections, even though he had never wanted to develop his own political movement within it. Above all, he rediscovered his freedom of speech and a real personal political independence. By deciding to not run for president in 2007, he managed to preserve whatever little political capital he had left. Certainly, under his leadership, the party experienced some defeats, but it did not suffer any electoral catastrophes. In addition, the image he projected as a unifier and man of synthesis was not perceived entirely negatively in the period of profound internal division that plagued the party beginning in 2008. After all, throughout his mandate as first secretary, he had built a reputation as a moderate Socialist who was up to speed with the needs of the Socialist electorate. Isolated, but at the same time free of the partisan hustle, he finally made the fundamental choice to become a presidential candidate in the 2012 elections.

Despite the fact that this was a mature and calculated decision, based on Hollande's determination and self-confidence—qualities which are indispensable for embarking on such an arduous journey—the presidential election was above all a personal adventure for him, even if gaining the support of one of the two major parties remained essential.

The Open Primary, A Propitious Innovation

Despite the fact that it was limited to party members, the 2006 primary contest to designate the Socialist candidate for the presidential elections of the following year raised a strong interest among voters, particularly due to the campaign and personality of Ségolène Royal. Media and opinion polls transformed this closed primary election into a political event of national significance.[2] In the wake of Ségolène Royal's defeat in the presidential elections, she along with other Socialist leaders pronounced herself in favor of introducing an open primary system to designate the Socialist candidate for the subsequent presidential elections. After long hesitating, Socialist leaders and Martine Aubry herself approved this procedure in 2009, and it was adopted in 2010 by an overwhelming majority of party members. Every voter who signed a declaration of principles committing himself or herself to supporting the values of the left—"I acknowledge the values of the left of the republic, the project of a society of liberty, of equality, of fraternity, of secularism, of justice, and of joined progress"—and donated the minimum contribution of €1 could henceforth participate in this consultation.

The introduction of the open primary benefited the PS and particularly François Hollande in a number of ways. First, it permitted the party to survive, without serious damage, the forced withdrawal of Dominique Strauss-Kahn, who had been widely seen to this point as the only Socialist candidate capable of defeating the incumbent president. No other candidate had solidified his position, but the fact that the party had already adopted the principle of the open primary assisted Hollande at this crucial juncture. In fact, even before Strauss-Kahn's withdrawal, a number of Socialist figures had confirmed their intention to run in the primary. Most prominent among them was François Hollande, despite the desire of the party machine to transform this competitive process into a unanimous ratification of Strauss-Kahn's candidature, that was to be legitimized through the primary process. François Hollande appeared most determined to confront the former in the primary. The fact that his decision was announced so early proved, once Strauss-Kahn was out of the race, a decisive advantage since voters interpreted it as a sign of true commitment. In turn, even before Strauss-Kahn's withdrawal, François Hollande had improved his public image. In the wake of the former's withdrawal, he headed the list of potential presidential candidates from the left in opinion polls conducted by the French Public Survey Institute (SOFRES), coming ahead of Martine Aubry who, pressed by the party machine, prepared her campaign without much enthusiasm.

Moreover, the innovation of the open primary provoked public interest as well as strong media coverage and increased electoral participation: more than 3 million voters voted in at least one of the primary's two rounds. French voters of all political persuasions found this primary to be a success for the PS. And to the extent that on the left only the PS was capable of organizing such a consultation, this innovation further strengthened its status as the left's only viable presidential party.

In turn, the introduction of the open primary permitted François Hollande to effectively launch his campaign long before the presidential elections, thus developing his themes and affirming his personality among voters. Six candidates presented themselves in this primary, including a leftist radical, thereby transformed the primary into a citizens' primary. This procedure permitted Hollande, who had been relatively isolated inside the party, to set off on an equal footing with candidates drawn from the party's leadership. In fact, the public even preferred his independence. The opinion polls continuously ranked him as a favorite, securing his position throughout the primary campaign. In the first round, on October 9, he thus garnered a clear lead.[3] In the second, he prevailed decisively with 56.6 percent of the valid votes. A nomination convention was organized on October 22, the goal of which was to demonstrate in American fashion that the party stood united behind its candidate.

Alone but determined to face down the party machine, Hollande relied entirely on personalizing his campaign, a move typical of presidential elections and from which he benefited greatly. The primary allowed him to prevail without support from party insiders and to acquire the personal credibility that thus far he had been missing. Finally, his victory in the primary transformed Hollande into a legitimate and irrefutable candidate of the PS and allowed him to accrue legitimacy on the party's left. Despite the continuing division within the PS, this gave him an important advantage in the presidential election itself.

Though his political association with the center left was decisive in his primary victory, it also crucially contributed to his presidential win. Certainly, his sixty campaign commitments contained some symbolic leftist measures, such as increasing taxes on high incomes and capital, returning the retirement age to sixty (for workers who had entered employment early), and refusing to ratify, in case of victory, the Fiscal Stability Treaty (the Fiscal Compact) signed by twenty-five member states of the EU in March 2012. These commitments allowed him to unify the party behind his campaign. But at the same time, his principal commitment, which he reiterated on multiple occasions, was to reduce the budget deficit to 3 percent by 2013 and bring it into balance by 2017—a commitment identified with a pro-European stance that also gave him a centrist appeal.[4] As opinion polls indicated, this unifying position allowed Hollande to claim an advantage over Nicolas Sarkozy from the outset, which meant that he remained the favorite throughout the campaign. In addition, François Hollande refused to question the agreement negotiated between the PS's leadership and the Greens (Europe Ecology), which, while very favorable to the latter, allowed the Socialists to neutralize the environmentalist current and to subordinate it to Socialist leadership. Correlatively, in regard to the Front de Gauche, of which the PCF was the principal component, Hollande adopted François Mitterrand's 1981 position, according to which any government agreement between the two parties would necessarily depend on the acceptance by the latter of the commitments made by the Socialist candidate during the campaign. Finally, in the course of this campaign, François Hollande was doggedly effective in discrediting accusations by the right of his indecision and weakness of character. His debate with the incumbent president between the two rounds was decisive in this respect because it presented the image of a future president that his competitor could not counter by invoking his authority and experience. Thus, François Hollande managed to present himself as a credible alternative to Nicolas Sarkozy.

Hollande's Presidential Victory and its Parliamentary Spillover

In the first round of the presidential elections on April 22, the Socialist candidate led the polls with 28.6 percent of the valid votes (table 5.1). He overtook the other candidates from the left by a significant margin. The Front de Gauche candidate, Jean-Luc Mélenchon, obtained 11.1 percent of the votes, a disappointing and unexpected result; the Green candidate, 2.3 percent, and the Trotskyist candidates (the NPA and Lutte Ouvrière (Worker's Struggle)) together received only 1.7 percent. The Socialist domination of the left was, therefore, confirmed. In the second round, then, the old rule of republican discipline drove the candidates from the Front de Gauche and the Greens, who were eliminated, to redirect their votes to the Socialist candidate or, at least, take them away from the incumbent president. François Hollande's victory was rendered possible by the massive shift (80 percent) of support by the first round of Jean-Luc Mélenchon

Table 5.1. 2012 Presidential and Parliamentary Election Results

	First round of presidential elections (%)	Second round of presidential elections (%)	First round of parliamentary elections (%)	Second round of parliamentary elections (%)
Participation	80.4	80.3	57.2	56.3
Blank and invalid votes	1.9	4.7	1.6	3.9
Far-left (Arthaud+Poutou)	1.7	–	1.0	–
Left Front/ Communist Party (Mélenchon)	11.1	–	6.9	1.1
Socialist Party (Hollande)	28.6	51.6	29.2	40.6
Radical Party of the Left	–		1.7	2.5
Miscellaneous Left	–	–	3.6	3.3
Europe Ecology— The Greens (Joly)	2.3	–	5.6	3.8
Centrist, including Democratic Movement (Bayrou)	9.1	–	2.3	0.5
Union for a Popular Movement UMP (Sarkozy)	27.1	48.4	26.6	37.0
New Center and Radical Party	–	–	2.1	3.0
Radical Party—PRV	–	–	1.2	1.5
Miscellaneous Right (Dupont-Aignan)	1.8	–	4.2	2.5
Far-Right, including National Front (Le Pen)	18.0	–	13.8	3.8
Miscellaneous (Cheminade)	0.3	–	1.8	0.4
Total	100.0	100.0	100.0	100.0

Source: Ministère de l'Intérieur

and Eva Joly voters to his candidacy in the second round, while Nicolas Sarkozy collected only about half of Marine Le Pen's votes. In the second round, Hollande won against the incumbent president with 51.6 percent, thereby becoming the seventh president of the Fifth Republic.

Similarly to 1981, 1988, 2002, and 2007, the elected president benefited from the spillover effect of the presidential elections in the ensuing parliamentary elections (table 5.1). With 29 percent of the votes cast, the PS arrived on top, followed by the UMP, the party of the incumbent president, which obtained close to 27 percent. In total, during the first round the candidates from the PS and left-wing radicals as well as those of the Greens who were supported by the PS—which allotted them sixty districts in which to compete—obtained close to one-third of the vote, their best result since 1988, thereby securing a win against the UMP and its allies. By contrast, the Front de Gauche, essentially comprising Communist candidates, garnered only about 7 percent of the votes. Hence, the Socialists' domination of the left was even more pronounced than in the presidential elections. Similar to the parliamentary elections of 2002 and 2007, Socialist votes represented almost two-thirds of the left's votes. But the Socialist victory in 2012 was even more pronounced than in these two elections, exceeding 30 percent of votes cast (see table 5.2).

Round Two of the Parliamentary Elections: Socialist Supremacy and the Vote

In the first round, twenty-two Socialists were elected. And the Socialists or their allies from the first round, the environmentalists and left-wing radicals, were present in all 541 voting districts, with the Socialists holding the vast majority. On the other hand, candidates from the Front de Gauche were only present in twenty-two districts as compared to the 558 districts in which they had been represented during the first round. The effects of the two-tiered majoritarian system and the withdrawal on the left also ensured the Socialist candidates' victory. Thus, in the second round (table 5.3), the Socialists and left-wing radicals obtained 46.4 percent of the votes, that is to say eight points more than candidates from the UMP, the Greens (3.8 percent), and the Front de Gauche (1 percent). The Socialist candidates, the left-wing radicals, and miscellaneous leftists obtained 90 percent of the votes of the left, with the other 8 percent for the Greens and 2 percent for the Front de Gauche. There was, thus, a near total Socialist domination. The translation of these results into seats gave the PS an absolute majority of seats in the National Assembly for the second time in the history of the Fifth Republic, the first being in 1981. After the formation of political groups in the National Assembly, the Socialist group represented 88 percent of all left-wing MPs. In the government, the left (which excluded the Front de Gauche after it decided not to participate in a government under Socialist leadership) included 328 delegates (an

Table 5.2. First-Round Presidential Election Results (2002–12)

Candidates' Political Association	2002 (%)	2007 (%)	2012 (%)
Far-Left	10.5	7.2	1.7
French Communist Party (PCF)/ National Front	3.4	1.9	11.1
Socialist Party (PS)	16.2	25.9	28.6
Radical Party of the Left	2.3	–	–
Greens	5.3	1.5	2.3
Left	**27.2**	**29.3**	**42.0**
Left + Far-Left	**37.7**	**36.5**	**43.7**
Union for French Democracy (UDF)	6.8	*	*
Union for a Popular Movement (UMP)	19.9	31.2	27.1
Miscellaneaous Right	5.1	2.2	1.8
Right	**31.8**	**33.4**	**28.9**
National Front	16.9	10.4	18.0
Far-Right	2.3	–	–
Right +Far-Right	**51.0**	**43.8**	**46.9**
Center	–	18.6	9.1
Union for French Democracy (UDF) 2007/ Democratic Movement (Modem)			
Miscellaneous (neither Left, nor Right)	9.4	1.1	0.3
Other greens	1.9	–	
Total	**100**	**100**	**100**
% PS+UMP/total	**36.1**	**57.1**	**55.7**

*In 2007, results for the Union for French Democracy's candidate, François Bayrou, were classified outside the Right.
Source: Ministère de l'Intérieur

absolute majority requiring 289 seats) (table 5.4). These numbers attested to the unconditional victory of the PS and defeat for the Front de Gauche, which could not form a parliamentary group. Indeed, the latter lost nearly half of its members, without calling on five representatives from overseas, with the necessary minimum to form a group being fifteen members. The French partisan system remains structured, therefore, on the opposition of the large presidential parties—the PS and UMP. Between them, these account for nearly 90 percent of the seats in the National Assembly.

Table 5.3. Second-Round Parliamentary Election Results (2002–12)

Candidates' Party Association	2002 519 ballots (%)	2007 467 ballots (%)	2012 541 ballots (%)
French Communist Party	3.3	2.7	1.1
Socialist Party (PS)—The Radical Party of the Left—Miscellaneous left	38.7	46	46.4
Greens	3.2	0.5	3.8
Union for French Democracy (UDF)/Democratic Movement (Modem)	3.9	0.6	0.5
Union for a Popular Movement (UMP)—Radical Party	47.3	47.8	38.5
New Center (PSLE)	–	1.8	3.0
Miscellaneous Right	1.5	–	2.5
National Front	1.9	0.1	3.8
Miscellaneous	–	0.5	0.4
Total	100	100	100
Socialist Party (PS) + Union for a Popular Movement (UMP)	84.7	93.8	85.0

Source: Ministère de l'Intérieur

Table 5.4. Parliamentary Groups in the National Assembly (June 27, 2012)

SRC (Socialist, Radical, Citizen, and Miscellaneous Left)	279+ 16 related = 295
UMP (Union for a Popular Movement)	185 + 11 related = 196
UDI (Democrats and Independents Union)	29
ECO (Greens)	18
GDR (Democratic and Republican Left) (among which the Left Front)	15
RRDP Radical, Republican, Democrat, and Progressive	15
NI Unregistered (among which 2 from National Front and 1 from Democratic Movement	9
Total	**577 (absolute majority: 289)**
Left from the government SRC+ECO+RRDP	328
Total Left SRC+ECO+RRDP+GDR	343
Right UMP+UDI	225
Left + Right	568

Source: Ministère de l'Intérieur

Like his predecessors in 1981, 2002, and 2007, the new president thus enjoyed an absolute majority in the National Assembly and could select the prime minister of his choice. (see table 5.5). He named Jean-Marc Ayrault, former president of the Socialist group at the National Assembly, mayor of Nantes, and a close personal and political ally who like him was both a reformist and a pro-European. The new majority, which includes the PS, the Greens, and radicals of the left, is nevertheless divided over certain key issues. For example, during the vote on the Fiscal Compact that was conducted on October 9, 2012, the law was approved by 264 Socialist MPs, 3 Greens, and 14 radicals, while being opposed by 20 Socialists, 12 Greens, and 2 radicals. Moreover, all the parliamentary members from the Front de Gauche voted against. In turn, out of the 70 votes against the compact, 47 came from the left. In the senate, the government needed the votes of the right for the proposition to pass. Thus, the European question continues to divide the left and the Greens' affiliation to the majority is not clearly established. Certainly, the Socialist group constitutes a numerical majority in parliament, but politically, the government is not guaranteed, even in the National Assembly, a favorable vote on all of the legislative proposals that it presents.

In addition, contrary to François Mitterrand in 1981 and Lionel Jospin in 1997, François Hollande could not easily put forth a candidate for the party's leadership. At the Toulouse Congress in October 2012, the roll supported by the head of state and the incumbent first secretary collected only 68 percent of the votes with only one of the candidacies surpassing the 50 percent mark, the left's motion amassing 13 percent, and the remainder of the vote divided among three other propositions. And the new first secretary, who was supported by the president, obtained only 72 percent of the vote versus 28 percent for the left-wing candidate. François Hollande is therefore far from enjoying the unanimous authority over his party that

Table 5.5. Cumulative Results of the 2012 Parliamentary Elections

	First round (%)	Second round (%)
Far-Left	1.0	–
Left	47.0	51.3
Center	2.3	0.5
Right	34.1	44.0
Far-Right	13.8	3.8
Miscellaneous	1.8	0.4
Total	100.0	100.0
Total Left + Right	81.1	95.3

Source: Ministère de l'Intérieur

François Mitterrand possessed in 1981. Moreover, it should be noted that after six months in power, the new president's popularity has considerably weakened. There is no doubt that his term will not be smooth sailing!

Epilogue: François Hollande and the Return of the Mitterrandian Compromise

Much like François Mitterrand in 1981, during his campaign François Hollande questioned the excessive powers of the incumbent president of the right. He condemned Nicolas Sarkozy's "hyperpresidency" and promised to counterbalance the powers of the executive in favor of the parliament and to grant actual power to the prime minister, an old demand of the PS, which had never fully accepted the Fifth Republic's institutions. But in reality, the logic of the regime, which was reinforced by the establishment in 2000 of the five-year presidential term and then by the institution of the Socialist open primary system, pushed the new president to become, much like his predecessors, the uncontested head of the executive. Indeed, Hollande sought, in contrast to Nicolas Sarkozy's image, to create an image for himself as the "normal president." However, in reality, his method of exercising power will most likely not fundamentally differ from that of his predecessors, even if every president holds a personal conception and practice of his role. Therefore, what this question will possibly boil down to is the new president's reaffirmation of François Mitterrand's compromise with regard to the institutions of the Fifth Republic during his presidency. Everything points to the prediction that François Hollande will in reality serve out his term as the Fifth Republic's seventh president, even if some members of his party had promoted in the run-up to the election a fundamental constitutional revision and the establishment of a sixth parliamentary republic in which the prime minister would hold the executive power. In his inaugural speech, Hollande declared, "At this moment, when I bear responsibility for our country's destiny and for representing it in the world, I pay tribute to my predecessors—all those before me who have held the responsibility of leading the Republic: Charles de Gaulle, who put his prestige at the service of France's greatness and sovereignty, Georges Pompidou, who made the industrial imperative a national challenge, Valéry Giscard d'Estaing, who re-launched society's modernization, François Mitterrand, who did so much for freedom and social progress, Jacques Chirac, who marked his commitment to the values of the Republic, and Nicolas Sarkozy, to whom I extend my best wishes for the new life that opens up before him."[5] How can one not see this declaration as a refusal to make any changes to the republic!

François Hollande finds himself in a particularly difficult situation both domestically at the European level. He has demonstrated his determination to become president. He has extensive power at his disposal. What is left to see is what kind of captain he will be in these tumultuous times. It is too early to deliberate conclusively on such conjectures. Machiavelli believed that the prince should simultaneously exhibit the cunning of the fox and the strength of the lion. Throughout his career, François Hollande has shown real skill, but not without cunning. Will he be the leader that the French expect in the difficult times ahead? Will he be able to transform himself into a lion once the moment comes?

Notes

1. Alain Bergounioux and Gérard Grunberg, *Le long remords du pouvoir. Le parti socialiste français, 1905-1992*. Paris: Fayard, 1992. Republished as: *Les socialistes français et le pouvoir. L'ambition et le remords*. Paris: Hachette, 2007.)
2. See Gérard Grunberg, "I paradossi dei socialisti francesi." In *La Francia di Sarkozy*, edited by G. Baldini and M. Lazar, 127–142. Bologna: Il Mulino, 2007.
3. Results of the first round of the primary:
    Voters: 2,665,013
    Valid votes: 2,650,259
    Arnaud Montebourg: 455,609 votes or 17.2 percent
    Martine Aubry: 806,189 votes or 30.4 percent
    Jean-Michel Baylet: 17,055 votes or 0.6 percent
    Manuel Valls: 149,103 votes or 5.6 percent
    François Hollande: 1,038,207 votes or 39.2 percent
    Results of the second round:
    Voters: 2,860,157
    Valid votes: 2,841,167
    Martine Aubry: 1,233,899 votes or 43.4 percent
    François Hollande: 1,607,268 votes or 56.6 percent
4. For the economic aspects of the program and presidential campaign of François Hollande, see Jacques Fayette's contribution to this edition.
5. François Hollande, "Discours d'investiture de Monsieur François Hollande," May 15, 2012. http://www.elysee.fr/declarations/article/discours-de-m-le-president-de-la-republique-ceremonie-d-investiture/.

Chapter 6

The Pyrrhic Victory of the Radical Left

Philippe Buton

In the 2002 French presidential election, the highest tally obtained by a candidate politically to the left of the PS was 5.7 percent of the total vote. These votes were for the candidate backed by the Trotskyist organization Lutte Ouvrière, Arlette Laguiller. In 2007 this tally was 4.1 percent, with the highest number of votes received by Olivier Besancenot, the candidate of another Trotskyist organization, the Ligue Communiste Révolutionnaire (Revolutionary Communist League). In 2012, however, the highest result obtained by a candidate situated, as per the traditional expression "on the left of the left," was 11.1 percent of the vote, for Jean-Luc Mélenchon. Mélenchon was a candidate for the party Front de Gauche, an electoral coalition uniting a few smaller far-left groups, in particular the Parti de Gauche, the name of the faction formed by Mélenchon's followers after he left the PS in 2008, and the PCF, which was created in 1920, led for a long time by Maurice Thorez and Jacques Duclos, and which, for decades, dominated the French left. Moreover, Jean-Luc Mélenchon obtained 11.1 percent of the vote after reaching nearly 15 percent in multiple preelectoral polls. There has therefore been a temptation for certain observers to determine that there is a new radical surge in the French electorate.[1]

In the first part of this chapter, we will test—and invalidate—this hypothesis. In order to do so, it is first necessary to contextualize, if not decrypt, the electoral success of Jean-Luc Mélenchon, and for this purpose to reinsert it into the history of the radical vote in France, a vote that has always been high but whose internal components have been transformed over the past few decades. Such a retrospective analysis allows for the conclusion that the recent breakthrough of Jean-Luc Mélenchon completes

Notes for this chapter begin on page 97.

a third stage of the electoral expression of French radicalism: the disappearance of an identity-based and ideological vote in favor of a media-based one.

The Strong Tradition of the Radical Left Vote

First, it is correct not to limit oneself to the analysis of this or that campaign or of this or that election, but rather to consider the entirety of the radical vote and analyze it within a certain time frame.[2] Table 6.1 reveals that the *vote de rupture* (radical left vote) has always been a real force in France and, as such, the perceived radical surge of 2012 should be appropriately nuanced: it is valid relative to the preceding presidential election (+5.3 percent), but less so in the medium term (–2.3 percent relative to the 1969–2007 average, and –0.2 percent relative to the 1981–2007 average).

In reality, the important novelty of 2012 was less the radical vote than its mutation, that is, the reversal of the balance of power between its two traditional components: the Communist and the Trotskyist vote. Table 6.2 elucidates this point and shows the progressive transformation of the radical vote in France. The PCF's electoral crisis (with 15.3 percent of the vote in 1981, i.e., -6 percent relative to 1969), followed by its decline (6.8 percent in 1988), and ultimately its marginalization (3.4 percent in 2002), were not

Table 6.1. The Radical Left Vote in Presidential Elections (1969–2012)

Presidential Election Year	Total radical votes (% of total votes)
1969	25.9
1981	18.7
1988	11.3
1995	13.9
2002	13.9
2007	7.6
2012	12.9

The number of registered voters combines the results obtained by the following candidates: Duclos (PCF), Rocard (PSU), Krivine (Trotskyist) in 1969; Marchais (PCF), Bouchardeau (PSU), Laguiller (Trotskyist) in 1981; Lajoinie (PCF), Juquin (PCF dissident), Laguiller (Trotskyist), Boussel (Trotskyist) in 1988; Hue (PCF), Laguiller (Trotskyist) in 1995; Hue (PCF), Laguiller (Trotskyist), Besancenot (Trotskyist), Gluckstein (Trotskyist) in 2002; Buffet (PCF), Laguiller (Trotskyist), Besancenot (Trotskyist), Schivardi (Trotskyist) in 2007; Mélenchon (Front de Gauche), Artaud (Trotskyist), Poutou (Trotskyist) in 2012. The PCF having already called for votes for François Mitterrand in the first round, 1974 Presidential Election cannot be taken into account. That year, the revolutionary candidates were Laguiller (Trotskyist) and Krivine (Trotskyist).

Source: Ministère de l'Intérieur

Table 6.2. The Weight of the French Communist Party in the Radical Left Vote in French Presidential Elections

Presidential Election Year	Total radical left vote (%)	Communist vote (%)	Trotskyist vote (%)	Relative weight of the PCF (%)
1969	25.9	21.3	1	82
1974		–	2.7	
1981	18.7	15.3	2.3	82
1988	11.3	6.8	2.4	60
1995	13.9	8.6	5.3	62
2002	13.9	3.4	10.5	25
2007	7.6	1.9	5.7	25
2012	12.9	11.1	1.7	87

Source: Ministère de l'Intérieur

representative of the disappearance of the radical vote, but rather of its mutation: within it, orthodox communism lost, step by step, its relative importance (going from 80 percent, to 60 percent, to finally 25 percent), to the benefit of the Trotskyist movement which has seen consistent growth: with 1 percent of the votes in 1969, an average of 2.5 percent between 1974–88, and a 7.2 percent average between 1995–2007. This progressive marginalization of the PCF was ostensibly reversed in 2012, given that the alliance to which the PCF belongs (Front de Gauche) obtained 87 percent of the radical vote, that is, 87 percent of the votes given to parties politically to the left of the PS. The PCF did not spare any effort or compromise in achieving this result. The principal compromise was to accept, for the first time (with the exception of the episode of 1974, which was of a very different nature)[3] to fall into line behind a non-party member: Jean-Luc Mélenchon, a former Socialist minister. This choice was particularly wise given that Mélenchon proved to be an excellent candidate.

A Charismatic Orator

The Front de Gauche candidate knew how to play in the big leagues. Far from the approved speeches, unattractiveness, and double-talk that Communist leaders often present, Jean-Luc Mélenchon knew how to use the most modern forms of political communication. First, he rode the Internet wave and used social media, including Twitter and Facebook. He also rejuvenated seemingly outdated forms of political communication, such as posters and meetings. Some of Mélenchon's posters are direct and original. For example, one makes an explicit reference to May 1968—"Citoyen, ceci est ton pavé (Citizen, this is your paving stone [the projectiles used by protestors against the police during the May 1968 riots]),"[4] indicating the voting ballot—or one which takes up Sarkozy's curse at a critic—"Casse toi, pov'con" (Get lost, asshole).[5] Mélenchon also invented a new form of assembly that met with real success: the outdoor campaign meeting, perhaps drawing on the traditional speech of the annual Communist grand assembly, that of the celebration of *L'Humanité*. He also perfectly mastered diverse oratory techniques, from speeches at meetings to televised debates to interviews with journalists. In each situation, his remarks, adapted to include the sound-bites intended to be taken up in audiovisual summaries, and often pronounced with a dramatic touch—whether by maintaining a certain suspense or by feigning righteous indignation—were reproduced.[6] At the same time, Jean-Luc Mélenchon forced the PCF to adopt a type of propaganda distant from its usual tactics, in particular through the personalization of political debate.

Upon examination of the posters produced by the Parti de Gauche for the presidential election—and the same observation holds for the 2012 legislative elections that followed it—it is striking to see the hegemonic presence of the candidate: in most cases, Mélenchon's portrait takes up more than half of the visual surface of the posters. In this respect, it is useful to compare the three official campaign posters of the presidential campaigns of 1981 (Georges Marchais), 2002 (Robert Hue), and 2012 (Jean-Luc Mélenchon).[7] In the first, Georges Marchais is photographed at the head of a group of workers in a combative and dominant position, complementing the text of the poster: "L'anti Giscard." In the second, Robert Hue is shown with two other people (of nondefined social status, the words "the people" having replaced the words "the workers") and in a posture of dialogue, rather than of leadership. But in the last, only Mélenchon is present, with a conquering posture, taking on a presidential and quasimartial attitude—upright, photographed from his torso and above, in suit and red tie, gazing into the distance to better represent the future he incarnates with the slogan, "Prenez le pouvoir" (Take the power). Mélenchon broke neatly from the customary reticence of the left, preferring personalization. This reticence was largely shared by the far-left candidates: in her first campaign, the Trotskyist candidate Arlette Laguiller went so far as to not appear visually on some of her posters. Following this decision, the Trotskyists knew that they should at least in part play the personalization game, though never to the degree of Mélenchon in the 2012 campaign.

Moreover, the acceptance of this personalization is in sync with the institutional and emotional sentiments of the French. Since the 1958–62 period, which saw the creation of the Fifth Republic followed by de Gaulle's reform instituting direct universal suffrage, the French have known that the personal role of the president they choose is crucial. This translates into high voter scrutiny of the presidential candidates, in contrast to other elections, in particular those held at the regional and, especially, European levels. This institutional factor is compounded by a second, emotive one. France has experienced for many years a crisis in its social organizations (parties, unions) and representative institutions (the parliament, and political groups in general). This crisis has been accompanied by a strong depoliticization and weakening of collective mobilization movements (strikes, protests, etc.). In this situation, the temptation, typical of the French, toward Bonapartism and its Gaullist resurrection—i.e., of waiting for a savior to arrive and resolve France's problems[8]—contributes to the easy popular infatuation for this or that personality. At the time of the previous presidential election, this same emotional factor had benefited (though in unequal proportions) both candidates in the second round (Nicolas Sarkozy and Ségolène Royal), who were both out of sync with the political and cultural habits of their parties, and who were appeasing the taste for the miraculous that a large part of the French electorate thirsts for. And now, at last, two obstacles that for a long time had opposed strong personalization of political debate on the left have disappeared. After the unfortunate examples of Jacques Doriot and Marcel Déat,[9] a fear of populism and Caesarism had infiltrated leftist parties. Moreover, excessive tributes to Stalin and Thorez during the years of Stalinist triumph had rendered these parties immune to the cult of personality. However, the historic culture of the left largely evaporated as time went on, and so limits to developing a potential cult of the leader were ipso facto eradicated. For all of these reasons, the personalization of Mélenchon's candidacy has had a more beneficial than negative impact on the campaign.

Mélenchon also knew how to be serious, to persevere, and reach the necessary degree of importance to reinforce the credibility of his candidacy. Accordingly, after a few months his candidacy had surpassed the realm of simple testimony—like the usual Trotskyist candidacies—to enter the realm of virtual reality: the importance the campaign developed was perceived not as a sort of warning directed at the Socialist alternative, but rather as an affirmation, on the left, of this alternative. Starting in March 2012 (the time of Mélenchon's breakthrough in the polls, when he moved from less than 10 percent to close to 15 percent, with a peak in one survey of 17 percent), what one could call the useful radical vote was cast in favor of Mélenchon to the detriment of the Trotskyist candidates,[10] with three leaders of the NPA even calling for their constituents to vote for Mélenchon instead of the candidate from their own organization. Naturally, these points also revealed the significant fragility of the electoral results achieved by the Trotskyist candidates.[11] While the total votes for the Trotskyists had been at a significant level since 1995—with 5.3 percent in 1995, 10.5 percent in 2002, and 5.7 percent in 2007—they went back to being marginalized in 2012 with a modest 1.7 percent.

Recovering the Communist Heritage

However, beyond the alliance with its partners (Parti de Gauche, Gauche Unitaire [from the NPA, itself an offshoot of the Ligue Communiste Révolutionnaire]; Fédération pour une Alternative Sociale et Ecologique; République et Socialisme; Convergences et Alternatives [another NPA offshoot]; and the older pro-Albanian Parti Communiste des Ouvriers de France), it is the PCF that ensured the organizational power of the campaign. Certainly, the PCF no longer has the same political strength that it held in the 1970s and 1980s. Nonetheless, it retains a respectable number of municipal and union strongholds, as well as a corps of activists that it can mobilize during an electoral campaign. Jean-Luc Mélenchon knew how to mold himself into this old Communist culture, which has been largely dormant since the party fell into crisis starting at the end of the 1970s.

Returning to Mélenchon's campaign posters, let us examine their color scheme. Viewers can see a double register therein. In a secondary sense, a series of posters reproduce black-and-white photos of Mélenchon. They play off the human factor and a sense of closeness, two elements tied to the personalization of the political battle by Mélenchon, a phenomenon already examined above. However, the majority of these posters also choose another, dominant chromatic choice: bright or dark, red bursts out in the posters of the Front de Gauche, while the PS had for a long time ceased to debate the symbolic use of this color with the PCF. The Front de Gauche posters also restored the five-pronged star, symbol of the Red Army that for decades had been commonly used to represent the violent dimensions of the Communist revolution. Nevertheless, Mélenchon's graphic artists moderated the violent revolutionary symbol by coloring the star yellow rather than the original red.[12] In general, Jean-Luc Mélenchon systematically takes up an oxymoronic discursive posture as with his trademark red tie. He chose red to preserve the Communist reference but, unlike the Trotskyist candidates, he actually wears a tie. The same could be said about his favorite expressions: "civil insurrection" or "citizen revolution." They recall both a subversive side with their roots in Communist political culture—with a preference for the 1789 reference rather than the overused 1917 reference—as well as a pragmatic side, given that the ends of insurgency in reality pass through institutional means.

Mélenchon's reclaiming of the Communist heritage is confirmed by an analysis of the geographic correlations of his electorate. Two scenarios were possible: Mélenchon's electoral map could resemble either the Communist electoral map or the Trotskyist one. Of course, these two maps are not necessarily in conflict because the far-left vote was more easily implanted in traditionally Communist zones than in prospective areas of support targeted by the left.[13] However, despite this partial overlap, the maps remain different enough that comparison is still useful and examining them leaves no room for doubt. Mélenchon's electoral map is very close to the Communist electoral map, and largely different from the Trotskyist electoral distribution. The Trotskyist electoral map is distinct from the Communist electoral map in two principal ways. First, it is far less southern and Parisian than the Communist electoral map. Second, its zones of strength are constituted by the wide coastal strip and border extending from the Finistère in the North to the Moselle, as well as a zone in the Massif Central overflowing, surprisingly, to areas foreign to the Communist tradition: to the west toward the Poitou-Charente region and to the north toward the center region.[14] However, these two geographic features do not appear on the electoral map of the Front de Gauche which, conversely, recovers the traditional strongholds of the PCF: the western and northern part of the Massif Central, the Mediterranean coast, the entirety of the North-Pas-de-Calais-Seine-maritime area, the Côtes-d'Armor, and a portion of the Parisian region.[15]

A Pyrrhic Victory?

Of course, behind this apparent victory of the PCF, there is a strong probability that what appears to be a Communist resurgence in fact represents only a Pyrrhic victory. This is because the price to be paid by the Communist party is likely to be heavy. In particular, this cost reflects the PCF's abandoning the spotlight of its propaganda to a man who will most likely not be as docile toward the as are the PCF's usual companions. In fact, the great historical irony is that this return of orthodox communism was facilitated through the help of a Trotskyist. Indeed, Jean-Luc Mélenchon has the peculiarity of having been trained as an activist in the ranks of the Lambertiste branch of French Trotskyism, so named after its former leader, Pierre Boussel [1920–2008], who went by the name Pierre Lambert. But Trotskyism for Mélenchon was not a simple lesson in agitprop. As the regional leader of the Organisation Communiste Internationaliste for close to a decade, Trotskyism gave him an orientation that he has maintained throughout his career, one of critical support for the left, as well as one that he assumed both within the PS—where he invigorated his leftist supporters—as well as outside the PS since his break with the party in 2008. Whereas Trotskyists officials—Lutte Ouvrière and the Ligue Communiste Révolutionnaire, which became the NPA in February 2009—abandoned the critical support/outburst posture to distance themselves in advance from the PS's expected social-democratic betrayals, Mélenchon himself rather took up a conventional Trotskyist tactic counseled by Trotsky himself in the transitional plan of 1938: to mobilize the masses around a program—granted, a program of reform, but of reform that is unattainable under the capitalist regime.[16] Mélenchon's great victory was to be able to rally toward this "critical support/outburst" tactic a PCF adrift with a stalled strategy.

Beyond betting its future on a potentially uncontrollable and particularly charismatic leader, this Communist victory also appears fragile because it is purely a protest vote and does not entail much commitment from voters. The French have not been converted, whether to communism, Trotskyism, or to the Venezuelan model.[17] The polls show that a break with capitalism is no longer a dream, that responsibility for the economic crisis is no longer solely to be placed at the feet of political executives, and that the slogan "les patrons peuvent payer" (the bosses can pay) is no longer the panacea projected by the majority of the French left.

This contradiction between the polls and the strength of the radical vote can be explained by the nature of the radical vote. An important fringe of the French left is concerned that the future Socialist government justly distribute its efforts and will attentively monitor the likely hesitations, inevitable compromises, and possible betrayals of the new government. These voters are moved more by a reformist vigilance, however, than by the search for a revolutionary alternative. A Front de Gauche poster during the 2010 regional elections already reflected this perspective: "Marre de la gauche qui se traîne? Allez plus vite: votez Front de gauche" (Sick of a lagging left? Go faster: vote Front de Gauche). And so, within the radical camp, Mélenchon's victory over his Trotskyist competitors reflects a move away from extremism and a move toward, rather than away from, the PS. This is because, despite all his departures from the party's platform, Mélenchon was always clear—unlike the Trotskyist candidates—that he was going to vote, without qualms, for the Socialists in the second round. Thus, he proclaimed, "I call upon you to unite on May 6, without asking for anything in return, to beat Sarkozy! I ask you not to drag your feet, I ask you to mobilize as if it were to make me win the Presidential election."[18]

Another weakness of the Communist victory is revealed by the paradox of the parliamentary elections that followed the presidential one. The Front de Gauche received more votes in the legislative elections in 2012 than in 2007, but it will still have fewer MPs. This inconsistency reflects the fact that, in certain leftist constituencies, the PCF (or, essentially, the Parti de Gauche) was defeated in the first round by the Socialist candidate, and so was eliminated from competing in the second round. This was the case for incumbent MPs Pierre Gosnat (PCF) and Martine Billard (Parti de Gauche), and of Jean-Luc Mélenchon himself in the Pas-de-Calais. However, this situation is only the result of another phenomenon that is very worrying for the PCF: the further disintegration of its strongholds. Those of the Massif Central and of the Pyrénées have eroded and, in the strict sense of the word, only the isolated Thiers (Puy-de-Dôme) and a few rare constituencies in the north or the Seine-Saint-Denis are still worthy of being called strongholds. The comparison between the results of the parliamentary and the presidential elections is not reassuring, either. In a few weeks, the Front de Gauche lost close to 5 percent (more than 40 percent of its initial tally), signifying that the votes for Front de Gauche did not enjoy the same degree of stability as those for the PCF once did.

Above all, this Communist victory seems like a sham because Mélenchon's breakthrough is neither of an ideological nature nor even of a political one. Rather, it was the product of the media sphere, which ultimately reflects the great evolution that the revolutionary vote has experienced over the past century. For decades, this vote has been represented, semi-exclusively, by the PCF. The nature of this vote was fundamentally identity-based: small social, familial, and local communities formed a kind of Communist antisociety within capitalist society that, at election time, voted without qualms for "le parti de la classe ouvrière" (the party of the working class).[19] This model, while relatively stable, fell into crisis starting at the end of the 1970s, which culminated at the beginning of the 1990s.

Meanwhile, parallel to this crisis of the Communist vote, the revolutionary Trotskyist vote slowly began to gain strength over the past three decades. The nature of this vote was fundamentally ideological. Individuals—and no longer communities—chose these extremist affiliations purely out of revolutionary fervor. This permanence of Trotskyism reflected the particularity of France, always prone to verbal radicalism, but unlike the Communist vote did not correspond to a significant, stable, and organized fraction of French society in a state of internal secession. It rather indicated an ephemeral sensitivity that surged at election time, to then disappear almost completely thereafter, except in diffuse episodes of social protest.[20]

The social evolution of the vote in favor of Jean-Luc Mélenchon is particularly revealing in this regard. Until February 2012 two social groups were overrepresented among voters saying they would vote for Mélenchon: retirees and the middle class. Conversely, blue-collar workers were not receptive to Mélenchon's proposals. However, a reversal began in February, which was translated by Mélenchon's breakthrough in the polls, which rose from an average of 8 percent to 14 percent, with Mélenchon surpassing Marine Le Pen in terms of the blue-collar vote. However, unfortunately for the Front de Gauche candidate, this rallying of blue-collar workers was transient and not maintained at the time of the actual vote. Thus, even if unionized workers and those close to the unions did actually vote for Mélenchon, most workers ultimately returned to the FN candidate. This inconsistent nature of the radical protest vote suggests the volatility of the Mélenchon phenomenon: for two decades, the majority of these protestors voted for "une femme et une travailleuse" (a woman and a worker) (Arlette Laguiller) before moving on to "un jeune postier dynamique" (a young dynamic postman) (Olivier Besancenot), without the respective organizations of these two candidates, Lutte Ouvrière on one side and La Ligue Communiste Révolutionnaire (eventually the NPA) on the other, making gains proportional to their electoral surge.

These most recent elections have only confirmed this basic thesis, which points to the weakening of French radicalism. In fact, after the identity-based vote, after the ideological vote, we have witnessed the victory of the media-based vote. It is by mastering the forms of political communication that Jean-Luc Mélenchon was able to surpass his rivals "on the left of the left." But this is not to say that in the medium-term, *"l'effet tribun du peuple"* (the tribunary effect of the people) of Mélenchon will not falter as did *"l'effet travailleuse"* (the female worker effect) of Laguiller or *"l'effet jeune postier"* (young postman effect) of Besancenot. The radical vote suggests a desire to push the official left farther to the left without denouncing it, and even more without breaking from it. For thirty years those with this sensitivity have gathered in the ideological supermarket, favoring the highest-bidding mediator. There is nothing to say that this latest victory will not be transient like the others, and that it will be able to crystallize around real forms of political organization. Above all, everything indicates that it will not resuscitate the defunct antisocietal communism, which remains the only guarantor of a true and durable revolutionary left-wing alternative.

Notes

Translated from the French by Constance Wilhelm.
 1. In this chapter, the terms "radical" or "radicalism" are not used in reference to the old Parti radical [Radical Party], but are rather equivalent to the expressions "revolutionary

vote" or "anticapitalist vote" or *vote de rupture* and so on, all these expressions indicating the candidates situated to the left of the PS (which excludes the radical left vote—in terms of the Radical Party—as well as the *vote écologiste* [ecological vote]). On the radical left, see in particular Richard Dunphy, *Contesting Capitalism? Left Parties and European Integration* (Manchester, UK: Manchester University Press, 2004); and Jean-Michel De Waele, Daniel-Louis Seiler, eds., *Les partis de la gauche anticapitaliste en Europe* (Paris: Economica, 2012).

2. On the French radical movement, see Philippe Raynaud, *L'extrême gauche plurielle: Entre démocratie radicale et revolution* (Paris: Autrement, 2006). See also the contributions of Dominique Andolfatto and Fabienne Greffet, "Le Parti communiste français: une reconversion sous contraintes," Thierry Choffat, "Lutte Ouvrière, entre continuité et renouvellement," and Didier Bonnemaison, "De la Ligue Communiste Révolutionnaire au Nouveau Parti Anticapitaliste," in De Waele and Seiler, *Les partis de la gauche anticapitaliste en Europe*, 157–76, 292–304, 305–22, respectively.

3. In 1974, the call to vote in the first round for François Mitterrand was not a sign of weakness—the PCF searching for (as in 2012) a more high-performing vehicle than a candidate labeled "Communist"—but rather one of too much strength: the PCF was completely dominating the *Union de la gauche* Union de la Gauche and did not want this domination to be too crushing so as to scare off the French population, which desired change but did not want to install a pro-Soviet regime.

4. http://fdgaucherhone10e.canalblog.com/albums/affiches_de_campagne/photos/71230140-fdgpaveplein.html.

5. http://dominiquehasselmann.blog.lemonde.fr/2009/03/25/herve-eon-le-chevalier-et-le-moulin-avent/.

6. The often confrontational relations between Jean-Luc Mélenchon and the media, seen from the former's perspective, are analyzed in Denis Sieffert and Michel Soudais, *Mélenchon et les medias* (Paris: Politis, 2012).

7. These are respectively available from http://www.parismatch.com/Actu-Match/Politique/Photos/Quand-la-campagne-s-affiche/L-opposant-377479/; http://www.election-politique/resultats.php?cle1=FR&cle2=1&cle3=2002-05-05&cle4=pr percentE9sidentielle; http://bellasteelor.kazeo.com/news-du-jour/affiches-de-campagne-de-la-presidentielle-2012,a3095752.html.

8. On this issue, see the seminal work by René Rémond, *La droite en France de 1815 à nos jours: continuité et diversité d'une tradition politique* (Paris: Aubier, 1954); and in updated form, *Les droites en France* (Paris: Aubier-Montaigne, 1982).

9. These two leftist personalities were, during the interwar period, the potential right-hand men, respectively, of the PCF and of the PS. Absorbed into "la sphère magnétique du fascisme" (the magnetic sphere of fascism)" (Philippe Burrin), they both ended up as heads of far-right collaborationist parties during the German occupation.

10. *Le Nouvel Observateur* [online], "Sondage: Mélenchon devient le troisième homme," March 23, 2012, http://tempsreel.nouvelobs.com/election-presidentielle-2012/20120322.OBS4390/sondage-melenchon-devient-le-troisieme-homme.html.

11. This fragility, and sometime volatility, has already been observed in Bernard Dolez and Annie Laurent, "Marche et marges de la gauche," in *Le vote de tous les refus. Les élections présidentielles et législatives de 2002*, ed. P. Perrineau and C. Ysmal (Paris: Presses de Sciences Po, 2003), 251–273.

12. On this Communist artistic symbolism, see Philippe Buton, "Symbolique communiste," in *Dictionnaire du communisme*, ed. Stéphane Courtois (Paris: Larousse, 2007), 538–40.

13. For a similar reflection on the scale of Europe as a whole, see Daniel Boy and Jean Chiche, "La gauche radicale et les Verts: Des contestations hétérogènes," in *Le vote européen 2004–2005, De l'élargissement au référendum français*, ed. P. Perrineau (Paris: Presses de Sciences Po, 2005), 205–28.

14. The designation of the geographic structure of the Trotskyist vote is based on the analysis of the presidential elections of 2002 and 2007, by adding together the votes of the various Trotskyist candidates. Among multiple studies concerning the Trotskyist vote, see in particular Vincent Tiberj, "L'extrême gauche électorale: une résistible ascension ?" in *Présidentielle 2007: Atlas électoral: Qui vote quoi, où, comment?*, ed. P. Perrineau (Paris: Presses de Sciences Po, 2007), 41–44; and Frédéric Salmon, *Atlas électoral de la France, 1848–2001* (Paris: Le Seuil, 2001), 64–65.
15. Salmon, *Atlas électoral*, 66–67.
16. See Léon Trotsky, "Programme de transition: L'agonie du capitalisme et les tâches de la IVe Internationale," *Bulletin de l'Opposition*, no. 66–67 (1938), http://www.marxists.org/francais/trotsky/livres/trans/tran.htm.
17. Jean-Luc Mélenchon chose to spend his 2012 summer vacation in Venezuela, where he met Hugo Chávez, to whom he often made public reference (as he has in the past for Fidel Castro).
18. Cited by Lilian Alemagna, "Jean-Luc Mélenchon veut jouer les barrages," in *Libération*, April 23, 2012, http://www.liberation.fr/politiques/2012/04/23/jean-luc-melenchon-veut-jouer-les-barrages_813885.
19. See the classic work by Annie Kriegel, *Les communistes français: essai d'ethnographie politique*, 2nd ed. (Paris: Le Seuil, 1985).
20. For example, the rail workers' strike in 1995.

Chapter 7

In Search of the Center

Gilles Le Béguec

For the political center in France, presidential elections follow but do not resemble each other. The only continuity has been that failure has almost always been on the agenda. The only deviation from this trend occurred in 1974, with the victory of Valéry Giscard d'Estaing. However, we can discuss ad infinitum whether the founding president of the very moderate Fédération Nationale des Républicains Indépendants (National Federation of Independent Republicans) actually belonged to the centrist family in the sense usually attributed to this adjective.

In general, this centrist political family has faced the electoral test in a scattered way. There have been few elections placed under the sign of real commitment for unity and effective cohesion: 1965 (with the candidacy of Jean Lecanuet, in which can be seen the birth of the center in the sense this term has taken for almost fifty years now) and 1981 (most of the centrists having then, while integrated into the young UDF founded in 1978, dutifully played the card of the outgoing president Valéry Giscard d'Estaing's reelection). In all the other cases, the personality issues and/or divergences of a strategic nature have sown the seeds of division. In 1988 and 1995 the division resulted in the existence of strong reservations, more or less openly expressed, with regard to the candidate officially anointed by the groupings of the centrist factions. Neither Raymond Barre (1988) nor Edouard Balladur (1995) was able to take advantage of all the support on which they could have theoretically counted.[1] In 1969, 1974, 2002, and 2007, the objections were much sharper, although the comparison between the four elections soon reaches its limits. This picture can be completed with the help of three explanatory factors: divisions

---

Notes for this chapter begin on page 110.

have almost always affected both the electorate and the staff of political organizations;[2] they were able to manifest themselves already during the first round of the elections (in 1969, for example, Jean Lecanuet expressed strong support for the candidacy of Alain Poher, while Jacques Duhamel made the decision to rejoin Georges Pompidou) or during the decisive ballot (in 2007, when Hervé Morin and most members of the UDF disassociated themselves from François Bayrou by calling to vote in favor of Nicolas Sarkozy); they eventually led to a split in due form, as occurred in 1969 with the establishment of the Center for Democracy and Progress by Jacques Duhamel and Joseph Fontanet, and in 2007, with the birth of the New Center (Nouveau Centre) led by Hervé Morin. For centrists, as for other political forces, the presidential election is a necessary step. But for these same centrists, this necessary step is full of danger.

Second, the leaders of the centrist groupings did not always opt for the same strategy. In 1965, 2002, and 2007, the centrists—those, at least, who claimed loud and clear such an affiliation—were battling each other under their own flag. In 1974, 1981, 1988, and 1995, the choice was a center-right strategy—that is to say, the rallying around one personality— Valéry Giscard d'Estaing, Raymond Barre, or Edouard Balladur. They were on the outside of the centrist family in a strict sense, but were also considered able to switch in favor of their candidacy very large sectors of moderate opinion. Once more events turned out differently in 1969. The candidate, Alain Poher, president of the senate, was an almost chemically pure centrist. However, his supporters ranged from an anti-Gaullist right seeking revenge, to a moderate left—of radical or Socialist leanings. This moderate left was disoriented by the mishandling of May–June 1968, the disintegration of the Federation of the Democratic and Socialist Left (the FGDS of François Mitterrand), and the disastrous campaign of Gaston Defferre, the official candidate of a PS in full transition. In such a configuration, the center—in this case the Democratic Centre of Jean Lecanuet and its closest allies—could come to serve as the backbone of a majority coalition. Alain Poher had failed. Nevertheless, was his formula still not the right one?[3]

In 2002 François Bayrou's candidacy was conceived to make a statement—to be more precise, as a means to take time and mark a territory.[4] His candidacy in 2007 had allowed the centrist leader to achieve an almost unexpected electoral breakthrough and heralded his arrival in the major leagues.[5] Despite the many disappointments of the 2007–11 period, this acknowledgment was for Bayrou a powerful invitation to try his luck for the third time.

The Center, the Test of the Presidential Election, or the Time of Disillusionment

Like the Orient mentioned by General de Gaulle in his war memoirs, the center's history—one would probably rather speak of centers—is a terribly complicated story. What was true for the Third and Fourth Republics, particularly the end of the Fourth Republic, has been also largely true for the regime founded in 1958. This was due to both the weight of ideological and cultural traditions (the centrist tendency to cultivate first their differences and the reluctance to obey the imperatives of a strong collective discipline) and, in our opinion more decisively, because of the operating logic of a party system structured around the left-right cleavage, a cleavage that often passes directly through the so-called centrist electorate.

While largely dictated by the constraints of the political and institutional game, the campaign strategy adopted by the centrist side during the 2012 presidential elections was nevertheless very simple and without real surprise. François Bayrou's desire to be candidate to the presidency for a third time was never in doubt. In fact, all indicators show that this has indeed been the principal purpose (the only purpose?) of his political engagement since the impressive success he recorded in the 2007 presidential elections. As a matter of fact, the balance sheet of his campaigns was not exactly encouraging. The various elections held during the presidency of Nicolas Sarkozy have resulted in a cascade of failures, first and foremost the defeat suffered by François Bayrou himself in his native city of Pau, during the municipal elections. Most observers also noted that the MoDem—the group founded by François Bayrou in the aftermath of the 2007 election and led by him with a firm hand—was not in great shape. On March 23, 2011, at a research seminar held at Sciences Po, the political scientist Dominique Reynié presented a particularly bleak picture concerning Bayrou's electoral outlook, speaking of the latter's "organizational evaporation," "ideological dislocation," and "electoral inconsistency." However, François Bayrou never lost confidence in his star, and was even heard to say that he expected to do better in 2012 than he had in 2007.[6]

The situation was less simple in the camp of the former centrist majority. The game appeared indeed relatively open and the assumption of one (or even more) candidatures arising within this political family could not be excluded. However, in our opinion at least, the conditions for such an outcome were not met. We know that this eventful story unfolded in two principal phases; we can call them, for convenience's sake, the Borloo phase and the Morin phase. The possibility of a candidacy by Jean-Louis Borloo emerged from May 2011, at the Radical Party congress held in Lyon, the city formerly headed by Edouard Herriot, called the "pope of radicalism." The former ecology minister, who had failed to enter the Hôtel Matignon in the reshuffle of the end of 2010, had numerous strengths: his reputation, his extended experience in government, his winning image, the strength of his personality, and his moderate political positions. An arrangement was thus built around an organization, half committee of liaison, half draft confederation, named the Republican, Environmental, and Social Alliance (l'Alliance Républicaine, Ecologique et Sociale; ARES). But Jean-Louis Borloo had always been a great pragmatist, and he could not help but make two observations that worked against his candidacy: the relatively narrow window of opportunity that he enjoyed, and the reservations, if not hostility, of several of his natural allies, in particular Hervé Morin, the president of the New Center political group. At the beginning of October, the former ecology minister preferred to withdraw from the race, at the same time forcing ARES to put its activities on hold. Thus, the way was now free for the nomination of Hervé Morin whose campaign lasted only a little over two months, from November 27 (date of the official announcement of his candidacy) until February 16 (date of his withdrawal). In fact, the former defense minister under Nicolas Sarkozy was never able to convince his political party of the merits of his candidacy, with several of the heavyweights of the New Center making no secret of their hostility to the latter.[7] The surveys predicted that he could expect a score of little more than 1 percent of the vote, while collecting the requisite five hundred signatures proved more difficult than expected.

At the same time, in a somewhat incongruous fashion, the interests of François Bayrou and Nicolas Sarkozy converged on the eve of the campaign. The president of MoDem had everything to gain by appearing as the center's sole representative, which would free him from making any concession to the outgoing majority. Nicolas Sarkozy estimated, rightly or wrongly, that a candidacy issued by the centrist wing of his majority would likely damage his candidacy by preventing him from collecting the maximum votes during the first round of the elections.[8] Thus, by mid-February 2012, attempts to use the presidential competition to give the center the means of autonomous political expression ended with the candidacy of François Bayrou.

Ironically, this moment of grace roughly corresponded to a breakdown in the campaign, that is to say, a significant decrease in the voting intentions recorded by most surveys in favor of the centrist candidate. François Bayrou had started off at a fairly low level, with around 7–8 percent of the vote in surveys conducted in October and the beginning of November. Afterward, the rise in support seemed promising: from around 11 percent in December to 13 percent in early January, and 15 percent at the end of that month. The trend was then reversed: 13 percent in early February to 11 percent in late February. The campaign of the centrist candidate then entered a period that one of his chief advisers, the sociologist Robert Rochefort, qualified as flat. The month of April, with its ups and downs, rather confirmed the hypothesis of a settlement.[9] From that moment on, the die were cast.

The quality of the campaign was not the issue and we can see that the months of January and February 2012 were those of missed opportunities. In early February the successive pullout of the two champions of the centrist wing of the majority—Hervé Morin's pullout coming at that point in only a matter of days—and the doubts hovering on the right concerning the chances of Nicolas Sarkozy's reelection encouraged speculation on centrist voters rallying around François Bayrou's bid. In other words, the way might have been open for the adoption of a center-right strategy, focused on the call for the establishment of a new majority and the search for a better balance between the right and the center. However, the choice of such an option required not standing in the way of possible arrangements with Nicolas Sarkozy and, incidentally, also differently calibrating the attacks aimed at the left and the right.[10] This is what neither François Bayrou nor, it seems, key members of his entourage, had wanted.

The following events are well known to all and it suffices to recall the most revealing figures of the presidential election: François Bayrou received 9.1 percent of the vote, which represents, in percentage terms, less than half of his score in 2007 (18.57 percent). This was a major failure and the disappointment of his supporters was equal to the illusions they had too long entertained. Nevertheless, it would be excessive to speak of defeat. However, during the parliamentary elections of June 10 and 17 one can say that the MoDem literally collapsed. In the first ballot, the Centre pour la France (Center for France), essentially the MoDem and its allies within the centrist alliance, won 2.33 percent of votes cast, of which, according to some estimates, 1.8 percent went to the MoDem itself. After this decisive election, the MoDem had to settle for two seats in the National Assembly: that of the outgoing MP Jean Lassalle, who was reelected in the Pyrénées Atlantiques with the support of the UMP, and the seat of Thierry Robert, who was elected in the overseas department of the Ile de la Réunion. With a score of 23.63 percent of the votes cast in the first round, François Bayrou found himself in a difficult position in his district of Pau East and South. On June 17 he was beaten in a triangular election (PS-MoDem-UMP), obtaining only 30.7 percent of the vote. According to the cruel formula of the political scientist Sylvie Strudel, the hypercenter had become a hypocenter.[11]

On the eve of this election, the center was split into several factions: two elected from the MoDem, two from the members of the fragile centrist

Alliance, twelve from the deeply divided New Center, and nine from the Parti Radical Valoisien Radical.[12] The way was paved for yet another recomposition. François Bayrou was no longer able to play the leading role in this political enterprise, on which we will comment later.

Reflections on a Dual Failure

In my opinion, François Bayrou conducted a rather good campaign and his level of popularity remained high throughout the period between the declaration of his candidacy and the election's first round on April 22. The causes of his failure must thus be sought elsewhere. In line with the diagnosis of Dominique Reynié, we focus on three explanatory factors.

First, François Bayrou has emerged as a lonely figure, excessively anxious to cultivate his political uniqueness and to rely on a very small group of followers. His campaign thus greatly suffered from lack of grassroots support. Activists and UDF members had often been very active in 2007 and the use of the color orange—the color traditionally associated with Christian Democracy in France—gave this movement a moral and emotional dimension. Five years later, that presence had become extremely discrete, especially in urban areas.[13]

The divine surprise of 2007 was in large part due to François Bayrou's novelty appeal. Throughout the 2012 campaign, another François Bayrou was present in the media, embellishing indefinitely a small number of very general issues that he had already evoked in 2007. Curiosity therefore could no longer have the same impact, especially since Jean-Luc Mélenchon had taken up the role of challenger disputing the system's rules. At the risk of confusing those who see centrism as a synonym for supporting greater European integration, throughout the campaign Bayrou failed to make any proposals to remedy the eurozone crisis. Even more embarrassingly, his discourse stressed the need to produce and consume French—an incongruous statement coming from a leader claiming the pro-free trade tradition of Robert Schuman and Jean Lecanuet.

Finally, the presidential candidate of the MoDem did not seem to be aware of the blurring of his political strategy. We know that the strategy in question was in principle based on an attempt to redefine the rules of the political game and to allow an authentic and strengthened center to attract moderates from both mainstream parties—clearly, elements of both the PS and the UMP had tired of dealing with their respective extremes—and to occupy a pivotal role within a more open partisan system. In many respects, the position adopted by the MoDem candidate in 2012 was much stronger in this area than the position adopted by that of the UDF in 2007—a

UDF that had been represented in the previous government appointed by Jacques Chirac in the person of Gilles de Robien. Not coincidentally, this scheme was largely deprived of credibility. In fact, almost all the support for Bayrou's candidacy came from the center right, if only for reasons of thwarted personal ambitions (with, for example, the somewhat surprising support of Philippe Douste-Blazy, the last of the foreign ministers of Jacques Chirac, who had once advocated for the integration of the UDF into the UMP). At the same time, Bayrou's comments had increasingly focused on criticizing the policies, style, and choices of Nicolas Sarkozy, to the point of assuming an essentially center left rather than a centrist position. In other words, François Bayrou, probably without weighing the consequences, risked cutting himself off from the center right where his main reservoir of votes appeared to lie.

A few words remain to be said about the more specifically Christian Democratic component of the "Bayrouiste" electorate in 2007 and 2012. In 2007 François Bayrou presided over the destiny of a UDF that was the partisan heir of Jean Lecanuet's Center of Social Democrats, a group that had its roots in Christian Democracy. The UDF candidate was thus able to benefit from the revival of a Christian Democratic electorate that had been unreceptive to either Nicolas Sarkozy's or Ségolène Royal's message. Evidence of this was to be seen in the results obtained in several former zones of influence of the Christian Democratic Mouvement Républicain Populaire under the Fourth Republic. Almost all the departments gave the party a higher percentage of votes than its national average in these areas.[14]

Events unfolded very differently in 2012. The UDF had given way to a MoDem with a fuzzy ideological identity in which the Christian Democratic element was not represented. Meanwhile, the municipal, cantonal, and regional elections of the Sarkozy years had provided the Socialist left with the opportunity to strengthen its presence significantly in some of the former Mouvement Républicain Populaire region, particularly in the west of France. François Bayrou thus lost one of his most valuable assets, with the exception—or rather partial exception—of a small number of departments. One of these was the Mayenne of Senator Jean Arthuis, president of the small centrist alliance and former cabinet minister—a region where the support of particularly influential politicians could mobilize a significant number of votes. However, such clientelism only played a peripheral role at the national level.

Conversely, there is little to say regarding the causes for the severe failure suffered during the parliamentary elections of June 10 and 17, the reason simply being that a defeat was inevitable. Everyone was well aware that it would have taken a miracle to undo the effects of the poor results from the presidential election and the disorder caused by François Bayrou's support for François Hollande's candidacy in the second-round runoff. However, we can also take note of two additional explanatory factors. First, during the parliamentary elections, the MoDem disappeared in front of the Center for France, which appeared, rightly or wrongly, as a haphazard and improvised political grouping. This Center for France supported a little more than four hundred candidates belonging to and also not belonging to the MoDem. The majority of these candidates suffered from a telling lack of public exposure and among those who were the best known, a significant number had followed quite different political trajectories from 2007 to 2012. These were within the quasi-opposition embodied by François Bayrou, on the fringes of the majority, such as the centrist alliance of Senator Jean Arthuis, or within the majority itself, like former minister Rama Yade, also candidate of the Parti Radical Valoisien of Jean-Louis Borloo. Finally, one could observe that those members close to François Bayrou had generally preferred to abstain from the parliamentary election such as Marielle de Sarnez, who had foregone applying as a candidate in Paris. Second, the Center for France did not give itself the means to organize a campaign worthy of the name. François Bayrou, leader of MoDem, was engrossed by his election campaign in his stronghold of the Pyrénées Atlantiques, and events unfolded at the district level as if many candidates had considered it wiser to keep a low profile and economize their efforts. In a number of cases there was no campaign at all.

What Future for the Center?

The 2012 electoral cycle has cruelly revealed the weaknesses of the center: its divisions, its policy fragility, and the inability of its leaders to develop consistent political strategies. While the iron law of bipolarization asserts itself with renewed strength, the question regarding the future of the center has been well and truly posed. The problem arises in a different light in the case of the MoDem and the nebulous group that has tried to organize itself under the leadership of Jean-Louis Borloo, i.e., the disparate band of centrists who had belonged to the ex-majority on the one hand, and those who had intended to keep their distance from the UMP on the other.

It is not clear if the MoDem can survive for long following the failure of François Bayrou in the 2012 presidential election and its comprehensive defeat in the subsequent parliamentary elections. In my opinion, François Bayrou has without doubt a future, though what it will be is unclear. The prospects are different for the movement he created and led to defeat. In theory, one can imagine that a transformed MoDem relieved of its more moderate elements might become a backup for a left-wing majority confronted by an intensifying challenge and contestation from its radical wing. However, experience has shown that such a center left strategy faces many obstacles: first and foremost, the unwillingness of the PS and its representatives to cooperate in such a strategy.[15] In any case, the precedents are not encouraging: during the second seven-year term of François Mitterrand, the movement "France Unie" (united France) failed to impose itself even though its main leader, Jean-Pierre Soissons, demonstrated political skills at least equal to those of François Bayrou. Indeed, this enterprise quickly came to an end.

The centrist component of the former majority has better reasons for hope. In the weeks that followed the parliamentary elections, twenty-nine MPs, mostly belonging to the New Center born in 2007 or to the old Parti Radical Valoisien, formed a parliamentary group bearing the rather colorless name Union des Démocrates et des Indépendants (Union of democrats and independents, UDI).[16] During an interview with the January 26, 2012, issue of *Le Figaro,* Jean-Louis Borloo, president of the Radical Party and of the newly formed parliamentary group, explained the meaning of the maneuver. He formulated the diagnosis that "in the absence of a strong center, the outgoing majority was too narrow [and] one-legged" and set a goal: "to recreate a center right force, as Valéry Giscard d'Estaing did thirty years ago."[17]

Does the UDI have the means to fulfill this ambition? The comparison to the UDF shows that all in all it is limited by the fact that the confederation of Giscardian inspiration was dominated by the Republican Party and its satellites, i.e., by the liberal and moderate right. In fact, this new group suffers from two handicaps. The first is Jean-Louis Borloo himself, due to his very personal way of doing politics and the unpredictability of his decisions. The second is related to the partially blurred picture—if not outright confusion—offered by both the New Center and the Radical Party. The two, by the way, do not control a specific electorate which is distinct from that of the UMP, except for in a small number of districts. Finally, it is well-known that disagreements exist among the staffs of these representative groups.

Recalling these facts, however, does not preclude a more general reflection. First, in a way the past ten years have been beneficial in clarifying what it means in French politics to be a centrist. What was misused under the term "center" from 1962 to 1965 was actually a coalition born under the sign of an opposition to a triumphant Gaullism. It gathered forces that had ranged from the boundaries of the extreme right to the margins of the center left. Founded on the eve of the parliamentary elections of 1978, the UDF was the culmination of these efforts to build a common framework of action for all those who did want a union of the left, the Gaullists, or the neo-Gaullists. Created mainly through the rallying to the candidacy of Valéry Giscard d'Estaing in 1974, the establishment of this pseudocenter around the institutional rules of the Fifth Republic allowed it to aspire for a while to the possibility of becoming a majority political force in the country. Valéry Giscard d'Estaing's defeat in 1981 permanently destroyed this grand ambition.

By the same token, by encouraging the creation of the UMP, Jacques Chirac and Alain Juppé were probably right in assuming that no insuperable differences separated the neo-Gaullists of the RPR and the conservative liberals (former Giscardiens, if one prefers) from the right wing of a UDF whose leadership was crumbling. However, one wonders if they had been well advised in trying to associate the centrist component of the UDF—that is to say, the former Center of Social Democrats—with an initiative that de facto appeared like a new union of the right. The price to be paid was much greater than expected. On the one hand, this gambit ended up undermining the political identity that François Bayrou had been able to incarnate with real talent. In other words, he embodied the resurgence of a centrism situated in the beginning on the margins of the opposition, and later in quasi-opposition or outright opposition to the UMP. On the other hand, the rallying of many notable centrists to the UMP has gradually cut them off from a significant portion of their traditional electoral base. The result has been the rallying of large sectors of the formerly Christian Democratic electorate to the PS, particularly in the west of the country.

It is too early to comment on the prospects of Jean-Louis Borloo's attempt at reuniting the forces of the center. However, it is difficult to see how such reunification could lead to anything other than the emergence of a backup force expanding the political supply on the center right.[18] In other words, the reconquest of centrist voters who defected in spring 2012 is first and foremost a matter for the UMP itself. It depends on the ability of the latter to renew its appeal to a part of public opinion that is at the same time heterogeneous and volatile. It was understood that this would be one of the key issues of the internal debates animating the UMP and the rival factions competing for power within it.

Sisyphus and Janus

More or less constrained by the dynamics of a bipolar party system, the centrist Sisyphus tirelessly continues to push his rock up the hill for it to roll back down. Jean-Louis Borloo and his friends of the UDI have chosen to position themselves on the center right, drawing, at least in appearance, all the lessons from this iron law of bipolarity. The problem is that at the same time the center also derives its legitimacy and even its strength from the allergy on the part of some voters to the effects of this bipolarization. To continue with this metaphor, we might ask under what conditions Sisyphus can also stop being Janus.

Notes

Translated from the French by Catherina Pruegel.
1. Valéry Giscard d'Estaing, president of the UDF, had hence refused to support Raymond Barre in 1988. In 1995 he de facto granted his preference to Jacques Chirac, at the expense of Edouard Balladur, who was supported by the main components of the UDF (the Republican Party and the Center of Social Democrats).
2. According to some estimates, in 414 constituencies where the competition came down to a right-left duel, 42 percent of MoDem voters voted in favor of the left-wing candidate in the second round of voting.
3. The nomination of Alain Poher also created a dynamic that led a few years later to an ambitious attempt to reunite the forces of the center, including the reform movement bringing together the democratic center (Jean Lecanuet), the Radical Party (Jean-Jacques Servan-Schreiber), and two small groupings, the Republican Center and the Socialist Democratic Movement of France. It is likely that the reform movement served as a model for the Republican, Environmental, and Social Alliance (ARES), which will be discussed later.
4. François Bayrou garnered 6.3 percent of the votes cast in 2002.
5. This impressive score of 18.6 percent was higher than Jean Lecanuet's in 1965 (15.6 percent) and Raymond Barre's in 1988 (16.5 percent), but lower than that of Alain Poher in 1974 (23.3 percent). On the 1989 European elections, the centrist list led by Simone Veil—which already figured Jean-Louis Borloo—received 8.5 percent of the vote. François Bayrou did a little better in the 2012 presidential elections. Presumably this range of 8 to 10 percent roughly corresponds to the habitually low score of the independent center.
6. Seminar put on by Sylvie Guillaume and Jean-François Sirinelli, Centre d'Histoire de Sciences-Po, February 2, 2011.
7. These included in particular Jean-Christophe Lagarde, Maurice Leroy Sauvadet, and François Leroy Sauvadet who had all at one time or another held positions of authority within the New Center.
8. See the article on February 15, 2012, by former education minister Luc Ferry, "Un rôle historique pour Bayrou?" *Le Figaro* [online], February 15, 2012, http://www.lefigaro.fr/mon-figaro/2012/02/15/10001-20120215ARTFIG00660-un-role-historique-pour-bayrou.php.
9. See, in particular, the full dossier published by *Le Figaro* in collaboration with the Centre de Recherches Politiques de Sciences Po (CEVIPOF), in the February 28, 2012, edition.
10. This way, a number of tenors of the UMP tried to convince François Bayrou to moderate his attacks, suggesting that in case of the reelection of Nicolas Sarkozy the president of the MoDem could be appointed prime minister. See, for example, the statements made by Minister of the Budget Valérie Pécresse in *Le Figaro,* March 27, 2012. This hypothesis lost all credibility from the moment the polls in favor of François Bayrou started to decline significantly.

11. *Le Figaro* [online], "Bayrou réduit à l'hypocentre" June 19, 2012, http://www.lefigaro.fr/mon-figaro/2012/06/19/10001-20120619ARTFIG00531-bayrou-reduit-a-l-hypocentre.php. In the scholarly literature the term "hypercenter"—copied after that of "hyper-president" attributed to Nicolas Sarkozy—has tended to replace that of "extreme center." The author of this chapter remains a bit reserved.
12. *Valoisien* refers to the Place de Valois in Paris, the site of the Radical Party's headquarters since 1972.
13. The author has the habit of frequenting markets during election campaigns. Unlike what happened in 2007, he never met a single leaflet distributor in favor of François Bayrou throughout 2012 campaign.
14. While these former strongholds of the Mouvement Républicain Populaire still offered François Bayrou scores slightly higher than the national average—11.3 percent in the Bretagne region and 11.71 percent in the stronghold of strongholds that was Alsace—it remained largely a residual phenomenon.
15. One should also take into account the fact that the Radical Party of the Left (Parti Radical de Gauche, PRG) believes that its mission is to occupy all the political space on the center left. It has always shown itself to be ill-tempered toward attempts to enlarge left-wing majorities to incorporate centrist elements unless such an opening passes through the party itself, which has never really worked.
16. The group brings together the elected representatives of the New Center, two from the centrist Alliance, and radical representatives who have chosen, following Jean-Louis Borloo, autonomy with regard to the UMP. Other radicals like Jean Leonetti preferred to continue working within the UMP group. The new group was joined by a handful of UMP centrists and by deputies who considered it to be, perhaps only temporarily, more convenient to adopt this label.
17. Logically, the UDI group was to be extended into a political party. One can think of a reactivation of ARES. However, it is most probable that the centrists, yielding to one of their most cherished habits, wanted something new and to start a new organization. The former cabinet minister Maurice Leroy, a neo-centrist often at odds with Hervé Morin, appealed very clearly in this direction.
18. On this crucial point, Borloo's rhetoric is very clear: it is indeed about occupying the niche of the center right, and not to position himself at the center. And concerning this subject, the head of the New Center, Hervé Morin, is perhaps even firmer than Jean-Louis Borloo. We can appreciate the magnitude of this semantic evolution. The UDI speaks of the center right where twenty-five years ago it had just spoken of the center. In a sense, the hypercenter of François Bayrou and his defeat has tainted the reference to the center with suspicion. With the help of Maurice Leroy, Jean-Louis Borloo seems to have chosen to rush things by making public the project of creating, by the end of July, a "rassemblement des démocrates et indépendants," a rallying of democrats and independents. However, Jean-Christophe Lagarde, a leader of the New Center at odds with Hervé Morin, announced in parallel the establishment of a Force Européenne et Démocrate," a European Democratic Force, which would also be a component of this gathering.

Chapter 8

The Resurgence of the Front National

Gabriel Goodliffe

After suffering its worst electoral results since the early 1980s in the 2007 presidential and parliamentary elections in France, the FN reestablished itself as a powerful electoral force in the country in the 2012 national elections. The party's new leader, Marine Le Pen, achieved a record score of 17.9 percent (versus 10.4 percent in 2007) in the first round of the presidential election, eclipsing the historic record set by her father when he acceded to the second-round runoff in 2002. Meanwhile, the FN garnered 13.6 percent of the vote in the first round of the June 2012 parliamentary election (compared to 4.7 percent in 2007) and returned two deputies to the National Assembly, marking the first time it has gained parliamentary representation since 1988. This chapter seeks to account for this electoral resurgence of the FN. It argues that, particularly following the nomination of Ms. Le Pen at its head, the party has skillfully exploited favorable conditions of political demand and supply that came to the fore during Nicolas Sarkozy's presidency.

At one level, the present economic crisis, following on the heels of significant market liberalization and welfare retrenchment during Sarkozy's term of office, has exacerbated the social vulnerability of the middle- and working-class electorates that have gravitated to the FN since the mid-1980s. Faced with conditions of burgeoning unemployment and declining living standards that show no signs of abating, particularly given the incumbent government's adoption of a sweeping austerity program months prior to the election, a significant proportion of these voters, many of them erstwhile FN supporters who had defected to Sarkozy in 2007, flocked back to the party in 2012. Le Pen came first among industrial workers (at

---

Notes for this chapter begin on page 128.

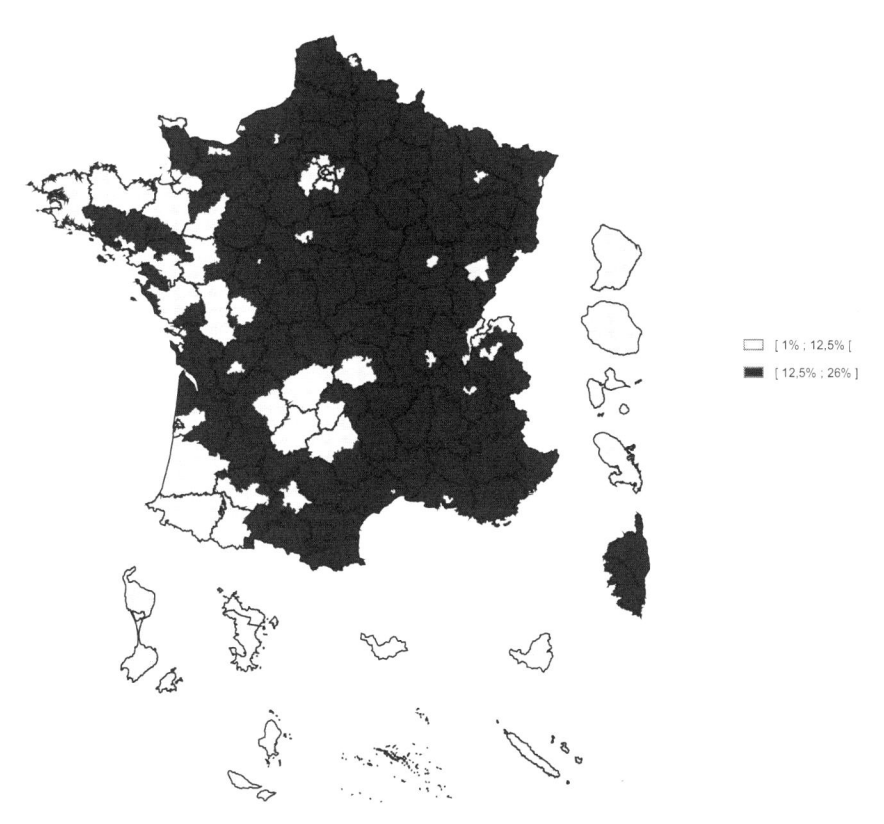

Map 8.1. Marine Le Pen's Performance in the First Round of the 2012 Presidential Elections.
Votes cast in favor of Marine Le Pen in the first round of the presidential election, 22 April 2012; parliamentary constituencies in which her score exceeded 12.5 percent of registered voters. *Source:* Centre de recherches politiques de Sciences Po 2012.

33 percent) and tied for first with François Hollande among *employés* (service sector workers) (28 percent) in the first round of the presidential election, while coming second to Sarkozy among employers (19 percent) and *petits indépendants* (artisans, shopkeepers, and owners of small and medium-sized enterprises, or SMEs (17 percent).[1] In turn, the failure of the Socialists to address this socioeconomic crisis, as reflected by their strategic ambivalence and internal divisions in the face of Sarkozy's economic reforms and social retrenchment, has enabled the FN to present itself as the principal defender of these crisis-ridden constituencies among the major parties. Meanwhile, Sarkozy's repressive discourse and policies on immigration have served to normalize the FN's exclusionary conception of the nation and anti-immigration agenda among growing numbers of voters.

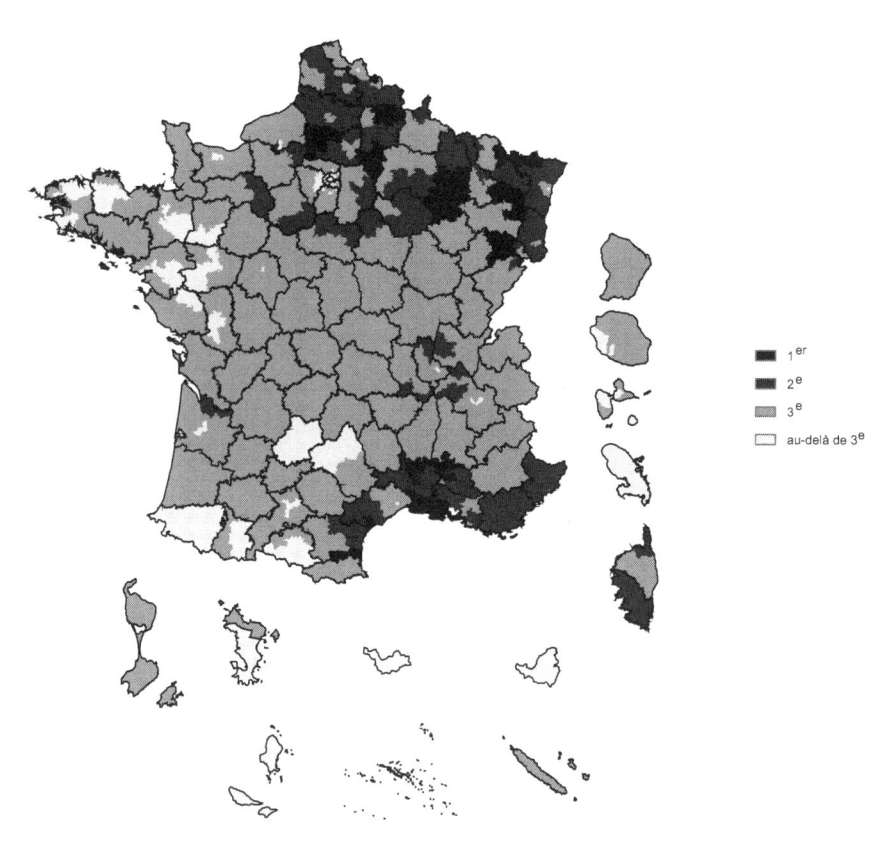

Map 8.2. Marine Le Pen's Performance in the First Round of the 2012 Presidential Elections.
Votes cast in favor of Marine Le Pen in the first round of the presidential election, 22 April 2012; her final ranking within each parliamentary constituency (1st; 2nd; 3rd; lower than 3rd.) *Source:* Centre de recherches politiques de Sciences Po 2012.

At a second level, the FN's adoption of an antiglobalization and anti-EU economic program, and its pursuit of a strategy of normalization under Ms. Le Pen's leadership, have provided an effective electoral platform on which the party was able to capitalize in 2012. In particular, its advocacy of populist economic policies in the form of statism, protectionism, and abandonment of the euro, combined with the sanitizing of its image through the downplaying of its extremist associations and rhetoric, enhanced the party's appeal among working- and middle-class voters who, after experiencing a steady deterioration in their socioeconomic position over the past quarter century, have been hardest hit by the financial crash of 2008–9 and European debt crisis of 2010–12. Thus, the results of the 2012 elections put paid to predictions that consigned the party to political oblivion following the reversal of 2007. Instead, the 2012 elections signaled the party's renewed electoral potency under Marine Le Pen's stewardship, and represent a significant step in her campaign to transform it from an antisystem into a governing party.

Explaining the Resurgence of the FN

Ideologically, the FN combines political antiliberalism, in the guise of an exclusionary, ethnocentric authoritarianism, with (at least since the mid-1980s) economic antiliberalism, in the form of protectionism and "welfare chauvinism."[2] Sociologically, the party continues to rely on the support of those strata—*petits indépendants* through the 1980s, industrial workers since the early 1990s—who are most threatened by economic and social modernization.[3] Thus, in terms of its ideology, program, discourse, sociological support, and spatial positioning within the French political system, the FN under Marine Le Pen remains essentially the same party that it was under her father. What needs to be explained, therefore, is how, from its precipitous decline in the 2007 elections, the FN was able to reassert itself as an electoral force in 2012. This will be done in two stages. First, we will focus on the favorable economic and societal context, notably the worsening structural and cultural crisis affecting French workers and a growing segment of the middle classes, to which the party is currently responding and that constitutes the principal factor of political demand for its support. In turn, we will examine how, under Marine Le Pen's leadership, the FN has repackaged its discourse and program in order to harness the grievances of these crisis-ridden constituencies while successfully rebranding itself from a protest party into a potential party of government—the factors of political supply accounting for its electoral resurgence.

Petits Indépendants and Industrial Workers in Crisis

The attraction exercised by the FN among *petits indépendants* and industrial workers highlights the similar conditions of crisis that have overtaken these groups within advanced capitalist society. Economically, such a crisis reflects the growing functional redundancy of *petits indépendants* and blue-collar workers within the processes of advanced capitalist production and the ensuing erosion of their material and social status in modern industrial society. From a sociopolitical standpoint, this crisis reflects the mounting social alienation and political irrelevance felt by members of these groups within advanced capitalist society. As the economic and social structures that underpinned their social roles and cultural norms eroded and their concerns went unaddressed by the French republican state, voters from these groups increasingly latched on to the FN's xenophobic and repressive discourse.

Through the 1980s, *petits indépendants* have constituted the principal base of support of the FN. Their attraction to the party reflected the combination of technological and social changes and economic crises that have impacted these independent strata throughout the postwar period. The latter saw the most sweeping economic modernization and rationalization the country had experienced to date, resulting in the dramatic sectoral decline of *petits indépendants*.[4] In less than fifty years, they went from being one of the most important economic groups in the country to representing an endangered species. Incapable of competing with concentrated and rationalized forms of industry and commerce, they grew increasingly susceptible to economic crisis, and hence became a significant reservoir of discontent that fueled the FN's electoral rise in the 1980s.

Since the early 1990s there has been a seminal shift in the composition of the party's electorate as *petits indépendants* were supplanted by industrial workers as its principal base of support. Accordingly, the FN came first to eclipse the PCF and then to outcompete the PS as the leading recipient of the working class vote. The migration of French workers to the extreme right reflects the profound social crisis that has overtaken the working class as a result of the structural transformation of the French economy since the late 1970s. Principally, it translates the worsening socioeconomic standing of French workers as a result of the spread of manufacturing unemployment and the ensuing erosion in their standard of living over the past twenty-five years. After peaking at 12.5 percent in 1995, by the turn of the millennium the country's aggregate unemployment rate had settled at between 9 percent and 10 percent. Industrial workers were the worst affected, with their living standards suffering a dramatic decline since the 1980s.[5]

The rise of unemployment among industrial workers and deterioration of their incomes over the past quarter century can be attributed to the strategies of *déplanification* (state disengagement from the economy) and deregulation that were followed by the French state in order to meet the challenges of globalization and European economic integration. In terms of macroeconomic policy, this entailed privatizing state-owned firms or subjecting them to market forces, while abandoning the Keynesian focus on growth and employment in favor of monetary targeting and inflation control so as to remain within the EMU. In microeconomic terms, price, wage, and credit controls were lifted; restrictions on layoffs and temporary and part-time employment were relaxed; and occupational safety laws and worker participation rules were ignored in order to make it easier for businesses to cut their labor costs.⁶ The ensuing wage deindexation and employer initiatives to maximize profits significantly eroded workers' living standards. At the same time, increased labor market flexibility made it possible for employers to restructure their operations by resorting to mass layoffs. Finally, the exponential rise in capital flows, in combination with unprecedented access to cheap labor and minimal taxes and regulations abroad, intensified the outsourcing of French manufacturing. In short, the country's economic liberalization, deindustrialization, and shift to a services-based economy starting in the 1970s and 1980s underscored workers' growing redundancy within the new postindustrial economy.

In turn, the social crisis that enveloped the French working class was accompanied by the correlative collapse of their principal sectoral and partisan organizations, notably the trade unions and the PCF. The transformation of the French economy since the 1970s has eroded these dual loci of working-class organization and representation. From a peak of 35 percent in 1949, the unionization rate fell to only 7 percent in 2007.⁷ Similarly, the PCF parliamentary vote declined from almost 50 percent in the early 1950s to a mere 2.5 percent in 2007.⁸

At one level, the decline of the unions and PCF was the result of deindustrialization and the transition to a service economy, whereby industrial workers went from accounting for around four in ten members of the total workforce during the late 1960s and early 1970s to fewer than one in three by the end of the 1990s.⁹ However, of equal importance has been the sweeping transformation of industrial production since the 1970s, which eliminated the structural conditions that had facilitated workers' economic and political organization. The growing unsuitability of large productive units to the demands of global competition and the individualization of consumer tastes spurred a movement away from the concentrated factories of the Fordist era. These were replaced by diffuse or flexible forms of production characterized by automation, flow-process production, just-in-time inputs and outputs, and the subcontracting of subordinate or peripheral tasks.¹⁰ In turn, the transformation of productive structures and processes was supported by a juridical framework that codified this shift to more flexible and adaptive modes of production, legislation such as the Auroux Laws (1982), the thirty-five-hour work week (1998), and the Fillon Law (2004) progressively increasing employers' leverage over their workers.¹¹

Through the transformation of production and corresponding legislation of labor market flexibility, the process of capitalist restructuring during the 1980s and 1990s fractured the industrial workforce and dissolved the solidarities that had formerly instilled a collective sense of identity among

French workers. Consequently, the latter were increasingly unable to recognize themselves in the unions and PCF that had appealed historically to the Fordist labor aristocracy concentrated in large factories and traditional heavy industry. In turn, the PS failed to adequately address workers' anxieties and to arrest their economic and social decline. Complicit in the structural reforms that eroded their sectoral clout in the economy and accepting the neoliberal rationale for widespread privatization and deregulation while embracing European economic integration, the PS abandoned any programmatic attempt to reverse the decline of the working class.[12] Thus, deprived of their traditional corporative and collective markers of identity and considering the left and the unions to be unwilling or unable to defend their social *acquis* (achievements), French workers sought new sources of political identification and turned in growing numbers to the FN.

Sarkozy's election in April 2007 did little to allay the social crisis affecting a growing proportion of the French middle and working classes. Indeed, the structural transformation of the French economy that continued apace during his presidency served only to intensify this crisis. Under the guise of maintaining the country's international competitiveness and fulfilling its eurozone obligations, his government pursued a strategy of economic liberalization while reducing the costly social anesthesia state that was put in place in the 1980s and 1990s to dampen the pain of *déplanification*.[13] Thus, after attempting to shrink the public sector through natural attrition in 2007, it proposed to cut the public sector by 30,000 posts in 2008 and again in 2010. In turn, public sector cuts were complemented by the privatization of the last remaining state enterprises and the opening of certain public services to private capital.[14]

By the same token, following the retrenchment strategy put in place by his predecessors, Sarkozy sought to diminish the economic costs of the welfare state by implementing substantial cuts in social spending. At one level, he tried to shift the burden of social security financing away from firms toward consumers by offsetting a reduction in the share of the payroll tax levied on employers with an increase in the value-added tax—the so-called *TVA sociale* (social VAT). Similarly, he also attempted to further reduce social spending by increasing individual health-care liabilities as well as diminishing unemployment benefits for those who refused to take a job. Finally, his government complemented these retrenchment measures with policies to stimulate saving and encourage people to work more, while seeking to reduce the fiscal burden on the wealthiest French people. In this vein, it exempted employers and employees from paying social security taxes on overtime work, increased the *bouclier fiscal* (tax shield) the cut-off above which income is taxed at the highest marginal rate), reduced the capital taxes on inheritances, and cut the supplemental *impôt de solidarité sur la fortune* (ISF wealth tax).[15]

The 2008–9 financial crash and the 2010–11 European sovereign debt crisis failed to deflect the course of these policies. After the passage of a timid and short-lived stimulus package at the end of 2008 and 2009, the Sarkozy government resumed its course of public sector and welfare retrenchment.[16] This strategy gained particular urgency in the midst of the ongoing European sovereign debt crisis as financial markets lost confidence in the country's ability to service its debt, culminating in the downgrading of its AAA credit rating in January 2012. In December 2010 the government pushed through a pension reform that standardized public sector pensions with those in the private sector by making retirement benefits for both categories of workers contingent on paying into the social security system for forty-one years. In turn, in August 2011 it introduced an austerity budget that sought to reduce government expenditures by €1 billion in 2011 and another €11 billion in 2012. This plan was revised in November 2011 to take account of falling growth projections, calling for €65 billion in budget cuts by 2016, including €7 billion in 2012 and €11.6 billion in 2013, with the ultimate goal of achieving €100 billion in savings and balancing the budget by 2016. Since these cuts will accelerate the course of public sector retrenchment and welfare reform, they are bound to disproportionately impact those worst affected by the economic crisis.[17]

Finally, the ongoing disarticulation of the workplace and continuing erosion of professional and social identities that has been wrought by globalization threatened new, previously unaffected professional and social categories, including service-sector *employés*, members of the intermediary professions, and even the previously secure category of *cadres* (management executives). As we saw, these new losers from globalization provided the additional tinder that helped fuel the FN's electoral resurgence in 2012.

The Front National's Aggiornamento

In addition to the context of crisis adumbrated above, the FN's electoral resurgence also reflects the favorable conditions of political supply that the party has cultivated since Marine Le Pen's accession to the leadership in January 2011. Central to these conditions of political supply is the programmatic and discursive aggiornamento that the "new" FN has undergone. At one level, this aggiornamento can be seen in the ideological positions and policy stances adopted by the party since 2007. Through its elaboration of a holistic critique of globalization, the FN has derived a program that renews its appeal to the sectoral losers of the latter. Second, the party's aggiornamento has implied a normalization of its image and discourse. By following a strategy of *dédiabolisation* (dedemonization), the party has sought to broaden its appeal to voters who might agree with its conception of contemporary French society and the policy solutions it proposes, but who were heretofore reluctant to vote for it due to its extremist reputation. Thus, armed with this critique of globalization and working to soften its image, the FN under Marine Le Pen is seeking to break out of its marginal position as an antisystem party and present itself as a potential party of government.

Beginning with the programmatic dimension of this aggiornamento, the FN has developed a coherent theoretical framework for analyzing French social relations. On the basis of this framework, the party has shifted its critique of French society and the policy proposals it derives from it away from the organic ethnonationalism that formerly underpinned its program toward an economic and cultural nationalism couched in the language of political pluralism and universal rights. Thus, though the new FN in effect proposes the same policies, these are presented in a very different light, downplaying their xenophobic character and instead affirming their practical necessity as a function of the deleterious impacts of globalization. As we shall see, even the central plank of the FN's program since the 1970s, the fight against immigration, has been repackaged in terms of this critique of globalization rather than by reproducing the racial hierarchies posited by the FN and extreme right historically. Thus, this critique provides the party with a universal explanatory key for understanding the country's current social and economic ills and to distilling the policy responses by which to arrest the deleterious effects of globalization on French society.

The political program elaborated by the FN as a function of its critique of globalization posits the advent of a new fundamental division in French politics. The latter is no longer conceived in terms of the traditional opposition between left and right, but instead in terms of the irreducible conflict between the advocates of globalization on the one hand and the defenders of national identity on the other.[18] Indeed, in contrast to the critique of globalization developed by movements and parties of the left, that advanced by the contemporary FN is undertaken on nationalist rather than socioeconomic grounds. It connects the growing economic interdependence and integration synonymous with globalization to the leveling of cultural and national differences. Accordingly, Marine Le Pen focuses her attacks on "a capitalism without frontiers" and the neoliberal philosophy that justifies it on the basis that these empower financial speculation and maximize corporate profits at the expense of the economic well-being and social stability of countries.[19] In turn, globalization is criticized as culturally reductive and morally debasing due to the materialist and consumerist values it propagates.[20]

The FN's critique of globalization leads it to take aim at two of its principal manifestations in France. First, it subtends the FN's attack against the EU, which is portrayed as the principal vehicle through which neoliberal globalization has been imposed on the country by the dominant economic and political elites. In the first place, the EU's baleful impact is to be seen in terms of the socioeconomic costs of harnessing the French economy to its liberalizing policies and monetarist strictures, notably monetary union. The result has been to put French workers into increasingly direct competition with low-wage labor in the developing world, while hastening the country's deindustrialization by facilitating the outsourcing of French industry. Meanwhile, small and medium-sized French firms are incapable of competing with the cheaper goods produced by multinational firms in low-cost economies, condemning them to bankruptcy and their workers to unemployment.[21] Second, the fiscal and monetary strictures of EMU have deprived the French state of its sovereign control over economic policy. Instead, the state defers to the European Central Bank and the European Commission to set macroeconomic policy and hence direct French economic development.[22] Third, as the purveyor of a rootless philosophy that seeks to transform the world's peoples into consumers within a seamless global marketplace, the EU is seen as the destroyer of the cultural and linguistic specificities that underpin French civilization and identity.[23] Finally, politically, the EU is excoriated for its antidemocratic character because it strips the French people of their sovereign control over their economic, social, and cultural destiny. Instead, it forces laws on them in the formulation of which they have no say and about whose acceptance they are not consulted.[24]

Second, the FN's critique of globalization is extended to the phenomenon of immigration, which is conceived as its human face. This critique is no longer presented in terms of the rejection of the other but rather as an economically and culturally destabilizing force wrought by the "global financial mega machine."[25] Accordingly, immigration is portrayed as simultaneously exploitative of immigrants of the developing world and economically disastrous for native workers in the developed countries.[26] In turn, the promotion of immigration by the stewards of globalization is held to threaten French national identity, which is being overwhelmed by culturally inassimilable foreigners who have been welcomed into the country under the banner of multiculturalism.[27] By presenting its opposition to immigration from the developing world in terms of the imperatives of economic self-defense while dwelling on its immoral dimension for the immigrants who are held to most benefit from it, the FN has repackaged its opposition to immigration by situating it within a holistic critique of neoliberal globalization. It is thus able to deflect the accusations of racism and xenophobia while continuing to oppose immigration in the name of preserving France's economic sovereignty and cultural identity.[28]

Programmatically, the critique of globalization in its institutional, political, and social guises provides the basis for the FN's assertion of the principle of national sovereignty. However, instead of positing this principle as before in relation to an exclusive national identity or ethnocultural *différencialisme* (differentialism), this is done by evoking the principle of democratic accountability so as to legitimize the state's reassertion of control over the forces that affect the nation. At an economic level, this reassertion of the prerogatives of national sovereignty leads the FN to call for a middle path between the savage liberalism advocated by the centrist UMP and PS, on the one hand, and the anticapitalism of the far left internationalist parties on the other.[29]

This implies reordering French economic life around two principles. First, it translates into a reaffirmation of *étatisme* (statism), the resurrection of a strategic role for the state in coordinating the country's economic development and presiding over its social stability.[30] This entails reendowing the state with financial and administrative competencies to steer the French economy toward maximizing the well-being of the society and shielding it from the depredations of globalization. In practice, the state becomes responsible for directing investment in order to safeguard French industry and jobs while seeking to enhance economic productivity and performance. Thus, dirigisme in a *frontiste* guise would reverse the course of shrinking the public sector that was engaged by Sarkozy, even countenancing the nationalization of certain enterprises so as to preserve them from bankruptcy or foreign takeover.[31]

Second, the adoption of a strategy to shield the country from globalization implies a recourse to economic and social protectionism. At a first and most obvious level, this involves enacting commercial policies to protect French enterprises and workers against competition from foreign firms and labor, particularly in the developing world. By the same token, it also implies providing support to nationally bound *patrons responsables* (*petits indépendants* and SME owners) against rootless *patrons commis* (multinational corporations traded on the Paris bourse). In both cases, this requires reasserting the country's monetary sovereignty—leaving the euro and reestablishing the franc—on the grounds that participation in the single currency is not only economically ruinous for French industries and workers, but also profoundly antidemocratic as well.[32] Contrary to the expanding and seamless world market envisioned by the advocates of globalization and EMU, then, the FN's goal is to reestablish a Europe of nations capable of feeding and producing for itself while providing jobs to its own people and consumers for its firms. Organized according to the principle of economic subsidiarity, this organic economic system would entail creating a nationally autarkic space in which goods are locally or regionally produced and consumed within a country, and in which national producers are protected and supported so as to sustain these local markets.[33]

Finally, the advocacy of protectionism is extended to the social realm under the principle of *la préférence nationale* (national preference). At one level, this would involve stopping the largely illegal inflow of immigrants who compete with French workers for jobs and push down their wages and living standards. In turn, access to jobs, benefits, and housing would be predicated on the criterion of national appurtenance in order to prevent foreigners from taking advantage of the country's welfare and social security system.[34] Of particular note is that these arguments for controlling immigration and allocating social benefits are advanced on economic rather than racial or ethnonationalist grounds. They fit into the FN's assertion of the principle of national sovereignty as a means of resisting the socially leveling and politically disempowering impetus of globalization, while reasserting the democratic prerogatives and legitimacy of the French state. Thus, the party has repackaged its former ethnonationalist program in a more palatable guise in the hope of breaking down the reticence of French voters toward it and securing their support in 2012 and beyond.

In this respect, the couching of its policies in terms of a broad struggle against globalization rather than a closed exclusionary nationalism connects to the second key factor in the discursive aggiornamento undergone by the FN under Marine Le Pen: the transformation of its image from a raucous fringe party to a normal party ready to assume the charges of government. At a first and most obvious level, this attempt to recast itself in a normal guise has led the new FN to rid itself of its most extreme followers. Accordingly, the assorted neofascists, Vichyistes, fundamentalist Catholics, and erstwhile defenders of l'Algérie française who were present at the FN's founding and accompanied its rise have been pushed to the margins of the party if not expelled outright. This *assainissement* (cleaning up) of the FN's image has gone hand in hand with Le Pen *fille's* determination to purge it of *les zozos* (clowns): the skinheads and other tenants of extreme right-wing folklore who were fellow travelers to the party in her father's time but whose violent demeanor frightened potential voters away.[35]

By the same token, the FN under Marine Le Pen has been much more forthright in condemning the German occupation and the Holocaust during World War II than it was under her father. Shortly after being elected party leader, she condemned "what happened in the camps [during the Second World War as] the height of barbarism," contrasting sharply with Jean Marie Le Pen's notorious quip that the "gas chambers were a minor detail in the history of the Second World War." More broadly, anti-Semitism has been officially disavowed by the new leadership as having no place in the party's discourse, a significant evolution from Jean-Marie Le Pen's reign.[36]

Finally, following in the image of its leader, a divorcé and working mother of two who is unabashedly pro-choice and living out of wedlock with her current partner, the new FN presents itself as much more culturally tolerant than it was under her father.[37] Once again, however, its defense of the progressive values of feminism, abortion rights, and homosexual rights is presented in contradistinction to the supposed cultural benightedness of Muslim immigrants whose cultural and religious origins render them fundamentally inassimilable into the French cultural mainstream. In this way, these progressive values are identified as part of France's or Europe's cultural patrimony and thus are portrayed as irreducibly at odds with the value systems of immigrants from non-European cultures.[38]

This affirmation of progressive values as preternaturally French dovetails with the second principal element of the FN's discursive aggiornamento: the affirmation of the party's democratic convictions and congruence of its prescriptions with France's republican heritage. Most obviously, as we have seen, this involves toning down the exclusionary nationalist tenor of its anti-immigrant discourse and replacing it with an attack on multiculturalism in general and Islam in particular as fundamentally incompatible with the nation's republican values. Multiculturalism is cast as the inevitable byproduct of immigration and portrayed as an agent of division and fragmentation that threatens France's cultural coherence, social unity, and, ultimately, republican identity.[39] In turn, due to the disproportionate presence of Muslims among these immigrants, Marine Le Pen warns against the impending threat of the Islamicization of French society that is being facilitated by the lax immigration policies of successive French governments. Denouncing Islamism as a totalitarian ideology that would seek to impose sharia law in France, she is thus able to cast herself as the "last defender" of the foundational republican principle of *laïcité* (secularity), the affirmation of the secular identity of the French state as the guarantor of equality under the law, and to present the FN as "the only true movement capable of defending this good and great principle of the French republic."[40]

The defense of *laïcité* is central to the FN's discursive aggiornamento for two reasons. First, it situates the party in the republican tradition, thereby making it possible to occlude or at least blur the antidemocratic and antirepublican associations with which it is historically identified. Second and perhaps more importantly, the defense of *laïcité* allows the FN to present itself as the guarantor of the French republic and its core values. This enables it to pursue the fight against immigration under ostensibly republican auspices, thereby defusing the charge of racism and xenophobia with which its anti-immigration program was formerly associated and hence making it more palatable to voters who might share the FN's diagnosis that there are too many immigrants in France but who could not bring themselves to vote for it due to its extremist pedigree.[41]

Finally, Marine Le Pen seizes on the core republican principle of equality in order to assert her populist credentials as a woman of the people who will fight on behalf of women against the privileges of the economic and political elites that subjugate and exploit them. Hence her denunciation of the "caste," conceived as a loose conglomeration of these elites who have exposed the country to the depredations of globalization, economic liberalization, and uncontrolled immigration, for the benefit of oligarchical capital and at the expense of the common man.[42] Politically, this caste is embodied in the collusion of the major parties who, while engaging in a simulacrum of democratic competition, share a deep ideological and economic stake in globalization. Hence Le Pen's designation of the UMP and PS under the moniker "UMPS."[43]

In contrast to this UMPS analogous to the despotic and sclerotic Ancien Régime,[44] the FN casts itself as the agent of republican and democratic renewal. In true populist fashion, it calls for the instauration of direct democracy in the form of popular consultation by referendum so as to bypass the corrupted instances of representative democracy, the mainstream parties, and their oligarchical backers, and to restore the power of the vox populi.[45] Correlatively, on the economic front, the new FN seeks to burnish its populist credentials by calling for measures to moralize French capitalism. Hence Le Pen's condemnation of "the powers of money" and her call for greater "sharing of the value added" and a "more equitable redistribution of super profits."[46]

In short, the FN under Marine Le Pen portrays itself as a progressive and democratic party that aims to reassert the republican ideals of patriotism, *laïcité*, and equality instead of the ethnonationalism that had subtended its discourse in her father's time. As a result, the party has been able to broaden its appeal to attract voters who agree with its critiques of immigration and globalization but were alienated by the party's former identification with ideas that were identified with the extreme right historically, such as Vichyisme, colonialism, Catholic *intégrisme* (fundamentalism), or biological racism. This does not mean that the FN's ethnonationalist program has changed in practice. But by couching this program in a holistic critique of globalization and legitimizing it through the evocation of republican principles, the FN under Marine Le Pen has been very effective in mounting, in the words of one commentator, "an appeal to populist fears [based on] dressing up intolerance as common sense."[47]

Conclusion

The success registered by the FN in the 2012 elections naturally raises the question of where the party goes from here. Is it poised to build on this success and further progress toward its goal of exercising power or, as in the past, is it condemned to suffer reverses that will restore it to its formerly marginal position on the French political scene? On this score, it is worth noting that despite its gains in 2012, the FN failed to achieve its objective of splintering the mainstream right and forcing a reconfiguration of the latter around itself. Indeed, despite a handful of instances to the contrary, the overwhelming majority of UMP candidates respected the party leadership's injunction not to enter into electoral alliances with the FN in the parliamentary elections.

Yet, just because it failed this time around does not mean that this strategy will not be more successful during the next electoral cycle. The FN is bound to profit from the factional divisions that have emerged within the UMP following Sarkozy's departure, not to mention the economic fallout from the eurozone debt crisis and the failure of the major parties to resolve the country's endemic unemployment crisis. Likewise, barring a U-turn by the Hollande government, the FN seems poised to continue capitalizing on the PS's abandonment of industrial workers and *employés* over the next electoral cycle.

Meanwhile, in the longer term, the party's prospects are brightened by the growing number of voters who agree with its positions. At one level, this could be seen in the attempt of the mainstream candidates, principally Nicolas Sarkozy, to coopt the FN's electorate by campaigning on the party's signature issues of immigration, crime, and Europe. In the 2012 campaign, Sarkozy pandered to FN voters by claiming that "France has too many foreigners," calling for the labeling of halal meat, and threatening to pull France out of the Schengen customs union unless its other members clamped down on illegal immigration.[48] Thus, though Marine Le Pen failed to accede to the second-round runoff in 2012, she was inordinately successful in setting the terms of the electoral debate not only on the immigration issue, but also regarding the questions of economic, social, and European policy.

In turn, the FN's growing influence over the French political debate can be seen in the *droitisation* (shift to the right) of the general electorate, with recent polling data showing that an increasing proportion of French voters share the party's positions on key issues. According to a rolling survey on political attitudes that was last conducted in October 2011, on the immigration issue fully 60 percent of the French believed there were too many immigrants in France. On the economy, the same survey found that 49 percent of the French believed that the capitalist system should be fundamentally reformed and 46 percent that it should be reformed in some of its aspects. Meanwhile, articulating with the FN's critique of globalization, an exit poll taken on the day of the first round of the presidential election found that 60 percent of voters believed that France was too open to the world and should protect itself more, while only 22 percent thought that the country should open itself more to the world. Finally, at the political level, in October 2011 60 percent of the French believed that democracy in France does not function very well or that it does not function at all, while only 39 percent had any confidence in the EU. Only 13 percent had confidence in the political parties, while 52 percent claimed that they trusted neither the left nor the right to govern the country.[49]

In short, a substantial reservoir of support exists for the FN's positions. The normalization of the party's image and correlative couching of its program in opposition to globalization in the name of the republican ideals of sovereignty, equality, and *laïcité* singularly equip it to harness this potential support. When one combines this updating of the party's discourse and image with the worsening social crisis hitting industrial workers and a growing segment of the French middle class, the electoral prospects for the FN under Marine Le Pen appear bright beyond 2012.

This diagnosis was confirmed by the party's groundbreaking results in the 2014 municipal and European parliamentary elections. In the former, the FN won an unprecedented eleven mayoralties in cities of over 10,000 inhabitants—the previous highest tally being four in 1995. In the latter, the party won 24.86 percent of the vote in front of the UMP with 20.81 percent and the Socialists with 13.98 percent. This marked the first time in the history of the Fifth Republic—even arguably going back to 1871—that a far right party has come first in a nationally contested election. Beyond attesting to the effectiveness of the FN's discursive and programmatic aggiornamento, these results bring the party closer to its new goal of achieving and exercising political power than ever before.

Notes

1. IFOP, "Premier tour de l'élection présidentielle 2012: profil des électeurs et clés du scrutin," April 22, 2012, 9–10, http://www.ifopelections.fr/resources/Downloads/290/Documents.pdf.
2. See Gabriel Goodliffe, *The Resurgence of the Radical Right in France: From Boulangisme to the Front National* (New York: Cambridge University Press, 2012), chap. 2.
3. Ibid., 24–26.
4. Ibid., 64–69.
5. Ibid., 282.
6. See Jonah Levy, "Redeploying the State: Liberalization and Social Policy in France," in *Beyond Continuity: Institutional Change in Advanced Political Economies*, ed. W. Streeck and K. Thelen (New York: Oxford University Press, 2005), 103–26; and Stéphane Beaud and Michel Pialoux, *Retour sur la condition ouvrière: Enquête aux usines Peugeot de Sochaux-Montbéliard* (Paris: Fayard, 1999), 423–24.
7. Dominique Andolfatto, "Syndicalisme," in Lau, *L'État de la France*, 231.
8. CEVIPOF, "Résultats des élections législatives des 10 et 17 juin 2007," *Baromètre politique français: Elections 2007*, http://www.cevipof.com/bpf/; and Michel Verret, *La culture ouvrière*, 2nd ed. (Paris: L'Harmattan, 1996), 235.
9. Nonna Mayer, "Du communisme au Front National," *L'Histoire*, no. 195 (1996), 111.
10. Danièle Linhart, "Travail: Grandes tendances," in Lau, *L'État de la France 2010–11*, 65–9; and Beaud and Pialoux, *Retour sur la condition ouvrière*, chap. 1.
11. Beaud and Pialoux, *Retour sur la condition ouvrière*, 422–24; and Chris Howell, "The Dilemmas of Post-Fordism: Socialists, Flexibility and Labour Market Deregulation in France," *Politics and Society* 20(1) (1999):71–99.
12. See, for example, Bruno Jeanbart and Olivier Ferrand, "Gauche, quelle majorité électorale pour 2012?," *Fondation Terra Nova: Projet 2012*—Contribution no. 1 (2012), http://www.tnova.fr/sites/default/files/Rapport%20Terra%20Nova%20Strat%C3%A9gie%20%C3%A9lectorale.pdf.
13. Levy, "Redeploying the State."
14. Norbert Holcblat, "Politique macroéconomique:Une mise en perspective," in Lau, *L'Etat de la France 2011–2012*, 175–77.
15. Jean-Marie Monnier, "Politique fiscale: Une mise en perspective," in Lau, *L'État de la France 2010–2011*, 179–88.
16. Jonah Levy, "The Return of the State? French Economic Policy under Nicolas Sarkozy," paper presented at the annual conference of the American Political Science Association, Washington, DC, September 2–5, 2010.
17. *Le Monde* [online], "Fillon dévoile un plan de 11 milliards d'euros de réduction des déficits," August 24, 2011, http://www.lemonde.fr/politique/article /2011/08/24/francois-fillon-devoile-son-plan-de-11-milliards-d-euros-de-reduction-des-deficits_1563069_823448.html
18. Caroline Monnot and Abel Mestre, *Le système Le Pen : Enquête sur les réseaux du Front National* (Paris: Denoël, 2011), 115.
19. Ibid., 117.
20. Ibid., 120.
21. Marine Le Pen, *Pour que vive la France* (Paris: Grancher, 2012), 76–77.
22. Ibid., 57.
23. Ibid., 77–78.
24. Ibid., 78–79.
25. Monnot and Mestre, *Le système Le Pen*, 48.
26. Le Pen, *Pour que vive la France*, 82, 85.

27. Ibid., 86.
28. Sylvain Crépon, *Enquête au cœur du nouveau Front national* (Paris: Nouveau Monde Éditions, 2012), 178.
29. Monnot and Mestre, *Le système Le Pen*, 114.
30. Le Pen, *Pour que vive la France*, 220.
31. Ibid., 222.
32. Ibid., 91.
33. Monnot and Mestre, *Le système Le Pen*, 118.
34. Ibid., 158.
35. Ibid., 135–51.
36. Ibid., 147, 148.
37. Crépon, *Enquête au cœur*, chap. 5.
38. Ibid., 257.
39. Ibid., 181–87.
40. Monnot and Mestre, *Le système Le Pen*, 130.
41. Crépon, *Enquête au cœur*, 213–14.
42. Le Pen, *Pour que vive la France*, 116–20.
43. Ibid., 134–42.
44. Ibid., 90.
45. Ibid., 180.
46. Monnot and Mestre, *Le système Le Pen*, 154.
47. *The Economist*, "France's Far Right: They can't keep her down," March 19, 2011, 59–60.
48. Harriet Alexander, "France election 2012: Islam takes center stage in battle for France," *Daily Telegraph* [online], April 8, 2012, http://www.telegraph.co.uk/news/worldnews/europe/france/9191923/France-election-2012-Islam-takes-centre-stage-in-battle-for-France.html; and IFOP, "Premier tour de l'élection présidentielle 2012," 71.
49. See CEVIPOF [online], "Le Baromètre de la confiance politique : Vague 3–Octobre 2011," October 2011, http://www.cevipof.fr/fr/2012/recherche/barometre/; and IFOP, "Premier tour de l'élection présidentielle," 71.

Part III

The Electoral Campaign and Hollande's Challenges

Chapter 9

Hollande's Economic Agenda

Jacques Fayette

The year 2012 was marked in Europe by stagnation or recession and an unemployment rate of 11.3 percent, but the difficulties faced by France began in the year 2000 with a collapse of industrial production. In 2007, candidate Nicolas Sarkozy believed and maintained that political will alone would allow France to fully recover; in 2012 François Holland held a similar belief. By examining the 2007–12 period we will present the policies of the Sarkozy-Fillon administration, analyze the role of the economy in the 2012 electoral campaign, and assess the policies of the Hollande-Ayrault administration during its first seven months of office.

The Economic Policies of President Sarkozy

On the night of his election on Sunday, May 6, 2007, Nicolas Sarkozy said in his acceptance address, "The French people have chosen to break with the ideas, habits and behavior of the past. I want to rehabilitate the values of work, authority, morality, merit."[1] For the new president, France had to move forward again and to break with the status quo of the twelve years of the Chirac presidency, even if, in his mind, the status quo dated back twenty-five years to when François Mitterrand was elected.

The defining characteristic of the newly elected president was voluntarism. In the sole economic arena, it translated into a conviction that France's loss of market share in international trade, deindustrialization, and its effects on unemployment and living standards could be tackled by setting out guidelines that would inspire energetic action.[2] On the eve on the first round of the election, the *Economist* gave an analysis of his campaign: "On the evidence of his career and his campaign, Mr. Sarkozy

---

Notes for this chapter begin on page 149.

is less a principled liberal than a brutal pragmatist. Yet he is the only candidate brave enough to advocate the 'rupture' with its past that France needs after so many gloomy years. It has been said that France advances by revolution from time to time but seldom, if ever, manages to reform. Mr. Sarkozy offers at least a chance of proving this aphorism wrong."[3]

The interventionist attitude of the former interior minister had become more and more intense during the campaign, as was illustrated by his attack on one of the pillars of liberalism: the open borders within the EU. Those attacks were aimed at the European Commission with regards to its competition policy and the laxity it demonstrated within the framework of the World Trade Organization (WTO). The European Central Bank was also held accountable for not promoting a weak euro as a factor of competition on world markets.

In his May 6 victory speech, he issued a plea to his European partners: "I urge them to hear the voice of the peoples who want to be protected. I urge them not to ignore the anger of the peoples that perceive the European Union not as a protection but as a Trojan horse of all the threats carried by the transformations of the world."[4] The concerns of the *Economist* would find repeated justification over the following five years.

The first significant initiative was to entrust Jacques Attali with the presidency of a commission for the liberation of French growth (the Attali Commission). The association of the two terms "liberation" and "growth" was in itself a very strong signal. The presence of seven foreigners including Franco Bassanini and Mario Monti (Italy), Theodore Zeldin (United Kingdom), and Ana Palacio (Spain) was hailed as an unusual token of openness. Three hundred and sixteen reforms were listed in the report that was published in January 2008 and the European Commission supported those reforms while (already!) considering the French fiscal adjustment to be very slow to materialize. Among the emergencies identified by the Attali Commission was the projected failure during the 2007–12 period to bring the budget deficit below 3 percent of GDP in conformity with the Stability and Growth Pact. A second emergency the report highlighted was the need to decrease labor costs by reducing the social security charges paid by employers and compensating for the lost revenues through a VAT increase. In May 2010 it was estimated that 60 percent of the measures proposed by the Attali Commission had been implemented, while at the same time a second Attali Commission was charged with drafting another report dedicated to finding a way out of the economic crisis.

The second initiative of June 2007 was the launching of the General Revision of Public Policies (Révision Générale des Politiques Publiques, RGPP), a program that would clearly define the state's fields of intervention and specify the best ways for it to act. The component that attracted the most media coverage (and that sparked the most controversy among the opposition) was the nonreplacement of one out of every two civil servants that would retire between 2009 and 2011. This rule was implemented with exceptions such as in universities and in the Justice Ministry. In total, around 150,000 civil servant jobs were scrapped during Nicolas Sarkozy's five-year term.

Third, on August 21, 2007, the Travail, Emploi, Pouvoir d'Achat (work, employment and purchasing power; TEPA) Act was enacted. This TEPA legislation was essentially fiscal in nature. It established the so-called *bouclier fiscal* (tax shield) protecting taxpayers against taxation that surpassed 50 percent of income. Other measures included reducing taxation of property assets for gifts and inheritances, and allowed individuals to deduct 75 percent of the solidarity tax on wealth (*impôt de solidarité sur la fortune*; ISF) by investing in SMEs. These measures all weighed heavily on the public finances and the opposition did not miss the opportunity to present this as a symbol of Sarkozy acting as president of the wealthy.

Tax Exemption for Overtime

The issue of work time and of state intervention in its determination is a very good illustration of French-style dirigisme.[5] Under the Socialist administration of Lionel Jospin, the Aubry Law of June 13, 1998, reduced the legal work week from thirty-nine to thirty-five hours so as to distribute labor and decrease the number of unemployed. In order to limit the costs of the measure for companies (thirty-five hours paid at the previous thirty-nine hour-wage), a set of fiscal devices and reduction of social security charges shifted some of these costs to the state. In 2007 it was expected that the Sarkozy-Fillon administration would have the legislation annulled. This did not happen and in the name of the "work more to earn more" motto, they exempted employees and, partially, companies from taxes and social security charges on overtime hours exceeding the legal thirty-five-hour limit. Thus, while a first fiscal exemption compensated firms for the shift from thirty-nine to thirty-five hours, a second contradictory one allowed employers and employees to work more than thirty-five hours! And as the first aid exemption progressively disappeared, it was French firms who had once again to bear the costs: "Between 2000 and 2008, the hourly cost of labor force in the industry has increased by 38 percent in France, 17 percent in Germany and 19 percent in the European Union. ... This was due to Lionel Jospin and Martine Aubry who were the initiators of the catastrophic reform and to Nicolas Sarkozy who did nothing to erase what was indeed a huge mistake."[6] Tax exemption of overtime was the subject of fierce criticism from the left and the unions who interpreted it as incitement to avoid recruiting more and as a gift to the wealthy. This explains why it was removed as early as August 2012, even though high-school teachers were among the principal beneficiaries of the measure.

Initiatives to Face the Crisis

In the summer of 2007, the international crisis called into question the projects of the new president and the conditions in which the TEPA Act was to be drafted. This crisis inspired the doctrinal speech that was given by Sarkozy in Toulon on September 25. The president promised that the state would come to the rescue of the French people by expanding the public finances. In 2007 it was expected that the budget would be balanced in 2010; in his Toulon speech this date was pushed back to 2012, and in November 2011, it was pushed farther back to 2016!

On October 12, 2008, eurozone leaders gathered in Paris expressed a willingness to commit €1,700 billion to save the financial system of the zone. France was developing a rescue plan for its banks that would guarantee interbank lending up to €320 billion and giving €40 billion to recapitalize banks that were facing difficulties. The Socialist opposition was considering supporting this plan but did not vote for it in the end. "We cannot give the impression, through the approval of a technical measure, that we support a system that amplifies the crisis."[7] Ultimately these loans, granted at superior rates than those of the market and quickly reimbursed, allowed the Banque de France to make a profit of hundreds of millions of euros. This would however not stop some commentators from later denouncing the gift made to the banks in 2008.

The recovery plan presented at Douai on December 4, 2008, included tax relief measures, income supplements for households worst affected by the crisis, loans to car manufacturers, and most importantly, a public infrastructure investment program, including in public housing, roads, and railway works, the total cost of which would run to €34 billion. According to the administration, this plan explained why in 2009 France was suffering one of the least severe recessions in Europe (figure 9.1).

With this recovery plan financed through deficit spending, tax revenues covered only 53.3 percent of spending in 2009 and 57.6 percent in 2010. In January 2009 the Socialist opposition would present a counter-recovery plan based in part on consumption (increase of salaries and VAT decrease) and in part on investment favoring regions, hospitals, and SMEs. The measure in this plan to reduce the VAT rate from 19.6 percent to 5.5 percent in the catering sector was the subject of bitter debate during

Rate of growth

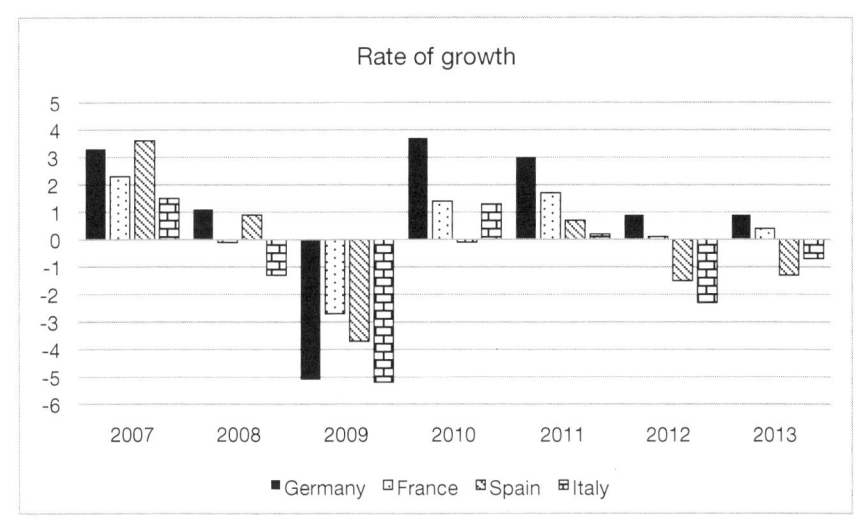

Figure 9.1. French Growth Compared to Select European Countries. *Source:* Eurostat, IMF for 2012 and 2013.

the 2012 campaign. In total, the national Court of Auditors estimated that the growth generated by this recovery plan amounted to 0.5 percent.

From the foregoing, it appears necessary to specify the main characteristics of the French tax system. Table 9.1 gives the principal fiscal resources in billions of euros for 2009.

Table 9.1. French Taxation Structure

VAT	CSG	IT (people)	CT (companies)	ISF
165	85	59	65	4

Source: Insee Comptes nationaux—Finances publiques

We can see how weak the income tax is in France, many households being exempted from it or benefiting from reductions called fiscal niches that are subject to endless political debates. Conversely, in November 1990 the Rocard administration created the Contribution Sociale Généralisée (general social contribution; CSG), a flat tax deducted at the source and the returns from which are particularly high.

The Fight Over Pensions

The pension debate constitutes one of the key moments of tension between the government and public opinion. The right to retire at age sixty had been a key factor in François Mitterrand's victory in 1981. The French system is pay-as-you-go, which is to say that active workers pay social premiums that finance pensions. This general system also includes numerous special regimes aimed at specific categories of workers. The public sector in particular is strongly unionized and benefits from more generous pension regimes, an advantage that was historically considered as a payoff for lower salaries.

In 1995 violent protests forced the Alain Juppé administration (May 1995–June 1997, under the presidency of Jacques Chirac) to abandon a reform that aimed at bringing the special regimes closer to the general one. The government of cohabitation headed by Lionel Jospin (June 1997–May 2002) brought no change to the situation, but when the right returned to power in 2002, it managed to adopt a first reform, the so-called Fillon law, after the name of the labor minister and future prime minister. This reform made the contribution period longer for the general regime (up to a duration of forty-two years) and for the civil servants regime (up to forty years), penalizing (through a system of *décôte* [haircut]) those who retired early.

The reform proposed in 2010 was no longer aimed at increasing the number of contribution years, but at raising from sixty to sixty-two the legal retirement age and from sixty-five to sixty-seven the age at which an employee is not penalized by the system of *décôtes*. As early as March 2010 protests and strikes began to break out in opposition to the reform. Eight consecutive waves of protests took place with several million employees from both public and private sectors taking to the streets. Students from universities and high schools, claiming that this reform threatened their futures, joined the trade unions supported by the left. By the end of October, however, the movement had run out of steam. On the one hand, those who opposed the plan knew that the government would not give in; on the other, public opinion was aware that in France, like everywhere else, the increase in life expectancy gave the government no choice but to push back the legal retirement age. After having said that he would renegotiate the reform in case the left came back into power, in December 2011 the Socialist candidate François Hollande abandoned the idea of reestablishing the retirement age at sixty.

The Fillon Plans

Slow growth and tax exemptions provoked the public debt to explode by more than 40 percent during the five-year term of Nicolas Sarkozy. In 2011 the government had to back off spending under pressure from its

European partners and the European Commission. In August a first savings plan of €12 billion was launched, then a second one in November to save €7 billion by 2012, and aiming for a balanced budget in 2016. The tax shield was abandoned, taxation of financial gains was increased, and the reduced VAT rate was raised again, with a few exceptions, from 5.5 percent to 7 percent. Simultaneously, health spending was tightened.

These measures were successful. In the spring of 2012, the government, which had predicted a deficit of 5.7 percent of GDP for 2011, congratulated itself on having reached 5.2 percent (versus 7.1 percent in the previous year) and was considering getting to 4.4 percent in 2012 and 3 percent in 2013, so as to finally reach a balanced budget in 2016. One of the symbols of these measures was the preservation of the AAA rating attributed to France by the credit rating agencies. However, on Friday, January 13, 2012, Standard & Poor's downgraded the debt of several European countries, including France. *Le Monde* analyzed this as "a sanction likely to be interpreted, a hundred days before the first round of the presidential election, as a verdict on the presidential term."[8] Finally, during the electoral campaign, a belated policy measure was taken: from October 1, 2011, the VAT was increased from 19.6 percent to 21.2 percent in order to further reduce the social security charges for companies by more than €10 billion. This measure had first been advocated by the Attali Commission in 2007 and was aimed at enhancing French industry's competitiveness following the country's attainment of a record current account deficit of €70 billion in 2011. On the eve of the elections, the government thus found itself on the defensive.

The Economic Themes of the Election Campaign

It is somewhat arbitrary to try to separate the economic debates that were conducted during the five-year term of Nicolas Sarkozy from the broader political debates that emerged during the electoral campaign, particularly since the latter had begun as soon as 2007.

Only a few words need be said about the economic programs of the candidates who were competing in the first round. Besides the usual advocates of collectivism, Jean-Luc Mélenchon's program seduced a lot of people because it preferred political voluntarism over the accounting logic of economists. It included measures such as the reestablishment of the retirement age at sixty with full pension, an increase of the minimum wage to €1,700 a month, and the full reimbursement of all health spending. At the same time, Mélenchon advocated that France remain in the EU but renegotiate its treaties. Another group of candidates was characterized by their willingness to take France out of the European system, starting with the single currency (Dupont-Aignan, Marine Le Pen) and even withdraw from international trade agreements—the infamous theme of deglobalization evoked by Arnaud Montebourg during the Socialist primaries. François Bayrou, whose European convictions had been commended in 2007, made the "made in France" theme one of his major strengths. Faithful to his opposition to excessive public debt, however, he advanced of all the candidates the most rigorous plan to consolidate the public accounts.

Focusing on the economic programs of the two candidates in the second round of the election, the PS launched an outright attack on Nicolas Sarkozy's poor economic results: stagnation, unemployment, deficits, loss of purchasing power, and policies that favored the wealthy. Leaving the core of the attack to his party, Hollande summed up his economic program in a document published on January 26, "My 60 Commitments to France," under the slogan "Change is now."[9] In a speech given on January 22 at Le Bourget near Paris, François Hollande identified his opponent: "My true adversary has no name, no face, no party, it will never be a candidate and yet he is the one who governs ... , it is the world of finance."[10] At that time, the progress of Jean-Luc Mélenchon in the polls had shifted the debate to the left. Conversely, on February 14, on the eve of a trip to London, he told the *Guardian:* "The Left was in government for 15 years in which we liberalized the economy and opened up the markets to finance and privatizations. There is no big fear."[11]

In the Bourget speech he detailed some of the measures he would adopt were he to be elected: a separation of credit and speculating (that is, market) activities in banks, the prohibition for French banks to operate in tax havens, and the establishment of a tax on financial transactions. All of this would be accompanied by sweeping tax reform, raising the superior marginal cap to 45 percent on incomes above €150,000, while in the meantime efforts would be made in terms of competitiveness and budgetary rigor to balance the public accounts by 2017. With regard to the state budget, this rigor signified that "state expenditure would be managed, any new spending would be financed through savings."[12] He stated, however, that he wanted to put an end to the rule of the nonreplacement of one out of every two civil servants (contained in the RGPP) by holding the public service workforce constant and favoring reassignments. To foster growth and employment, he committed himself to creating a public investment bank and to recruiting 150,000 young people through jobs that would be partially financed through public assistance. Finally, with regard to savings he stated that he aimed to multiply twofold the maximum amount of deposits in savings banks (*caisses d'épargne*), since those deposits were used in particular to finance social housing. This set of policies was couched as part of a broader progrowth European perspective: "France must rekindle the ambition to change the orientation of Europe."[13] (Needless to say, critics have not failed to point out that a country benefiting from the possibility of living with €1,700 billion of debt because of global finance would be well advised not to declare war on it, at the risk of paying a very high price after the elections). Finally, François Hollande managed to create a media tour de force with his proposal to marginally tax incomes above to €1 million a year by 75 percent. Added to the CSG and other taxes on dividends, this 75 percent rate could become more than 90 percent for about five thousand French taxpayers. Nicolas Sarkozy dismissed the proposition as "appalling amateurism" but on the electoral front, success was guaranteed.[14]

As the incumbent, Sarkozy was naturally placed on the defensive and was reduced to singling out "the lies" of his opponent: the new expenditures that would stem from returning the retirement age to sixty for about 20 percent of the working force and recruiting 60,000 civil servants in the education sector. Another theme was the unavoidable consequences of the confiscatory increase in taxes, namely an incitement to the wealthy to expatriate themselves. Media coverage of the issue showed Swiss or Belgian tax havens receiving French citizens that were looking for less hostile environments, which would be illustrated in December 2012 by the move of famous actor Gérard Depardieu to Belgium.

In the meantime, economic problems were still very much present. More and more European meetings were held following the signature of the budgetary treaty that François Hollande was committed to renegotiating. There was a gap between the true nature of France's, and more generally Europe's, economic problems and anecdotal or ideological issues on which the media and the voters chose to concentrate. One of the harshest opinions voiced on the economic contents of the 2012 presidential campaign could be found in the *Economist*.[15] In an article entitled "France's Future: A Country in Denial," the British periodical wrote, "It is not unusual for politicians to avoid some ugly truths during elections; but it is unusual, in recent times in Europe, to ignore them as completely as French politicians are doing," before concluding, "France's picnickers are about to be swamped by harsh reality, no matter who is president." Commenting on this article, one French member of European parliament (MEP) noted, "Apparently, there's nothing new in the French presidential election campaign. The agenda is driven by French obsessions: like Asterix's village against the Roman Empire, France will 'hold out alone' against globalization and foreign influence."[16]

This, however, did not stop the *Economist,* in its edition of April 26, from supporting Nicolas Sarkozy, François Hollande being considered as a dangerous man for France and Europe. Ultimately, the man who wished to embody the rupture suffered the same fate as all the other European leaders of the economic crisis. He failed to reconcile French people with the popular liberalism he had praised during the 2007 campaign and that had alienated a part of his electorate and his European partners, more as a result of his political style than because of the effective content of his policies.

The Economic Policy of the New Majority

As soon as he took office, the visits made by the new president to Berlin, Brussels, Rome, London, and so on, reassured the markets. Similarly, the choice of ministers he placed in charge of economic issues was seen in a positive light: Pierre Moscovici as finance and economy minister and Jérôme Cahuzac as budget minister. The only question mark concerned the transformation of the Ministry of Industry into a Ministère du Redressement Productif (Ministry for Production Recovery), which was entrusted to Arnaud Montebourg, an advocate of deglobalization. With regard to economic matters, the first seven months of the new administration can be divided into three phases: fulfillment of electoral promises, preparation of the 2013 budget, and reception of the Gallois report.

Among the promises made by the left-wing candidate figured the illusory renegotiation of the European fiscal pact. François Hollande managed to negotiate that funding amounting to around 1 percent of the GDP be grouped in a single program to support economic activity. Most of this funding had already been planned; the goal was only to save face in order to ratify the unchanged treaty that was criticized during the campaign. As Hollande had promised during the campaign, as soon as the new administration was formed the Court of Auditors was solicited to audit the public finances. The conclusions were given to Prime Minister Jean-Marc Ayrault on July 2, 2012. In addition to contrasting with the accusations of lack of transparency that were levied against the previous administration, the document gave details, and most importantly gave details as to the conditions France would need to meet in order to lower the budget deficit to 4.5 percent of GDP in 2012 and to 3 percent in 2013. The Court estimated that the measures would amount to €6 billion to €10 billion for 2012, but need to reach more than €33 billion in 2013, a huge amount that would mainly have to come from cuts in public spending but that would also unavoidably result in increases in the CSG or VAT.

However, rather than follow the report's recommendations, the new administration chose to order new expenditures, abrogate cost-saving measures that had been adopted by the previous government, and to introduce additional taxes to compensate for the increase in spending. Among these new expenditures, it is worth mentioning the increases of the new-school-year allowance and of the minimum wage, and the partial return of the retirement age to sixty. Through Wolfgang Schäuble, Germany voiced its irritation over these measures. Pierre Moscovici addressed these concerns by stating that he would not be caught commenting on the German administration's policies. However, nothing can get on Germany's nerves more than pleading for a European pooling of debts while giving free rein to every country to spend however they like.

The termination of measures taken by the previous administration consisted of the end of tax exemptions for overtime pay—an unpopular measure that penalized 9 million employees—and the termination of the decrease of social security charges that had been compensated by an increase in the VAT. Social security charges were even increased to pay for the partial return of the retirement age to sixty. The measure to lower social security charges had been meant to come into force in October 2012 and had been highly anticipated. One of the specialists of French industry and adviser of the new majority, Elie Cohen, claimed in a note on the PSA Peugeot Citroën case that "only a supply shock with a changeover of a significant share of employer contributions towards a CSG tax base can reduce the cost of labor and provide a booster shot in competitiveness for the companies located in France."[17]

As was noted before, France is the European country that was most affected by deindustrialization. The creation of a Ministry for Production Recovery is a symbol of this willingness to give France back part of its former industrial fabric, an omnipresent theme in the sixty propositions of François Hollande as candidate. The production recovery minister was rapidly absorbed by severance schemes, that is to say large-scale dismissals, like the case of PSA Peugeot Citroën and the loss of several thousands of jobs. His style was aggressive, as was the president's in his Bastille Day interviews, which resulted in both of them being severely criticized in one of *Le Monde*'s editorials.[18] The government proposed a recovery plan that included subsidies for purchases of electric cars, which form 0.2 percent of the sector. Other issues appeared in the food processing, electronics, pharmaceuticals, call centers, and steel sectors, to the point that Arnaud Montebourg came to be referred to as the "palliative care minister."

Concerning revenues, the new administration's novelties were an increase of taxes on gifts and inheritance, the establishment of an exceptional contribution in 2012 for households that pay the ISF, the subjection of housing revenues of nonresidents to social security contributions, an increase of the taxation of stock options and distribution of bonus shares, the establishment of a tax on oil stocks, and new taxes on banks as well as a tax on financial transactions decided by the previous government that was doubled by the new one. On top of these changes, technical measures aimed at fighting tax optimization by businesses were adopted and even tightened by parliament. The whole of these measures should raise 7.2 billion in new revenue and make it possible to reach a deficit of 4.5 percent of GDP in 2012.

All of these measures were part of the Amending Finance Law (Loi de Finances Rectificative; LFR) that was prepared by the Council of Ministers held on July 4, 2012. It was adopted by parliament and came into force after it was validated by the Constitutional Council on August 9, along with the decision not to make the "golden rule" part of the Constitution.[19] The main targets of the LFR measures are big companies and the wealthiest social classes. Without accounting for the risk of emigration to avoid taxes and the possibility of having big companies set up their head offices in other European countries, the general concern resulted from the penalization of savings destined for businesses. Contrary to a widespread belief that was repeated during the campaign, capital revenues are not taxed less than work revenues; indeed, ever since the legislation adopted in July, they are even more taxed According to the National Institute of Statistics and Economic Studies (Institut National de la Statistique et des Etudes Economiques; INSEE) data from June 2012, profit margins of corporations have fallen to 28.6 percent in 2011, the lowest rate in twenty-five years, against 41.7 percent in Germany. These low profit margins limit the possibility for firms to finance themselves and contribute to a higher tax burden for companies. The tone and content of some speeches together with these new tax measures provoked a hostile feeling toward companies and the words of warning of the CEOs of Unilever and General Electric were widely echoed.

Preparation of the 2013 Budget

These measures taken in July were nothing but an appetizer for what was to be announced for the 2013 budget. It was not about finding €7.2 billion anymore but €33 billion, and in the meantime, the budget minister announced that he would increase neither the VAT nor the CSG. Talking to three thousand managers gathered on August 29 at the University of HEC Paris the prime minister announced that the value of companies would enter in the calculations to determine the amount of the ISF tax for their owners, which the president of the business union denounced as a form of "hara-kiri for the French economy."[20]

Four examples illustrate the complexity of preparing the budget. The French government stated that the public service workforce would stay unchanged while announcing a jobs increase in the sectors of education, police, and justice services, which represent 60 percent of the total public service workforce. As a consequence, nonpriority ministries (including perhaps the health sector) will no longer have to deal with the nonreplacement of one out every two civil servants, a measure condemned by the opposition under Nicolas Sarkozy, but of two out of every three public sector employees. Second example: the 75 percent marginal tax rate on annual income surpassing €1 million was indeed a measure stipulated in the budget that targeted football and tennis players and musical artists. Third example: the freeze on oil prices. As a candidate, François Hollande had announced that he would block oil prices to protect purchasing power. However, the only possibility that was offered to him turned out to be a modest and temporary use of lowered taxes. In 2011 the domestic consumption tax on petroleum products (taxe intérieure de la consommation sur les produits énergétiques; TIPP) had yielded €14.6 billion, twice as much as the LFR of July 2012. After an intense media campaign at the end of August, the government, in consultation with industry, announced a tax decrease of 3 percent to 4 percent during three months, which increased the budget deficit by €300 million and was not to the taste of Germany. As the British say, this kind of initiative amounts to painting oneself into a corner. Fourth example: 150,000 *emplois d'avenir* (jobs of/for the future). With more than €1 billion, the government will finance up to 75 percent of the jobs in local administrations, associations, and, on a limited scale, companies. Similar programs have been pursued for thirty years. However, the Court of Auditors has demonstrated that though these public sector hiring programs in the public sector could provoke a temporary decrease in the unemployment statistics, they never actually manage to improve the overall job situation. During the month of August 2012, INSEE reported zero growth for the second trimester and a slight decrease in tax revenues in the budget. In the first semester of 2012, French external trade showed a €35 billion deficit. Inversely, French conditions for borrowing were such, with a spread under 1 percent and negative short-term interest rates, that the cost of debt financing was €3 billion below predictions.

The reactions to increased taxation were best illustrated by the revolt of the suckers (*les pigeons*). The government was desperately looking to make profits from capital and wanted to consider gains on business sales as revenue to be able to tax them up to 60 percent. In other words, an entrepreneur who had launched a start-up with a small capital investment and sold it a few years later after having transformed it into an economic success would have had to pay a 60 percent tax on the price of his company, which would be treated as a capital gain by the state while the entrepreneur considered it to be the fruit of his labor, imagination, and courage.[21] Within days, public uproar on the social networks forced the government to capitulate and cancel the project, thus angering the left wing of its majority.

In accordance with François Hollande's commitment, public deficits must be brought back to 3 percent of GDP as soon as 2013; this will have to be done in a context of almost zero growth. To reach this goal, a historic austerity plan was launched that called for €24 billion of additional taxes and €10 billion in spending cuts. After having examined the official documents, the liberal think tank iFRAP estimated this last figure to be closer to €5.7 billion.[22] The targets of the first tax increase under the LFR were for the most part the highest-income households and big corporations. However, under the 2013 budget the middle classes were also asked to contribute. Notably, savings were penalized with regard to their collection, holding, and levels of return when they should be put to the service of businesses to address the auto-financing deficiencies. At the beginning of October, the Group of Industrial Federations (Groupe des Fédérations Industrielles; GFI) that represents the biggest French corporations was pleading for both a competitiveness shock of €50 billion that would not be spread out over three or five years, but rather applied immediately; and, most importantly, a tax ceasefire. The decisions that were to be made as a reaction to the Gallois report would partially satisfy these demands.

The Gallois Report and Its Consequences

As soon as the new government took office, it announced that a personality from the world of industry would be entrusted with a mission to write a report on the competitiveness of the French economy and to put forward some recommendations to redress the situation. Louis Gallois, ex-manager of the Société Nationale des Chemins de Fer (National Railroad Company; SNCF) and European Aeronautic Defense and Space company (EADS), received this mission in July and submitted his report on November 5. This report does not include any major innovations; dozens of documents addressing the same issue having been published over the last few years. According to Elie Cohen, the relevance of the report does not reside in its content or in its pedagogical aims: "French companies' costs are too high for the middle-market products that they are selling (cost competitiveness) which reduces their margins and prohibits them from investing in higher-market products. In other words, French companies do not sell enough high-end products (non-cost-competitiveness) to make up for the costs they have to bear ... which amounts to the same thing."[23] The government refused to provide a supply shock and thought the best approach would be to adopt a productivity pact over three years and avoid penalizing private consumption.

The previous majority had decided to transfer some of the social security charges paid by the businesses onto the VAT paid by consumers. This measure was meant to come into force in the last trimester of 2012 but was cancelled. The government opted for a characteristic procrastination technique with a system qualified to be "opaque with major uncertainties and contributing to deter the much awaited social protection reform."[24] The system constitutes of a credit on corporate tax (*impôt des sociétés*; IS) of €10 billion to be implemented as soon as 2013, which, according to the prime minister, amounts to a decrease in labor costs of about 6 percent. As this credit will also apply in 2014 and 2015, its effects will only begin to be revealed later on, even if for SMEs it will be possible to ask the fiscal administration for advances as soon as 2013. (We can then ask ourselves how many demands will be made—tens of thousands?) Big companies can be charged against the corporation tax they have to pay: if the credit is higher than the tax, they can charge it against the tax for the following year. Firms that pay a very low corporation tax or none at all will have to wait for three years, after which the state will send them a check.

During the 2013–15 period, companies will have to account for "the use made of the margins that were obtained through this tax credit to invest or hire" to their works' council and will have to create a committee to monitor whether such commitments were fulfilled.[25] In other words, the chosen procedure will have no effect on companies' margins when in the meantime France has reached a historically low level of auto-financing capacity. Simultaneously, these procedures will result in hundreds of pages of regulation, which will translate into conflicts with the administrative services responsible for monitoring their application. The result is a typically French arrangement, which explains why some managers have announced that they would not ask to benefit from this new instrument in order to avoid dealing with the additional bureaucracy involved.

The announcement of these measures did not create the psychological shock that was expected by the government. Accountants who monitor companies noted that hiring, investments, and the search for new markets have come to a stop, thus explaining the dark prospects for the job market. Soon after the announcement of the government's measures, a former Socialist prime minister wrote, "[W]e have just lived through six months during which those who produce, the firms and their managers, felt like they were used as scapegoats for the new majority. ... [A] different signal was given this week, it was about time."[26] Undoubtedly, this signal was seen as only partially positive: a survey conducted by a radio station among tax consultants showed that candidates for tax exile were not older citizens trying to protect their assets, but young entrepreneurs looking for a less hostile environment.[27]

Conclusion

A very thick dossier could be compiled with articles from the international press, professional or popular, puzzling over the case of France. In the October 30 issue of *Bild*, the Paris correspondent slightly mocked the country through its title: "Mon dieu, Where is the "Great Nation" Going?"[28] By the end of November the unemployment figures were accelerating again but no one could say which of the new or the old policies were accountable for the degradation. The government admitted that this trend would continue and even reach historical levels in 2013 before new measures could take effect and reverse it. During the course of the same month, the *Economist* published a special number on France with a cover representing a pack of baguettes as sticks of dynamite about to explode.[29] This edition took several weeks to prepare with the help of a Parisian advertisement company and provoked heated debate and a reaction of annoyance from the government. It included widely shared appraisals of the loss of competitiveness of French companies, the administrative monster with an unbearable territorial structure, stultifying regulation, and an unsustainable welfare state. The conclusion was unambiguous: "Unless Mr. Hollande shows that he is genuinely committed to changing the path his country has been on for the past 30 years, France will lose the faith of investors. ... France rather than Italy or Spain could be where the euro's fate is decided. Mr. Hollande does not have long to defuse the time-bomb at the heart of Europe."[30]

Two days after the publication of this special issue of the *Economist*, Moody's was downgrading France's credit rating. According to Pierre Moscovici, this decision was punishment against the policies of the previous government, but the reasons behind Moody's downgrade were directed against the new presidency as much as the old one.[31] The special edition of the British weekly magazine and Moody's motivations echoed the conclusions of Nicholas Bavarez, a French economist whose book was published in October 2012. This book contained a gloomy prediction, shared by many other economists, that took the Italian experience and Mario Monti's braveness as a counterexample: "[T]he alternative is simple: either France reforms itself in a voluntary manner; or it will reform under the double constraint of markets on the one hand and of the IMF and our European partners on the other."[32]

The near future will tell us who of the pessimist Bavarez or the optimist Moscovici (whose eyes are fixed on the very low level of French spreads) will be proved right. One month before Christmas 2012, unemployment reached historic levels, the program for lowering oil prices was terminated, the senate refused to adopt the budget, external trade was showing a few signs of improvement but remained largely in deficit The Organisation for Economic Co-operation and Development (OECD) was revising economic forecasts downward, while only 35 percent of the French people gave their trust to François Hollande and 30 percent to the prime minister. The struggle over the Florange steel plant in Lorraine, owned by the Lakshmi Mittal group, reached its peak at the end of November. After the announcement of the closure of the blast furnaces, a very active union movement was formed. During the electoral campaign, François Hollande was acclaimed during a visit there and had promised that, contrary to Nicolas Sarkozy and the case of the plant of Gandrange (also owned by Mittal) four years earlier, he would fulfill his commitments. Seven months later, the hyperactive production recovery minister was battling against Mittal, who according to him "did not belong in France";[33] he even talked of a temporary nationalization that would end with the sale of the plant to another steel producer and was not contradicted by the government. On November 30 the prime minister finally announced that the government had reached an agreement with the Mittal group. There would be no layoffs, the blast furnaces could eventually be put back into service, and an innovative conversion project would be set up. The agreement was in accordance with the analysis of Elie Cohen[34] (who was probably involved in shaping the final decision) and the idea of nationalization, that had started to be the subject of numerous mockeries in the international press, was dropped. Unions, however, felt betrayed.

For France, the moment of truth will come sooner rather than later. It is highly likely that an alternative policy will be adopted by the Hollande administration before the European elections of May 2014 to that espoused by Hollande as a candidate during the 2012 presidential campaign.

Notes

Translated from the French by Maëlle Lena.
1. Nicolas Sarkozy, "Discours d'investiture de Nicolas Sarkozy," May 16, 2007. http://www.elysee.fr/la-presidence/discours-d-investiture-de-nicolas-sarkozy/.

2. Fayette, Jacques. "Il volontarismo politico di fronte al realismo economico," in *La Francia di Sarkozy*, ed. G. Baldini and M. Lazar (Bologna: Il Mulino, 2007), 193–206.
3. *The Economist* [online], "France's chance," April 12, 2007, http://www.economist.com/node/9005216.
4. Sarkozy, "Discours d'investiture."
5. Nicole Bricq, "Rapport d'information fait au nom de la commission des finances sur les prélèvements obligatoires et leur évolution," *Sénat: Session Ordinaire de 2011-2012*, 64 (October 26, 2011), http://www.senat.fr/rap/r11-064/r11-0641.pdf.
6. Jean Peyrelevade, *France, état critique* (Paris: Plon Coll. Tribune Libre, 2011), 213.
7. Nicolas Barotte, "Les socialistes se réfugient dans l'abstension," *Le Figaro* [online], October 15, 2008, http://www.lefigaro.fr/politique/2008/10/15/01002-20081015ARTFIG00282-les-socialistes-se-refugient-dans-l-abstention-.php.
8. *Le Monde* [online], "Triple A: La politique de Sarkozy est sanctionnée, selon le camp Hollande," January 13, 2012, http://www.lemonde.fr/election-presidentielle-2012/article/2012/01/13/triple-a-la-politique-de-sarkozy-est-sanctionnee-selon-le-camp-hollande_1629544_1471069.html?xtmc=triple_a_la_politique_de_sarkozy_est_sanctionnee&xtcr=3.
9. PS [online], "Les 60 engagements pour la France: Le projet de François Hollande," January 26, 2012, http://www.parti-socialiste.fr/articles/les-60-engagements-pour-la-france-le-projet-de-francois-hollande.
10. "François Hollande: Discours du Bourget," January 22, 2012, http://www.youtube.com/watch?v=up62HaC6cFI.
11. *The Guardian* [online], "François Hollande seeks to reassure UK and City of London," February 14, 2012, http://www.theguardian.com/world/2012/feb/17/francois-hollande-uk-city-london.
12. "Hollande: Discours du Bourget."
13. Ibid.
14. Thierry Arnaud, "Imposition à 75%: Sarkozy dénonce 'une impression d'improvisation,'" BFMTV [online], February 28, 2012. http://www.bfmtv.com/politique/imposition-a-75pour-cent-sarkozy-denonce-une-impression-dimprovisation-de-precipitation-et-damateurisme-assez-consternante-207041.html.
15. *The Economist* [online], "France's Future: A Country in Denial," March 31, 2012, http://www.economist.com/node/21551478. The same theme is taken up in Sophie Pedder, *Le déni français: Les derniers enfants gâtés de la crise* (Paris: J.C. Lattès, 2012).
16. Sylvie Goulard, "France must set aside the spirit of Astérix," *Financial Times* [online], April 18, 2012, http://search.proquest.com/docview/1002597323/fulltext/141AE7BEC4CBE6FC2F/1?accountid=40183.
17. Elie Cohen, "PSA : l'État ne peut pas tout," *Telos* [online], July 16, 2012, http://www.telos-eu.com/fr/societe/entreprise/psa-letat-ne-peut-pas-tout.html.
18. *Le Monde* [online], "Le Ministre du redressement contre-productif," July 24, 2012, http://www.lemonde.fr/idees/article/2012/07/24/le-ministre-du-redressement-contre-productif_1737617_3232.html.
19. Jean Pisani-Ferry, "Finances : les choix de M. Hollande," *Le Monde* [online], August 14, 2012, http://www.lemonde.fr/cgi-bin/ACHATS/acheter.cgi?offre=ARCHIVES&type_item=ART_ARCH_30J&objet_id=1202742&xtmc=jean_pisani_ferry&xtcr=36.
20. Laurence Parisot, "Où est la stratégie économique du gouvernement ? " *Le Monde* [online], August 28, 2012, http://www.lemonde.fr/politique/article/2012/08/28/laurence-parisot-ou-est-la-strategie-economique-du-gouvernement_1752169_823448.html.
21. Tens of thousands of French people are estimated to be leaving the country every year to create their own companies; London has been transformed into the fourth "French city" by its population. François Mitterrand was astounded during his visit to the Sil-

icon Valley in March 1984 to meet hundreds of French citizens who had created their companies in California.

22. Elsa Conesa, "Budget 2013: la réalité des économies est contestée," *Les Echos* [online], November 30, 2012, http://www.lesechos.fr/30/11/2012/LesEchos/21324-006-ECH_budget-2013—-la-realite-des-economies-est-contestee.htm.
23. Elie Cohen, "Gallois, la gauche et la compétitivité," *Telos* [online], November 8, 2012, http://www.telos-eu.com/fr/gallois-la-gauche-et-la-competitivite.html.
24. Ibid.
25. Ibid.
26. Michel Rocard, "Un signal a été donné aux entreprises. Il était temps." *Le Monde* [online], November 10, 2012, http://www.lemonde.fr/cgibin/ACHATS/acheter.cgi?offre=ARCHIVES&type_item=ART_ARCH_30J&objet_id=1214969&xtmc=michel_rocard&xtcr=120.
27. http://www.francetvinfo.fr/economie/impots/exil-fiscal/qui-sont-les-exiles-fiscaux_281947.html.
28. Von Dirk Müller-Thederan, "Mon dieu, wohin steuert die 'Grande Nation'?," *Bild Zeitung* [online], October 30, 2012, http://www.bild.de/geld/wirtschaft/frankreich/frankreich-krise-autobauer-peugeot-symbol-fuer-niedergang-26861190.bild.html.
29. *The Economist* [online], "France and the euro: The time-bomb at the heart of Europe," November 17, 2012, http://www.economist.com/news/leaders/21566640-why-france-could-become-biggest-danger-europes-single-currency-time-bomb-heart.
30. Ibid.
31. *Challenges* [online], "Ce que Moody's reproche à la France," November 22, 2012, http://challenges-magazine-digital.challenges.fr/profil/liseuse.html#mid1353538800.
32. N. Baverez, *Réveillez-vous!* (Paris: Fayard, 2012), 200.
33. *Le Monde* [online], "Montebourg déclare la guerre à Mittal," November 23, 2012, http://www.lemonde.fr/economie/article/2012/11/23/montebourg-declare-la-guerre-a-mittal_1795036_3234.html.
34. Elie Cohen, "Faut-il nationaliser Mittal?" *Telos* [online], November 29, 2012, http://www.telos-eu.com/fr/politique-economique/faut-il-nationaliser-mittal.html.

Chapter 10

Europe in the 2012 French Presidential Election

Renaud Dehousse and Angela Tacea

Europe has long been absent from French national electoral contests. Given the influence Europe can have on the policies decided by governing elites, it seems legitimate that the candidates to run the country would enlighten voters as to how they would position themselves with respect to the policies of the EU, or even how they envision the evolution of the latter, were they to be elected. Instead, presidential candidates have long preferred to ignore these sorts of questions—perhaps because the latter tend to diminish the role to which they can aspire to play in the national political arena.[1] We can nevertheless ask ourselves if things are not beginning to change. In the current political climate dominated by the systemic crisis that has struck the eurozone and the constraints that the latter has placed on the national economies, it has become increasingly difficult to talk about politics without mentioning Europe. This was the case in the spring 2012 elections in Greece and the fall 2012 elections in the Netherlands.

Even in a country like France, in which the concept of national sovereignty is deeply anchored in the political culture, the 2012 presidential election showed that the situation had evolved. A number of the principal campaign themes had obvious European ramifications, a fact that led the principal candidates to specify certain key aspects of the policies they hoped to pursue at the European level if they were elected and to suggest the types of alliances they would seek within the EU in order to fashion these policies. At the same time, the campaign was closely followed in the other member states, with several heads of state even going so far as to indicate the candidates they favored. Finally, considerations linked to

---

Notes for this chapter begin on page 164.

different aspects of the process of European integration also seemed to have informed the choices of different voting groups. If it is still too early to assess the consequence of François Hollande's victory for Europe, it is nevertheless obvious that it has contributed to a change in direction in France's European policy.

What Is a European Debate?

In order to properly frame the argument, a semantic precision is in order. What exactly do we mean by "Europe"? The most obvious answer to this question incorporates a number of relatively abstract themes: to speak of Europe means indicating the importance one accords to European integration, the manner that one believes the European political system should be organized, the tasks that it should assume, and the relations it should have to the national states and societies. If we hold to this relatively simple definition, we can see that Europe generally occupies a significant place, but never the first rank, among the issues addressed by the candidates in the presidential campaign. Dominique Labbé and Denis Molière have published lexographic studies of the presidential campaign that measure the relative weight of each theme (as a percentage of words) within the totality of the communications issued by the principal candidates throughout the course of the campaign.[2] Table 10.1 indicates the five principal campaign themes developed by the different candidates. It shows that out of a necessarily broad spectrum of issues, Europe figured quite prominently in what the candidates had to say, for either good or ill!

We also see that the relative degree of importance accorded Europe varied between the candidates. For Marine Le Pen, who made of the denunciation of the loss of national sovereignty an even more important issue than the FN's classic focus on immigration and crime, Europe was the second-most important theme of the campaign at 6 percent. By contrast, Europe only arrived in fifth place among the campaign themes advanced by the incumbent president, Nicolas Sarkozy, and his principal rival, François Hollande. This replicates a common motif in the campaigns for the European elections, in which it is often the opponents of European integration who most frankly address questions pertaining to its nature and its ends.

However, after nearly a half-century of integration, the nature of the European theme has itself changed. Even if the EU is still far from presiding 80 percent of the national law of the members states as is often argued,[3] it nevertheless has become an indispensable actor in a number of areas. National politicians know that the freedom of maneuver that they enjoy to implement policy can be diminished, and even reduced to zero,

Table 10.1. Principal Themes of the 2012 Presidential Campaign

Candidates	Themes	%
François Bayrou	Economy	6.02
	Education	3.83
	Budget Deficits	4.27
	Germany	4.33
	Europe	**3.93**
François Hollande	Economy	6.42
	Education	5.37
	Employment—Unemployment	4.44
	Europe	**4.27**
	Budget Deficits	3.83
Marine Le Pen	Economy	6.47
	Europe	**6.04**
	Nation	4.27
	Immigration	3.89
	Money	3.84
Nicolas Sarkozy	Economy	7.9
	Business	6.59
	Crisis	6.53
	Unemployment	6.09
	Europe	5.72

Source: Dominique Labbé et Denis Monière, *Radioscopie 10, La dernière ligne droite*, Annexes, https://docs.google.com/viewer?a=v&pid=sites&srcid=aWVwZy5mcnx0cmllbGVjfGd4O jFmYjNhY2MxNjQ1MTM4MmY.

by decisions that are made in Brussels. However, they generally tend to obfuscate this fact, because it diminishes the prestige of the leadership functions to which they aspire, thereby contributing to a lack of policy transparency at both the national and European levels.

In the particular case of the 2012 presidential campaign, this strategy of concealment was rendered even more difficult by the context of crisis that served as the background for the campaign. While successive "last-chance summits" were held in order to try to resolve the European sovereign debt crisis and avert the threat it poses to the euro, it was difficult for François Hollande to evoke the need for a reflationary program targeting the lower classes without taking into account the constraints placed as France by the new mechanisms of economic governance that have been put in place by European law, most notably the "budgetary pact," over the preceding months. By the same token, Nicolas Sarkozy, who chose to focus on the issue of Europe's borders in order to address the need for protection he felt among the French, could not ignore the fact that the right to free movement of citizens is central to European integration in its present guise. In short, whenever they chose to address these policy issues, the candidates were invariably called upon to situate their initiatives in respect to Europe, whether in terms of how they would respond to injunctions from Brussels, or the policies that they would seek to defend within Europe. The European discourse of the principal presidential candidates thus found itself transformed: it was no longer sufficient for them to pronounce themselves in general terms as to the way to ideally organize the continent, but to specify the manner in which they would manage France's relations to Europe in a series of concrete areas.

Viewed from this perspective, the 2012 presidential campaign assumed a much more European focus. Among the campaign speeches of François Bayrou, for example to the 4 percent evoked above that were dedicated strictly to Europe, can be added references to Germany (4 percent), to Greece (3 percent), or to the budget deficit (5 percent), thereby taking the references to Europe, more broadly understood, to 16 percent. Similarly, for the reasons suggested above, it seems reasonable to consider that themes such as the crisis (7 percent), finance (4 percent), and immigration (2 percent) that were raised by Nicolas Sarkozy, or of the economy (7 percent) and the deficit (4 percent) by François Hollande, also incorporate an important European dimension. If this conflation of issues is accepted, we thus see that the themes linked either directly or indirectly to Europe become the issues of greatest importance in the campaign. True enough, other issues were also important to voters, as was shown by the aforementioned studies, but these facts nevertheless bring into question the notion that Europe was absent from the internal French political debate throughout the campaign.

The Europeanization of the campaign was also reflected by the attempts of the leaders of the other member states to intervene in and influence its outcome. For example, at the start of the campaign, during a Franco-German ministerial meeting in Paris, German Chancellor Angela Merkel publicly announced her support for Nicolas Sarkozy, even though the latter had not yet officially declared himself as candidate, and went so far as to openly criticize the plans of his Socialist rival to renegotiate the European 'Fiscal Compact' during a joint television interview with Sarkozy. The possibility of Merkel attending Sarkozy's campaign rallies was even raised at one stage, before being abandoned by the incumbent president following a rally at Villepinte, a suburb north of Paris, during which he evoked the possibility of France's "withdrawal from the Schengen Agreement" (see below).[4] For his part, British prime minister David Cameron also took sides in the campaign in favor of Sarkozy, and the idea that the principal conservative leaders in Europe had agreed not to welcome the

Socialist candidate in their countries was also raised in the press.⁵ For his part, over the following days François Hollande, who was frequently criticized for his lack of international experience and contacts, made a point of appearing alongside the leaders of the European Socialist parties at a meeting to discuss the European implications of his program. The electoral impact of the association of both candidates with other European leaders cannot be known, but their mutual desire to symbolically project themselves and discuss their differences on the European stage was made amply clear to French voters.

Forms of Opposition

If Europe was frequently brought up in the course of the campaign, it was often as an indeterminate object and in a manner that most often underscored the opposition of the candidates to what was being done in Brussels. This opposition, however, assumed several different forms.⁶

The first type of opposition was radical and frontal. What was being rejected was the very idea of the political construction of Europe, along with its necessary corollary, the ceding of national sovereignty. During the campaign, this attitude was strongly enshrined by the sovereignist candidate Nicolas Dupont-Aignan, who chose for his party a name that captures well the anti-European essence of his program: Arise the Republic. But this attitude was also taken up with great success by the FN candidate Marine Le Pen who, while portraying herself as representative of the French people—one of the key phrases in her political discourse—made of the denunciation of Europe and of globalization a major theme of her campaign.⁷ Thus, she proclaimed her intention to abandon the euro and leave the EU in case of victory.⁸

A second form of opposition, which is less direct, concerns not the project of European integration to which one claims to broadly subscribe and accept, but the political choices of the EU. The candidate of the radical left, Jean-Luc Mélenchon, followed such a line. Without raising the possibility of France leaving the EU, Mélenchon projected a series of objectives that he knew were unlikely to meet with the approval of France's European partners, such as the abrogation of the Treaty of Lisbon or the assertion of political control over the European Central Bank. That the candidate from a radical Party should adopt this line was not that surprising. However, one of the novel aspects of the campaign was to see the candidates from the mainstream parties adopt a similar line. Without going as far as his former Socialist comrade,⁹ the principal candidate of the opposition, François Hollande, embraced a discourse that was extremely critical of the manner in which the eurozone crisis has been managed. But the real surprise came from the incumbent president, Nicolas Sarkozy, who was extremely critical of Europe, a fact all the more remarkable given that throughout the course of his term he had actively embraced a leadership role within Europe.[10]

A few days apart from one another, both Sarkozy and Hollande dedicated a significant part of their campaign communications to presenting their vision of Europe. Sarkozy took aim at Europe at a rally held at Villepinte, which officially launched his campaign. François Hollande responded in kind in the days that followed at a conference attended by several European Socialist leaders. If the respective tenors of their speeches were different, the symmetry of their arguments was remarkable. Each of them chose to unveil their ambitions for France, but also for Europe, Sarkozy even going so far as to address himself directly to European voters: "I want to say to all the French. But I also want to say it to all Europeans. If we want to preserve our lifestyle, if we want to preserve our model of civilization ... then Europe must not be a threat, but a [means of] protection."[11]

This theme of Europe as a means of protection led Sarkozy to strongly affirm Europe's boundaries, presented as the continent's ramparts against "undesirable" immigration and against "disloyal" competition. But this theme was developed in a tenor of determined opposition to Europe as it had been constructed up to that point. The oft-commented *droitisation* of Sarkozy's campaign took on in this sense a strongly Euroskeptic flavor: "Europe cannot be the only region in the world to so poorly enforce its borders, to so poorly defend its interests, to so completely ignore the fears of its citizens. A Europe that refuses to defend its frontiers, its interests, its citizens, that thinks only of the consumer, never of the producer, that forgets that behind the consumer there is the worker, that Europe would be condemned to disappear because it would be the cause of too many tensions, of too much suffering."[12]

For his part, François Hollande chose to focus his criticisms on economic issues, clearly affirming the link between the French national agenda and the European agenda: "When I defend here in France employment, growth, solidarity, fiscal justice, I am also serving the interests of a Europe that is expecting growth, employment, justice and solidarity."[13]

Here too, the analysis begins with a critique of Europe's current orientation, which is "perceived as powerless in the face of market forces, even obsessed with deregulation, incapable of resisting neo-liberal globalization. It is this Europe that I reject. It is of this Europe that I want to change the orientation."[14] Thus, while recognizing the necessity of fiscal discipline in order to address the sovereign debt crisis, Hollande denounces the line of austerity enshrined by the "fiscal compact" signed several weeks earlier under pressure from Germany: "There will be no return to equilibrium if the treaty ... is only a treaty of constraints, of sanctions that will quickly become new instruments of austerity for Europe's peoples. ... No one can imagine that if growth is absent, the objectives laid out in this [budgetary] pact, in this treaty, will be attainable. Even the credit rating agencies, even the [financial] markets know this and are worried about the threat of recession."[15] In short, each of the principal candidates chose to focus their discourses on themes central to the preoccupations of their core group of voters: immigration and crime for the right, unemployment and purchasing power for the left.[16]

Similarly, in both cases the critique of Europe was accompanied by indications of the European policies each of the candidates would try to pursue in the case of victory. For his part, Sarkozy promised to reform the Schengen Agreement in order to reinforce their sanctioning mechanisms or to unilaterally pull France out of the agreement. Meanwhile, Hollande reiterated his desire to renegotiate the Fiscal Compact by affixing to it new objectives—increasing growth and creating jobs—that would be attained through increasing spending. In short, the governing programs outlined by each of the candidates was not to be limited to France: the mandate that they asked for from voters also aimed to inflect European policies.[17] Likewise, their campaigns highlighted the methods that they would adopt in Brussels to achieve these aims—a resolutely intergovernmental approach for Sarkozy, or a more open communal one for Hollande who in passing criticized the heavy-handed behavior of the "Merkozy" tandem, which had shown disdain for the concerns of their European partners.[18]

How are we to explain the fact that all of the candidates chose to various degrees to espouse a line of opposition to Europe? If the causes of their disaffection with the latter varied, they all appeared to have made the same calculation: there were more votes to be won by criticizing Europe than by supporting it. This convergence of motives was no doubt explained by the state of public opinion throughout the campaign. We indeed know that since the failed referendum on the draft European Constitution that Europe is first and foremost a source of anxiety for voters.[19] Confronted in addition with an unprecedented economic and financial crisis, the public was preoccupied first and foremost with safeguarding its social benefits. Thus, asked about what should be done in order to respond to the great challenges of the times at the very moment that a European summit was being held that was presented as essential for the future of the euro and that the new "Fiscal Compact" was being announced, a majority of respondents indicated that they would rather see national sovereignty preserved than see the powers of the EU reinforced (figure 10.1).

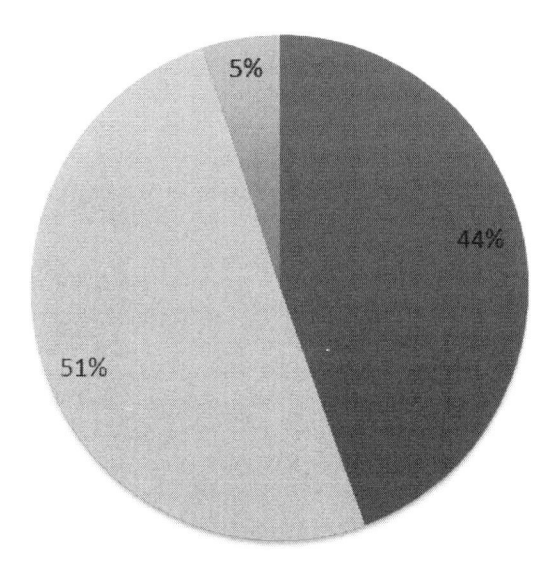

Figure 10.1. Public Opinion toward Europe at the Start of the Campaign

Question: "In order to effectively address the major problems of the coming years, what do you think is the best solution?"
—Blue response (44 percent): "We need to reinforce the EU's powers of decision, even if this means reducing the country's national sovereignty."
—Red response (51 percent): "We need to maintain the country's national sovereignty, even if this means reducing the powers of decision of the EU."
—Green response (5 percent): "No opinion."

Source: Enquête TNS Sofres – TriElec vague 3, Contexte politique à 5 mois de l'élection présidentielle, décembre 2011

The dominance of sovereignism must however not be confused with a wholesale rejection of Europe. In the same survey, a majority of respondents (51 percent) declared that they would have regrets if the dissolution of the EU was to be announced, with only 21 percent claiming that they would feel relieved.

The electoral system has no doubt contributed to a certain radicalization on the part of the candidates from the mainstream parties. In a majority runoff electoral system such as that governing French presidential elections, the mainstream candidates are forced to cast their net wide in the second round of the campaign in order to have any hope of victory. From this perspective, one of the singularities of the 2012 campaign was that the reservoir of votes for both of the candidates in the second round — FN voters for Nicolas Sarkozy; those of the Parti de Gauche for François Hollande — were much more wary about transferring new competences to the EU than were their own parties' voters.

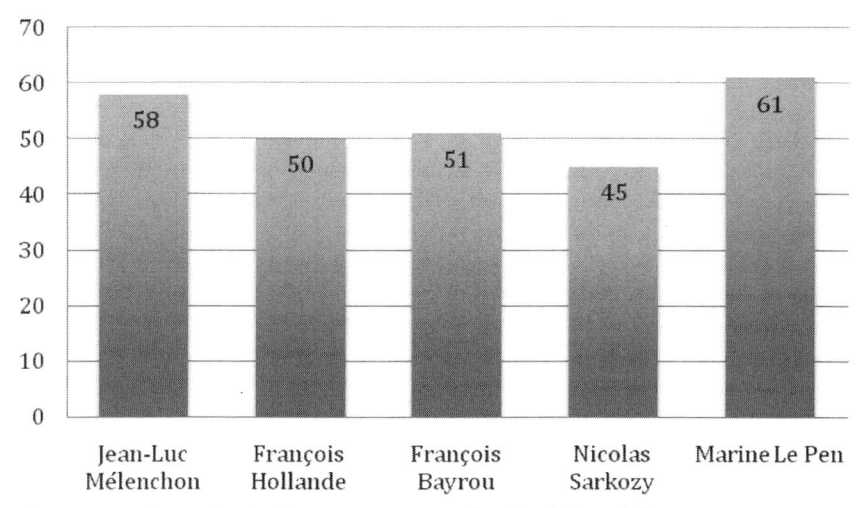

Figure 10.2. Sovereignist Sentiment among the Candidates' Electorates

The question posed was: "In order to effectively address the major problems of the coming years, what do you think is the best solution?" Two responses were proposed: maintaining the national sovereignty, even if this would limit the EU's powers, or reinforcing the powers of the EU.

Source: Enquête TNS Sofres – TriElec vague 3, Contexte politique à 5 mois de l'élection présidentielle, décembre 2011

Figure 10.2 effectively illustrates this predicament: if the two main candidates' supporters showed themselves to be (a bit) more favorable to a reinforcement of the EU's powers than the average French voter, sovereignist sentiment abutted 58 percent among Mélenchon supporters and reached 61 percent among those of Marine Le Pen. Given this fact, it is hardly surprising that the main candidates respectively campaigned on a line of opposition to European policy.

Europe and the Vote

What influence, then, did this Europeanization of the campaign have on voters' choices? The answer has several facets.

Asked about the themes that were most important to them, only rarely did French voters spontaneously evoke European issues: in the postelectoral European Economic Community (EEC) survey, these did not even reach 1 percent. However, when they were asked to choose between four themes—nuclear energy, immigration, reducing the number of civil servants, and the powers of Europe—it was by far this last issue that was uppermost in respondents' minds (43 percent vs. 27 percent for immigration).[20] This was particularly the case for Hollande voters, among whom this score reached 48 percent. Similarly, the issues that appear to have most influenced voters' choices were first and foremost economic and social in nature. This is shown in table 10.2.

However, the observation that was advanced above is also valid at this level: Europe often hides behind other issues. Throughout his campaign, the new president had explicitly tied the activities of the EU to the first two themes presented in table 10.2—employment and reduction of the deficit. Nicolas Sarkozy did the same with the themes of immigration and crime. If one adopts this broader concept of Europe, the latter indeed seems to have attracted the attention of large numbers of voters.

What was the impact of Europe on the outcome? Postelection surveys paint the picture of an anxious electorate that sees its identity as threatened (65 percent believe there are too many immigrants in France), and is pessimistic about the future. In such a context, Europe is often associated with negative changes: 67 percent of respondents feared that it would lead to an erosion of welfare protections in France and 53 percent that it would have a negative impact on the country's national identity and culture.[21] The election campaign, dominated as it was by negative portrayals of Europe, failed to diminish these fears. As figure 10.3 illustrates, the French emerged from the campaign less disposed to accept the transfer of more

Table 10.2. Issues that Influenced Voters in the First and Second Rounds of the 2012 Presidential Election

	April 22, 2012	May 6, 2012
Fight against unemployment	49	49
Reduction of the national debt and the budget deficit	31	35
Improvement of schools and teaching	30	32
Improvement of purchasing power	26	30
Financing of social security (pensions, health…)	25	28
Fight against inequality and injustice	24	23
Fight against poverty	19	18
Fiscal policy and taxation	16	15
Fight against insecurity	14	16
Fight against illegal immigration	13	18
Protection of the environment	11	7
International situation	9	9
Integration of minorities in French society	4	6

Source: Enquête TNS Sofres – TriElec Jour du Vote T1 et T2

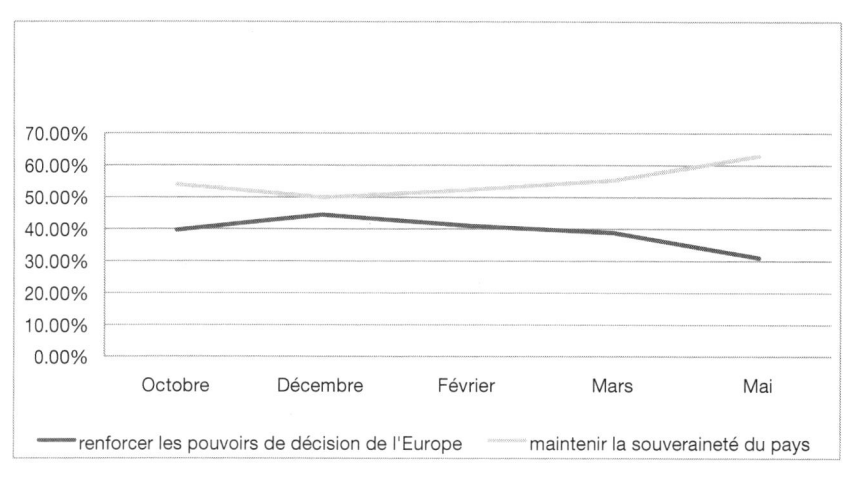

Figure 10.3. Progression of Sovereignism

Dark line: reinforce the powers of decision of Europe
Light line: maintain the national sovereignty of the country

Source: Enquête TNS Sofres – TriElec vagues 2 à 5 pour les valeurs d'octobre à mars 2012; Enquête post-électorale du CEVIPOF pour mai 2012.

sovereignty to Europe. The gap between the advocates of reinforcing Europe versus those in favor of preserving the nation's sovereignty, which had been of 14 percent in December 2011, reached 32 percent on the eve of the vote, without being able to say what this result owed to the candidates' anti-Europe rhetoric and the eurozone crisis.

As was mentioned above, this development must not be interpreted as an unconditional rejection of Europe, since a clear majority of respondents continued to indicate that they would regret to see it disappear. Nevertheless, in such a context it is no surprise that nearly one-third of the votes in the first round were cast in favor of candidates who, to different degrees, advanced discourses critical of European integration (Marine Le Pen, Jean-Luc Mélenchon, Nicolas Dupont-Aignan, Philippe Poutou, and Nathalie Arthaud). Though a general trend, the rise of sovereignism did not have the same impact on the electorates of the different candidates. Opposition to Europe appears to have been one of the principal motivations of the Le Pen vote.[22] Nicolas Sarkozy's Villepinte speech was also followed by a noticeable increase in sovereignist Euroskepticism among his supporters, which rose from 47 percent in February 2012 to 60 percent in March.[23] Evidently, the hardening of his discourse on Europe brought about a hardening of anti-European attitudes within his electorate.

By the same token, François Hollande's electorate eloquently captured the preoccupations of a significant part of the French left regarding European integration. Though it remained—though marginally, with 52 percent versus 59 percent of Sarkozy voters—in majority convinced that France had benefited from its EU membership, it nevertheless saw the latter as a threat to the welfare protections afforded the French (73 percent versus 59 percent among Sarkozy voters). On the other hand, Hollande's electorate was less preoccupied about the loss of cultural identity due to Europe (43 percent), and remained less critical regarding immigration than voters for the incumbent president: while 82 percent of the latter declared themselves totally or somewhat in agreement with the idea that there were too many immigrants in France, this percentage fell to 45 percent among Hollande voters. Another significant result, the latter were about as preoccupied about the need to balance the budget than voters on the right, the only difference being the relative importance which they attributed to this concern. Evoking the social divisions provoked by the 2005 referendum on the 2005 European Constitutional Treaty, Sarkozy clearly signaled in his Villepinte speech his intention to reconcile the France of the "*Non*" with that of the "*Oui*." Hollande tried to do the same thing on a more socially oriented register.[24] Neither of the two candidates really succeeded in this gambit, with 56 percent of "Yes" voters from the 2005 referendum voting for Sarkozy on May 6, while more than two-thirds of "No" voters cast their ballots for Hollande.[25]

Conclusion

If it was possible to speak of an invisible but omnipresent Europe in the 2002 presidential elections, this was no longer the case in 2012.[26] In a period that was dominated by the eurozone crisis and in which the weight of European issues was undeniable, it was difficult to hide Europe's electoral salience. This incontestable Europeanization of the vote in 2012 went hand in hand with the emergence of forms of resistance to Europe. Aware of the general climate of pessimism in which the election was held, the candidates as a whole structured their discourses by developing themes of opposition to Europe, each attempting to speak to the dominant fears of the voters. These discourses were effective. To a general reticence against the principle of integration could be added two forms of resistance to Europe—a left-wing variant, concerned with preserving the country's social acquis, and a right-wing variant, for which issues of national identity remain paramount.

François Hollande's victory has given rise to a number of questions. At a domestic political level, his room for maneuver has proved to be quite narrow: brought to the Elysée Palace by an electoral majority that is increasingly conscious of the weight of Europe in shaping French public policy, but also preoccupied with preserving the country's social acquis from change, he has found it difficult not to to disappoint his voters. The task was no easier at the European level where, at the behest of Germany and other northern countries, the rules of economic governance have been toughened. During his campaign, the new president had championed a political alternative at the European level. The European summit that followed his election was in fact marked by a shift in European economic policy, with the adoption of a reflationary program designed to dampen the effects of the crisis. Certain observers even went so far as to invoke the replacement of the "Merkozy" axis by a new "Latin alliance."[27] The hope was however short-lived and European fiscal supervision has been as tight as before his election. This was perhaps uanvoidable, since European decision-making is first and foremost the product of consensus.

The French election has confirmed the existence of a link between domestic political competition on the one hand and policy choices more or less determined at the European level on the other. It remains to be seen whether this phenomenon was first and foremost linked to the present context of crisis that has overtaken Europe or whether, on the contrary, it points to deeper structural changes that are also affecting other countries. If the latter is the case, we should ask ourselves what this Europeanization of French domestic politics bodes for the political system of the EU. Openly broaching European questions in national elections no doubt enhances the quality of the democratic debate by helping to clarify the central issues of the campaign. But if, failing to radically alter the course of European policy, each of the candidates chooses to adapt a logic of opposition to Brussels, the centrifugal forces that could be released would render European governance more difficult still.

Notes

Translated from the French by Gabriel Goodliffe.
1. Vivien Schmidt, *Democracy in Europe: The EU and National Polities* (Oxford: Oxford University Press, 2006).
2. These analyses have been published on the TriÉlec Web site, available from https://sites.google.com/a/iepg.fr/ trielec/.
3. Sylvain Brouard, Olivier Costa, Thomas König (eds), *The Europeanization of Domestic Legislatures: The Empirical Implications of the Delors Myth in Nine Countries* (New York: Springer, 2012).

4. Nicolas Sarkozy, "Discours de Nicolas Sarkozy à Villepinte," March 11, 2012. http://www.dailymotion.com/video/xpdrdw_discours-de-nicolas-sarkozy-a-villepinte_news.
5. Veit Medick, "Merkel Forges Anti-Hollande Alliance in Europe," *Der Spiegel* [online], March 5, 2012, http://www.spiegel.de/international/europe/meddling-in-france-merkel-forges-anti-hollande-alliance-in-europe-a-819297.html.
6. Peter Mair, "*Political Opposition* and the *European Union*," *Government and Opposition* 42, no. 1 (*2007*): 1–17.
7. Dominque Labbé and Denis Monière, *Radioscopies de la campagne présidentielle (X). La dernière ligne droite (8–21 avril)* (Paris: TriÉlec, 2012), http://hal.archives-ouvertes.fr/docs/00/71/87/44/PDF/ Radioscopie10.pdf.
8. Specifically, her program calls for "initiating a renegotiation of the treaties in order to break away from a dogmatic project of European integration that has totally failed." Marine Le Pen, "Mon projet. Pour la France et le Français," http://www.frontnational.com/pdf/projet_mlp2012.pdf, 15.
9. Jean-Luc Mélenchon was an elected representative of the PS until 2008.
10. On the ambiguities presented by Sarkozy's European policies, see Renaud Dehousse, "Nicolas Sarkozy l'Européen" in *Les politiques publiques sous Sarkozy*, ed. J. de Maillard and Y. Surel (Paris: Presses de Sciences Po, 2012), 153–66.
11. http://www.u-m-p.org/sites/default/files/fichiers_joints/articles/11_03_discours_villepinte.pdf.
12. Ibid.
13. http://www.jean-jaures.org/content/download/16559/161450/file/Discours_Hollande.pdf.
14. Ibid.
15. Ibid.
16. Viviane Le Hay, "Les thèmes importants dans le choix électoral au second tour de la présidentielle 2012," *TriÉlec* [online], May 10, 2012, https://sites.google.com/a/iepg.fr/trielec/resultats-analyses/enquetes-pre-electorales/vague-t2/lesthemesimportantsdanslechoixelectoralausecondtourdelapresidentielle2012.
17. François Hollande was most explicit in articulating such a demand, "I have therefore asked for a political mandate from the French people. If it makes the choice of electing me President of the Republic, I will then have the duty and the obligation to renegotiate this treaty because this will be the sovereign will of the French people" (speech in Le Bourget, *supra* note 13; authors' translation).
18. "France and Germany cannot pretend to lead Europe on their own. Europe is a common responsibility for France and Germany. Europe is not the common property of France and Germany" (speech in Le Bourget, *supra* note 13; authors' translation).
19. See Dehousse, *La fin de l'Europe* (Paris, Flammarion, 2005) ; Sylvain Brouard, Emiliano Grossman and Nicolas Sauger, *Les Français contre l'Europe?: les sens du référendum du 29 mai 2005* (Paris: Presses de Sciences Po, 2007).
20. Nicolas Sauger, "L'enquête électorale française 2012," November 20, 2013, http://www.cee.sciences-po.fr/en/research/election-analysis/lenquete-electorale-francaise-2012.pdf?format=phocapdf.
21. Ibid.
22. Nonna Mayer, "From Jean-Marie to Marine Le Pen. Electoral Change on the Far Right," *Parliamentary Affairs* 66, no. 1 (2013):160–78.
23. Annie-Claude Salomon, "Contexte politique à trois semaines de l'élection présidentielle," *TriÉlec 2012* [online], 8 April 2012, https://sites.google.com/a/iepg.fr/trielec/resultats-analyses/enquetes-pre-electorales/vague-5---avril-2012/resultatsdusondagetnssofrespourtrielec2012-vague5.
24. Sauger, "L'enquête électorale française 2012."

25. Annie-Claude Salomon, "Les thèmes importants dans le choix électoral au second tour de la présidentielle 2012," TriÉlec 2012 [online], May 11, 2012, https://sites.google.com/a/iepg.fr/trielec/resultats-analyses/enquetes-pre-electorales/vague-t2/lesthemesimportantsdanslechoixelectoralausecondtourdelapresidentielle2012.
26. Céline Belot and Bruno Cautrès, "L'Europe, invisible mais omniprésente," in *Le Nouveau Désordre électoral : les leçons du 21 avril 2002*, ed. B. Cautrès and N. Mayer (Paris: Presses de Sciences Po, 2004), 119–41.
27. Massimo Franco, "Una nuova guerra di religione," *Corriere della Sera* [online], September 7, 2012, http://www.presseurop.eu/it/content/article/2653351-una-nuova-guerra-di-religione.

Chapter 11

Hollande and Sarkozy's Foreign Policy Legacy

Frédéric Charillon

In a rare move for a president elect of the Fifth Republic, Nicolas Sarkozy chose to devote an important part of his victory speech of May 6, 2007, to foreign policy. In that speech, the new president and successor to Jacques Chirac (1995–2007) heralded sweeping policy departures that extended to the international domain. Addressing France's European partners, the United States, the countries of the Mediterranean, and Africa, Sarkozy concluded his speech by placing his prospective foreign policy under the banner of morality and human rights.[1] By the same token, the term of office of the new president, whom the media would soon portray as a "hyper-" or even "omni-president," came to be marked by a relentless and frantic activism that was defined by several overarching policy priorities, a broad commitment to political voluntarism, and a desire to change the consensual frameworks that traditionally underpinned French diplomacy.

Five years later and following his electoral defeat by François Hollande, what achievements can we attribute to Sarkozy's foreign policy, what were the principal debates that drove it, and what policy shifts can we expect? If it is still too early to render a full accounting of his foreign policy, a number of impressions—if not yet certainties—are already apparent. The first is that of a policy course so variegated and pragmatic that it is difficult to reduce to a simple interpretation. Sarkozy's decision-making process appears to have shifted at different times, the principles guiding his policy distancing themselves from both the expectations and the fears he inspired as a presidential candidate. As such, it was more by a reactive approach to crises than by the pursuit of a systematic course of action that his foreign policy came to be characterized.

Notes for this chapter begin on page 178.

In turn, the Sarkozy era helped crystallize at least three foreign policy debates that remain to be resolved. The first concerns France's relationship with its American ally and, following from this, France's relationship with NATO in particular and the West generally. The second has to do with France's freedom to maneuver to the south and, more specifically, to its traditional Mediterranean sphere of influence. Finally, the third debate concerns France's status as a power in the global system, the kind of power France aspires to be, and the means at its disposal to become that power.

A Sarkozian Foreign Policy?

Historians have alternately described the foreign policies of General de Gaulle as "sovereign," of Georges Pompidou as "subterranean," of Valéry Giscard-d'Estaing as "personal," and of François Mitterrand as "solitary."[2] More recently, political scientists have evoked the "affective" foreign policy of Jacques Chirac because it was determined in part by his personal attachments to certain world regions and leaders.[3] Is there such a qualifier that surmises Nicolas Sarkozy's foreign policy? The rather unscientific term "impulsive" is often used to highlight a policy that was conducted in fits and starts and guided by a capacity for reaction rather than a systematic framework. Certain defining foreign policy principles were in fact set down by Nicolas Sarkozy after taking office. However, faced with the difficulty of putting these principles into practice and holding to them given a shifting international context, it was the capacity for reaction and for adaptation—or inconsistency, in the word of his detractors—that became the hallmark of his foreign policy. This evolution can first be seen in the foreign policy team and decision-making procedures that were initially put in place in 2007. By naming several figures from the left to important foreign policy positions,[4] the new president showed himself to be an innovator. In order to fill posts to which close collaborators of the head of state had traditionally been named, Sarkozy chose, absent any political or institutional constraints, certain popular (Bernard Kouchner) or professionally competent (Jean-Pierre Jouyet) figures belonging to the political opposition, with all that this implied for the subsequent nomination of diplomats, their choice of collaborators, and the ministerial cabinets. In particular, this initiative was interesting because it asserted the novel principle that foreign policy was not the preserve of a single political party, but rather that of France as a whole. One might even have thought that it would set a precedent.

However, several factors invalidate the hypothesis that this principle was deliberately formulated and applied with such a purpose in mind.

In the first place, the new president's hesitation in choosing between such dissimilar candidates for the post of foreign affairs minister—Hubert Védrine, to whom the position was first proposed, and Bernard Kouchner, who was ultimately named—gives room for pause. The former, who had already served as foreign affairs minister during the cohabitation government of 1997 to 2002, was known for his penchant for realpolitik and his traditional approach to foreign policy: anti-Atlanticist and wary of media and humanitarian initiatives, as well as the involvement of non-state actors in the policy process. The latter, by contrast, exemplified exactly the opposite approach.

Perhaps more importantly, this opening of the instances of foreign policy to the left did not last, with each of the aforementioned actors being progressively replaced beginning in 2008 with figures drawn from the presidential majority. By naming Michèle Alliot-Marie to head the Quai d'Orsay in November 2010, followed by Alain Juppé in February 2011, the traditional pillars of Gaullism returned to the helm of French international affairs. Finally, the influence of ministerial nominees during Sarkozy's presidency seemed on a number of occasions to be offset by that of the president's entourage. First, key advisers in the Elysée Palace, notably secretary general to the Elysée, Claude Guéant (2007–11), and special presidential advisor Henri Guaino (2007–12), assumed an unofficial foreign policy role. Likewise, the president's more informal entourage also proved influential, notably with the responsibility attributed to (and self-proclaimed by) Bernard-Henri Lévy in managing the Libyan crisis of 2011, who remained throughout in direct contact with the commander in chief, to the great frustration of the foreign affairs minister.

Due to his reputation, previous statements, and purported affinities, Nicolas Sarkozy's assumption of office was met with hope by some and trepidation by others. He was said to be Atlanticist, less favorably inclined toward the Arab world and more sympathetic to Israel than were his predecessors. Finally, his early foreign policy speeches announced important reforms, notably regarding France's attitude toward authoritarian regimes, and called for fundamentally resetting relations with Africa. In nearly all these areas, however, and following a number of reversals, policy continuity has ended up trumping the proclaimed break with the past.

In the Middle East, despite delivering a speech that was well received by the Knesset in June 2008, Sarkozy ran up against Israeli intransigence during Operation Cast Lead in Gaza as well as the Jewish state's refusal to reconsider its settlement policy in the West Bank. Despite managing to reduce the tension in Franco-Israeli relations and to recast their differences in terms of a divergence of interest between the two states rather than a fundamental mutual antagonism, he was nevertheless unable to substantially alter the complex situation in the Middle East. Finally, his links with several Arab regimes exposed him to criticisms similar to those of his predecessors. This was notably the case when he chose to officially host Colonel Gaddafi in Paris in 2007, initiated a rapprochement with the Syrian regime with whom Jacques Chirac had cut relations in 2008, and hesitated to condemn the violent repression of popular protests by the dying Ben Ali regime in Tunisia in 2011.

In turn, Sarkozy's initial desire to revise France's traditional links with Africa was complicated by the poor reception elicited by his first major foreign policy address delivered in Dakar in July 2007.[5] This was followed by the negative reaction of several African countries—Gabon in the lead—to State Secretary Jean-Marie Bockel's January 2008 proposal to sign "the death certificate of *Françafrique*," which he qualified as an "ambiguous and self-satisfied relationship, from which some ... profit at the expense of the general interest of development."[6] The state secretary was quickly replaced. In respect to the question of how to treat authoritarian regimes, and after letting it be known that he would refuse to shake Vladimir Putin's hand and would be tough on China, the constraints of global power politics forced Sarkozy to cultivate closer relations with the former while the relationship with Beijing has alternated between critiques of the Chinese regime on human rights grounds and attempts at economic rapprochement on commercial grounds.

It is doubtless with regard to the United States that the most successful departure in French foreign policy was to be seen. Without resolving the differences of interest stemming from the divergent priorities of the two states (whether at the level of French participation in international military operations such as in Afghanistan, or regarding Turkish membership in the European Union), Sarkozy, whose November 2007 speech to congress was very well received,[7] was able, as in the Israeli case, to convince American policymakers that potential differences of views were the result of divergent interests to be discussed among allies rather than a priori French hostility toward the United States. Unburdened at least temporarily of the specter of this supposedly primal Gaullist anti-Americanism, the relationship between the two allies was much facilitated. And it would be even more so by France's return to NATO's integrated command structure, as will be seen later.

If revising the classic foreign policy tenets of the Fifth Republic turned out to be more difficult than anticipated and policy consistency through his *quinquennat* to be rare, most observers concur that Sarkozy's approach, simultaneously built on political voluntarism, impatience, and an obsession with quick results, was better adapted to responding to crises. The first context to which this approach was applied—on several occasions—

is Europe. Considerably restrained in its European initiatives by the failure of the 2005 referendum on the European Constitution, France was able to regain the initiative in European affairs following Sarkozy's election in 2007. Without resolving all the misunderstandings that have progressively emerged between Paris and Berlin over the intervening years,[8] as well as failing to reassure "small" members of the EU who have often viewed France as an arrogant partner calling for the attribution of "special responsibilities" to "large" members, the Fifth Republic's sixth president displayed remarkable dynamism, often in tandem with the German chancellor, in tackling the successive crises that struck Europe over his five years in office—first at the institutional level, then on the economic and monetary front. His willingness to react quickly through the holding of international summits and other fora or his—sometimes precipitate—announcement of decisive measures were also broadly perceived as the hallmark of a constructive voluntarism, even if they sometimes chafed with some of his European partners.

The same impression—and reservations—was also generated at a global level by his approach to major international crises. Three of these in particular provoked a forceful French response over this period: the Georgian crisis of August 2008 when Sarkozy, as titular EU president, imposed himself as a mediator to try to contain the effects of the Russian military intervention; the long crisis in Ivory Coast that came to a head in spring 2011 and saw Laurent Gbagbo finally leave power after refusing to accept his electoral defeat, a denouement in which the French army played a crucial supporting role; and, most obviously, the Libyan crisis of 2011, which saw Paris take the lead of the UN-sanctioned military intervention to protect the civilian population of Benghazi and ultimately led to the overthrow and death of Muammar Gaddafi. In these three cases, France's willingness to take immediate action, even if it was criticized at the time, met with success because the contextually specific and rapidly evolving circumstances of crisis favored such an outcome. Confronted with other global challenges that were more systemically rooted and whose resolution demanded action over the long term, such as in the case of the 2008 global financial crisis, a similar voluntarism was also on display but with much more mixed results.

Post-Sarkozy Debates

Through the initiatives he effectively led as well as the areas he left unaddressed because of his incapacity to act on a difficult international dispensation, Nicolas Sarkozy ultimately highlighted a number of key questions confronting French foreign policy. By effecting a return to most of NATO's integrated command structures and notably evoking France's appurtenance to the "Western family,"[9] he was de facto posing the problem of France's relationship to the Atlantic community. In turn, by defending the ambitious project of a Union for the Mediterranean (Union pour la Méditerranée, or UPM), he forcefully reopened the issue of France's potential role in its southern near abroad, including the countries of the Middle East. Finally, by commissioning the drafting of a new White Paper on defense and national security fourteen years after the last one was published, Sarkozy initiated a conversation on French military power at a time of tightening budgetary restrictions. His calls for reforming France's diplomatic structure, as well as for a separate White Paper on the country's foreign policy, were also made with a similar end in mind. The announcement at the April 2008 Bucharest NATO summit of France's return to the integrated command of the Atlantic Alliance, which was officially confirmed at the Ecole Militaire in March 2009 and then ratified the following April at a subsequent summit at Strasbourg and Kehl, as well as the reinforcement of the French military presence in Afghanistan in 2008, strengthened the bonds between France and the Atlantic Community. First contemplated by Jacques Chirac in 1996, this diplomatic-strategic shift had been forestalled by the latter's demands that a European country (i.e., France) be attributed a theater command, and then was indefinitely put on hold following the PS's victory in the mid-term 1997 parliamentary elections. Over a decade later, Nicolas Sarkozy successfully fulfilled this initiative without provoking a national outcry while nevertheless encouraging a serious and valuable debate that has continued beyond his departure from the Elysée.

Did this shift simply mark the formalization of a development that had already been years in the making and required French participation in the most important working groups of the Atlantic Alliance, or was it something more?[10] Did this evolution spell the end of France's privileged position, which had allowed the country to preserve its political and military autonomy without breaking with its NATO allies? A number of prominent political figures, including Laurent Fabius, Alain Juppé, and Hubert Védrine, strongly criticized the country's reintegration within NATO command. They argued that such a move gave the misleading impression of a fundamental French strategic realignment, created the illusion of greater participation in decision-making in an alliance that ultimately remained under American control, was unfavorable to creating a common European defense identity, was too costly in deployments, and finally made it harder for France to maintain its nuclear deterrent if NATO ever came to advocate, in keeping with President Obama's "global zero" option, a nonnuclear Europe protected solely by an American antimissile shield. On another front, the other great foreign policy initiative announced by Nicolas Sarkozy following his election, the creation of a UPM, stood to position France as a potential political leader in that region of the world. Justifiably taking stock of the stalled Barcelona Process that had been launched in 1995, this initiative nevertheless came in for severe criticism—and correctives—on the part of France's European partners before running aground on the harsh realities of the southern and eastern Mediterranean.[11] First, there was the Israeli operation in Gaza in December 2008 and January 2009, which proved as fatal to the UPM as the assassination of Yitzhak Rabin in 1995 and the Second Intifada of September 2000 had been to the Barcelona Process. In turn, the UPM was also jeopardized by ongoing Israeli settlement building as well as internal conflicts among the Palestinians. The final blow to the idea came with the Arab Spring revolts of 2011. How could such a process, which had been launched in Paris in July 2008 at a ceremony featuring President Bashar al-Assad of Syria as guest of honor and then subsequently presided over by President Hosni Mubarak of Egypt, be credibly pursued?

But the Mediterranean initiative, that these regional crises ended up reducing to naught, also raised some questions that remain relevant today. In the first place, it brought up the issue of whether France retained the capacity to launch initiatives in such a conflict-prone area, given the uneven support of its European partners and its lack of effective tools to act on this enormously complex and troubled region. In 2007–8, Lebanon again provided a telling illustration of French limitations in this regard.[12] It is thus the fundamental question of France's influence over its southern strategic ambit, often portrayed as the test case of its foreign policy, that is posed. The requisite management of the fallout from the Arab Spring, which caught France as much by surprise as it did everybody else, makes a resumption of the debate over this question unavoidable.

Finally, the commissioning of a series of analyses of France's place in the world,[13] the drafting of two White Papers—one on defense and national security by a committee presided over by Jean-Claude Mallet,[14] the other concerning France's foreign and European policy by a committee headed by Alain Juppé and Louis Schweitzer—exemplified a new willingness to launch the debate surrounding the state's foreign capacities and to render it more regular and permanent a fixture than ever before. In terms of defense, though Nicolas Sarkozy had already authorized a reduction in the scope of the military branches in 2008,[15] this trend would persist following the publication of a new report at the end of 2012. By the same token, the decision of whether to build a second aircraft carrier, difficult to avoid from a strategic standpoint but hard to contemplate from a budgetary one, has been indefinitely postponed.

Most importantly, a number of French military interventions and its contribution to joint operations over the period under consideration were a reminder that France's international responsibilities require maintaining high levels of military savoir faire and capability. This was underscored by French participation in combating piracy in the Indian Ocean (Operation Atalanta) and in the United Nations Interim Force in Lebanon (UNIFIL), the intervention in the Ivory Coast in 2011, and especially the intervention in Libya the same year in which French pilots, alongside the British and with substantial American support, had trouble overcoming the assorted forces supporting Colonel Gaddafi. Yet, how to maintain France's military capabilities in this period of budgetary constraint? How to safeguard the potential for military restoration until budgetary surpluses are achieved? The question remains apposite.

A similar debate is also warranted in terms of France's diplomatic capabilities, which the reform of the Ministry of Foreign Affairs launched by Bernard Kouchner failed to fundamentally change. France maintains the third largest diplomatic corps in the world, with around 160 embassies, 17 permanent delegations, 97 consulates general and consulates, and 154 organs of cooperation and cultural outreach. Embassies are now broken down into three categories: (a) around thirty multipurpose embassies, which are the most important; (b) around a hundred priority diplomatic missions; and (c) around ten minimally staffed diplomatic representations. The question remains whether this extensive global presence is still a guarantee of influence, and whether France needs to reconfigure its diplomatic apparatus, which currently extends from Washington, DC, to Saint Lucia and Trinidad and Tobago.

Toward a New Focus of French Diplomacy?

In his electoral campaign, the candidate who would defeat Nicolas Sarkozy in the April–May 2012 presidential elections sought first and foremost to differentiate himself from his predecessor's style, which was criticized for its agitation and ostentation (witness its infamous qualification as "bling-bling" in the media), and instead to place the emphasis on themes of social justice. International issues were conspicuously absent from the Hollande and Sarkozy contest and most notably from the debate that traditionally opposes the two remaining candidates prior to a presidential election's second-round runoff. One might have expected that some of Nicolas Sarkozy's foreign policy decisions would be attacked by the opposition, including the rapprochement with NATO, the troop increase in Afghanistan, and the botched initial response to the Arab Spring, among others. This did not happen for probably four reasons: (a) external constraints were so strong and the international situation so complex that the stakes involved militated against the opposition making any rash promises; (b) the opposition, including the PS, was itself divided on certain foreign policy questions, such as the split between Atlanticists and Europeanists; (c) Nicolas Sarkozy's foreign policy record—especially following the Libyan intervention as well as in terms of the numerous challenges to come, such as those in the Sahel—was not negatively regarded by the public; (d) and last but not least, foreign policy and defense issues tend not to sway electoral contests. Indeed, historical experience suggests that candidates who choose to play the foreign policy card do so at a high risk, for only a putative political benefit.[16] François Hollande thus wisely avoided making these themes the spearhead of his campaign while preventing Nicolas Sarkozy from translating them into a credibility gap that could play in his favor. To the incumbent president's claim of foreign policy experience and the support of several international leaders (including Angela Merkel), the socialist candidate opposed his willingness to mark a fresh start, beginning with a new style and approach, while promising to more forcefully assert the French perspective in dealing with Germany in Europe and China internationally.

In the wake of his election, how did François Hollande cope with the foreign policy legacy of his predecessor? Although a change in style was announced, how did this apply in practice to the area of foreign policy? A substantive change in policy content and direction was always unlikely, though the new president did enjoy some room for maneuver. Finally, on the domestic front, a calming of the debate over France's global capabilities and decision-making processes seemed desirable.

Empirically speaking, it was always unlikely that many of the foreign policy discourses deployed by Nicolas Sarkozy during his term of office would be reformulated in the same terms by François Hollande. (Indeed, it is probably unlikely that they would be by Sarkozy himself.) The tropes of the "African man" or the "Western family" come to mind, for example.[17] One could also imagine that the intense publicity and media scrutiny given to the figure and action of the president by Sarkozy meant that, under his successor, international crises impacting French citizens, either as hostages or as targets of prosecution, would not be managed in the same way.[18] On more explicitly political crises of broader import such as those in Georgia, Lebanon, or Libya, it is still too early to say what Hollande's style will be. However, the Syrian tragedy in the summer of 2012 provides an interesting first test. The former president, on the heels of meeting with the leader of the anti-Assad Syrian National Council, Abdel Basset Sayda, made an unusual public overture to his successor that he more proactively engage with the issue, while his party, the UMP, called on the new head of state to interrupt his summer vacation in order to address these questions. Quite clearly, then, the former president has persisted in his publicity-seeking style while his successor has continued in the desire to distance himself from the latter. What does this mean in substance? The very type of public policy implied by a foreign or defense policy—defined by the need to react to external events whose dynamics but not their timing can be anticipated—considerably reduces the scope for fundamentally modifying this field of policy. A lack of budgetary room for maneuver on the one hand and the international commitments of a responsible state on the other do not favor improvisation. It is therefore customary within the advanced Western democracies to see a relative continuity in the conduct of foreign policy, a few notable exceptions notwithstanding.[19] Consequently, even if some of the foreign policy choices adopted by Nicolas Sarkozy during his term were criticized by the new president's team, their out-and-out abandonment remains difficult to imagine.

On Europe, the renegotiation of the European Treaty and Fiscal Compact of March 2012, which had been advocated by François Hollande during his campaign (to the great consternation of the German chancellor), would be extremely complicated to see through in practice. And even though a report was commissioned in the summer of 2012 from former foreign affairs minister Hubert Védrine on France's role within the Atlantic Alliance, one can hardly imagine the country backtracking from its new position within NATO's integrated command structure. The predominant approach to the issue can be summarized by the following line: "We would not have done it, but now we are not going to undo it." What to do, by the same token, about the UPM? Ultimately, this initiative would not be attacked by Hollande during the campaign, particularly since it did not initially displease several Mediterranean specialists within the PS. And if it is now being reconsidered, this has more to do with recent developments in the region (see above) than it does with Hollande's desire to reverse his predecessor's foreign policy.

This leaves the question of new potential orientations that might inform French foreign policy under the new administration. On the diplomatic front, these remain more or less given and their contours self-evident.[20] They perforce include Europe and the Atlantic Alliance, while Africa and the Mediterranean also naturally top the list. A positing of French interests in Asia and Latin America might also be on the cards,[21] but these regions nevertheless remain remote even if they have assumed global strategic importance. In matters of defense judged in terms of concrete military strength and projection capacity (both material and human), the mechanism of redeployment offers greater latitude to reformulate priorities.

Taking advantage of the latter, Nicolas Sarkozy was thus able to move ahead with establishing a new military base in the United Arab Emirates. The possibilities open to François Hollande in this area, however, will very much depend on the straightened budgetary circumstances that he faces. A last possibility consists in announcing important policy departures, such as calling for a rapprochement with a given state or, conversely, opposing the designs of another. Nicolas Sarkozy did this by expressing his desire for a rapprochement with the United States, reaching a better understanding with Israel, showing less complacency toward Moscow and Beijing, resuming the dialogue with Damascus, and adopting a much tougher line with Tehran. Apart from the last objective, facts on the ground prevented him from achieving these aims.

One year after assuming power, François Hollande first attempted to distinguish himself from his predecessor in terms of the form of his policymaking by adopting a less "energetic" style, as Tony Blair had put it in 2007. Within the EU, he especially sought to distance himself from Germany, having previously criticized the drift of the "Merkozy" couple in which France was adjudged to have excessively deferred to its neighbor across the Rhine. Explicitly stating the French disagreement with Germany's advocacy of economic austerity, this new posture has also generated tensions with the German government and rhetorical excesses from both sides. By contrast, the criticisms that were formerly expressed by Nicolas Sarkozy vis-à-vis the European Commission and his tense relations with President Barroso have been broadly replicated during Hollande's first year in office. More interesting still, the interventionist military stance pursued by the former UMP head of state in Ivory Coast and Libya in 2011 has been perpetuated by his successor in Mali where François Hollande launched Operation Serval in January 2013 in order to dislodge the Islamists who had gained control of the north of the country. Thus, despite tightening budgetary constraints and shifts in the country's military structure (as commissioned by the White Papers of 2008 under Nicolas Sarkozy and 2013 under François Hollande—documents otherwise at odds on other issues), from one presidency to the next, France has confirmed that it remains today one of the powers most inclined to resort to military intervention.

There remains, however, one final point on which action by the new president is both expected and feasible: a general calming of the debate surrounding these questions both among the public as well as within the foreign policy establishment. Indeed, during the final years of Sarkozy's presidency (during 2010 and 2011, to be precise), the combination of budgetary constraints, military cuts, difficult deployments (such as Afghanistan), and unanticipated international developments (the Arab Spring) have fueled tensions and generated a noxious atmosphere within the instances of foreign policymaking.[22] The publication of signed or anonymous op-eds in the press in order to denounce the evolution of French diplomacy, the anxieties (once again attributed or nonattributed) expressed by the military establishment regarding the ongoing reforms or the situation in Afghanistan,[23] all of this suggested that a sense of malaise was spreading among the institutional actors responsible for carrying out these policies, that new ways of conducting policy debates, expressing concerns, and exploring options needed to be devised, and that decision-making should be restructured. On this score at least, the arrival of the new administration augurs a new beginning that is not solely dependent on external circumstances.

In the end, Nicolas Sarkozy illustrated in his own way an iron law of foreign policy, that the window of opportunity for states to push through dramatic changes in this area remains particularly narrow. He attempted to confute this law by combining a great sense of pragmatism with a political hypervoluntarism and manifold policy initiatives. He was sometimes lauded for these two last traits, but nevertheless failed to rise above this foreign policy principle. For his part, his successor has announced that he will embrace a different if not contrary policy style that seeks to build toward rather than impose his own goals. Initially, at least, this approach inevitably makes for a different impression. In terms of results, however, we shall have to wait and see what challenges international events pose to France as well as to its partners.

Notes

Translated from the French by Gabriel Goodliffe.
1. "I wish to appeal to those people in the world who believe in the values of tolerance, of liberty, of democracy and of humanism, to those who are persecuted by tyranny and dictatorship, to all the women and children who have been brutalized in this world in order to tell them that France will be on their side, and that they may count on her." N. Sarkozy, Speech of May 6, 2007, http://www1.rfi.fr/actufr/articles/089/article_51876.asp.
2. For recent studies, see M. Vaïsse, *Puissance ou influence ? La France dans le monde depuis 1958* (Paris: Fayard, 2009); and F. Bozo, *La politique étrangère de la France depuis 1945* (Paris: Flammarion, 2012).
3. F. Charillon, *La politique étrangère de la France* (Paris: La documentation française, 2011.)
4. Foreign Affairs Minister Bernard Kouchner was the first among these, but there were also Jean-Pierre Jouyet, appointed state secretary for European Affairs, and Jean-Marie Bockel, socialist mayor of Mulhouse since 1989, who was named state secretary for Cooperation and Francophonie.

5. Several passages in particular came in for harsh criticism: "The tragedy of Africa is that the African man has not yet entered history," or "Modern man ... has much to learn from the African man who lives in symbiosis with nature." N. Sarkozy, "Le discours de Dakar de Nicolas Sarkozy, July 26, 2007, http://www.lemonde.fr/afrique/article/2007/11/09/le-discours-de-dakar_976786_3212.html.
6. J-M. Bockel, "Discours de M. Jean-Marie Bockel : l'acte de décès de la Françafrique," January 15, 2008, https://appablog.wordpress.com/2008/01/16/discours-de-m-jean-marie-bockel-%C2%AB-lacte-de-deces-de-la-francafrique-%C2%BB-15-janvier-2008/.
7. In this speech, the French President expressed his admiration for the United States, evoking "the American dream," the liberation of France in 1944 ("America liberated us. We are eternally indebted"), and a French image of America sustained, according to him "by the conquest of the [American] West and by Hollywood." N. Sarkozy, Washington, DC, November 7, 2007, http://www.voltairenet.org/article152875.html.
8. Some of these misunderstandings have potentially serious consequences for the future, such as in the strategic realm with Germany's evolution of an increasingly noninterventionist position and its adoption of a nonnuclear stance for the continent.
9. "I first wanted to situate, frankly and clearly, and here is the first break with the past, France within the Western family. In a world that has lost its bearings ... it seems to me essential to clearly affirm where France situates herself and what values she feels are essential. ... By placing herself clearly within the Western family, France, and this was my goal, increases her credibility, her capacity for action, her means of influence." Nicolas Sarkozy, "New year's wishes to the diplomatic corps," January 18, 2008, http://www.ambafrance-uk.org/Voeux-du-President-Sarkozy-au.
10. In 2008 France was already the fourth greatest contributor to NATO's budget for civilian affairs after the United States, Germany, and Great Britain, accounting for 14 percent of NATO's military budget, and the third greatest military contributor in terms of personnel, with 4,800 troops earmarked for NATO operations.
11. Initially, the French president's idea had been of a Union *of* (and not *for*) the Mediterranean, that would include only the coastal Mediterranean countries. Germany as well as Italy and other EU members were opposed to what they construed as a potential move to splinter the EU, even though it was never made clear how the project would be financed.
12. Following the intense shuttle diplomacy with Beirut that was pursued by Bernard Kouchner to try to find a way out of the Lebanese impasse, it was the *coup de force* by Hezbollah in spring 2008, followed by the mediation of Qatar and signing of the Doha Accords, that finally brought a temporary resolution to the crisis and the formation of a new government in Lebanon.
13. For example, see the report commissioned in the summer of 2007 from Hubert Védrine: *Rapport pour le président de la République sur la France et la mondialisation* (Paris: Fayard, 2007).
14. A former member of Pierre Joxe's cabinet at the Ministry of Defense who was then given a brief over strategic affairs at the Ministry of Defense (1992–98), Mallet served as secretary general of National Defense from 1998 to 2004 and as *chargé de mission* to Jacques Chirac.
15. This called for eliminating a total of 54,000 jobs from the military budget over a period extending through 2015. See *Livre Blanc sur la Défense et la Sécurité Nationale*, http://www.defense.gouv.fr/educadef/defense-et-programmes-scolaires/enseigner-la-defense-textes-generaux/livre-blanc-sur-la-defense-et-la-securite-nationale-2013/(language)/fre-FR#SearchText=livre blanc sur la defense et la securite nationale#xtcr=1.
16. For example, Ségolène Royal, the socialist candidate in the 2007 presidential elections, saw her electoral standing substantially diminished following foreign trips to China and Lebanon.

17. Bockel, "Discours de M. Jean-Marie Bockel," January 15, 2008.
18. Nicolas Sarkozy played a very active role in obtaining the freeing of French citizens Ingrid Betancourt (held hostage in Colombia by the Revolutionary Armed Forces of Colombia (Fuerzas Armadas Revolucionarias de Colombia; FARC) and finally freed following a Colombian army operation in July 2008), Clotilde Reiss (accused of espionage in Iran and freed in August 2009), and Florence Cassez (sentenced in Mexico in 2009 to sixty years in prison for kidnapping and membership of a criminal organization who was freed in January 2013), communicating widely on these cases.
19. The coming to power of American neoconservatives in January 2001 is a striking example.
20. F. Charillon, *La France peut-elle encore agir sur le monde ?* (Paris : A. Colin, 2010.)
21. Such a reorientation was engaged during the presidency of Jacques Chirac, as well as by the new minister of defense Jean-Yves Le Drian, who announced at the Shangri-La Dialogue in Singapore in June 2012 that France was reclaiming its role as a Pacific power.
22. This deleterious atmosphere was underscored by a number of communications that appeared in the press over the span of a few months. These included a July 7, 2010, forum in *Le Monde* entitled "Stop Weakening the French Foreign Office!" ("Cessez d'affaiblir le Quai d'Orsay!") that was cosigned by Alain Juppé and Hubert Védrine, http://www.lemonde.fr/idees/article/2010/07/06/cessez-d-affaiblir-le-quai-d-orsay_1383828_3232.html; a particularly harsh interview given by Jean-Christophe Rufin, French ambassador to Senegal and close friend of Bernard Kouchner, on French diplomacy in Africa ("Le Quai d'Orsay est un ministère sinistré") in *Le Monde* [online], July 7, 2010, http://www.lemonde.fr/cgibin/ACHATS/acheter.cgi?offre=ARCHIVES&type_item=ART_ARCH_30J&objet_id=1129298&xtmc=quai_d_orsay&xtcr=2; a letter in the same newspaper cosigned by three former secretary generals of the French Foreign Affairs Ministry condemning the budgetary cuts targeting the French diplomatic corps (F. Scheer, B. Dufourcq, L. Hennekinne, "Le Quai, outil vital d'une diplomatie efficace") in *Le Monde* [online], August 24, 2010, http://www.lemonde.fr/idees/article/2010/08/24/le-quai-outil-vital-d-une-diplomatie-efficace-par-francois-scheer-bertrand-dufourcq-et-loic-hennekinne_1402148_3232.html; rumors of Minister Bernard Kouchner's impending resignation and his replacement in November 2010 by Michèle Alliot-Marie, who was herself forced to leave the government three months later following her botched handling of the events in Tunisia; and the publication of an article signed by the "Groupe Marly" entitled, "The Voice of France Has Disappeared in the World" ("La voix de la France a disparu dans le monde") in *Le Monde* [online], February 22, 2011, http://www.lemonde.fr/idees/article/ 2011/02/22/on-ne-s-improvise-pas-diplomate_1483517_3232.html.
23. See Groupe Surcouf, "Livre blanc sur la défense: une espérance déçue," in *Le Figaro* [online], June 19, 2008, http://www.lefigaro.fr/debats/2008/06/19/01005-20080619ARTFIG00011-livre-blanc-sur-la-defense-une-esperance-decue.php; and the director of the Inter-army Defense College (Collège Interarmées de Défense) General Vincent Desportes' very pessimistic interview in *Le Monde* on the situation of NATO in Afghanistan, in *Le Monde* [online], July 2, 2010, http://www.lemonde.fr/international/article/2010/07/02/afghanistan-un-general-francais-convoque-apres-une-interview-sur-la-strategie-americaine_1382449_3210.html?xtmc=entretien_vincent_desportes&xtcr=5.

Chapter 12

Immigration and the 2012 Elections in France

Ariane Chebel d'Appollonia

The 2012 presidential and parliamentary electoral campaign in France did not demur from the cardinal rule of French politics since the emergence of the Front National (FN) in the mid–1980s: the placing of the questions of immigration and of the integration of immigrants at the center of the political debate. Beyond the traditional left-right cleavage, proposing solutions to the "problems" posed by immigration has become a habitual exercise—to the point of coloring the debate on other political, economic, and social issues. In the 2012 campaign, the positioning of the candidates with respect to the EU, for example, included not only divergent views on the policies to adopt in response to the European financial crisis, but also triggered a heated polemic with respect to the Schengen Accords and the policing of Europe's external borders. Similarly, while advocates and opponents of electoral reform debated the introduction of proportional representation into the electoral system, the principal bone of contention remained extending the vote to immigrants. In turn, policies to address unemployment, pension reform, and the rights of the family have all more or less explicitly turned on the subject of immigration by addressing the situation of undocumented immigrants, their access to welfare benefits, and the reuniting of immigrant families. And last but not least, the security dimensions of police and judicial reform, the situation of the *banlieues* (deprived suburbs), and the threat of terrorism rekindled the debate regarding the supposed failings of France's republican model of integration.[1]

The centrality of immigration in the 2012 campaign was further accentuated between the first and second rounds of the presidential election.

Notes for this chapter begin on page 192.

Nicolas Sarkozy ramped up the nationalist tenor of his discourse, going so far as to prognosticate the death of French identity in case of a Socialist victory.[2] For his part, François Hollande made multiple references to the immigration issue to either denounce the disproportionate attention being given to it or to respond to the UMP's attacks, notably regarding the emergence of a pro-Muslim lobby within the PS.[3] In short, as was underlined by the virulence of the arguments exchanged by the two candidates in the televised debate of May 2, 2012, immigration has grown from being an important political issue into a quasi-existential one. Each candidate presented himself as the defender of the nation in a seminal confrontation that opposed their views of the supposed "communitarian and identity claims" emanating principally from Muslims living in France.

Three reasons have commonly been adduced to explain the unprecedented centrality assumed by immigration in French electoral campaigns and, more broadly, the country's political life: the growing weight of immigrants in French society, the growing preoccupation of the French with new immigrants and ethnic and cultural minorities in France, and, finally, the growing influence of the FN. In the first part of this analysis, these three factors will be analyzed in order to understand the dynamics of the French political debate on immigration.

An examination of the impact of the themes of immigration and integration in the 2012 elections reveals two significant paradoxes. On the one hand, the obsessive treatment of the immigration issue by the political elite very incompletely addressed voters' principal preoccupations, thereby explaining the inability of the mainstream parties to reclaim the vote lost to the FN. On the other hand, the growing attention given to immigration and the difficulty of integrating minorities into French society is proportionally inverse to the effectiveness of the measures being promulgated in order to achieve this aim, whether these be enhanced border controls or the imposition of stricter citizenship rules to ensure assimilation *à la française*. The result has been a sterile debate driven by a series of policy proposals that, in effect, have aggravated the "problems" they were designed to resolve. Future electoral campaigns are unlikely to depart from this pattern.

Immigration in the French Political Debate

As the FN's rhetoric on the "invasion" of France, the left's concept of a "baseline of tolerance," and the adage—employed by both right and left—according to which France cannot be a refuge for "all the misery in the world" suggest, if the various candidates and parties diverge in their specific approaches to the immigration issue, they are united in globally referring to the growing numbers of immigrants in France in order to justify their respective policy proposals. It is taken for granted by the principal parties that French society is being subjected to growing migratory pressures that are inducing ever-greater multicultural diversity. This general conviction, faithfully relayed by the media, is supposed to justify the outsized attention of which immigrants and minorities are increasingly the object—in particular during episodes of social violence, such as the 2005 urban riots, which have been interpreted through the prism of communitarian tensions.

Such an observation stands to be qualified, however. First, despite the evident centrality of immigration in the political debate, the state bureaucracy still does not dispose of a statistical organ that would make it possible to quantify immigration flows—let alone analyze their sources (i.e., for work or familial reasons) despite laws passed in 2003 and 2006 that highlighted the necessity of establishing "accurate immigration statistics" in order to "favor voluntary immigration."[4] The resulting arbitrary assessment of immigrant flows thus often ends up fueling a numbers battle relative to immigration during each election cycle.[5] The absence of reliable statistics on the number of citizens of foreign countries residing in France adds to this confusion. According to the 2009 census, there were nearly 5.3 million immigrants in France (of which 1.5 million were EU citizens), accounting for 6 percent of the population as a whole. To this can be added the population of immigrant origin or of partial immigrant origin living in France—immigrants or natives of France having at least one parent or grandparent of immigrant background—which can be approximated at between 13 and 15 million people, i.e., between one-fourth and one-fifth of the total population. Finally, there is no official quantification of illegal immigrants, which has allowed various political actors to extrapolate based on ancillary sources such as the number of beneficiaries of state medical assistance (Aide Médicale d'Etat; AME), the number of asylum seekers who have been turned down, or the number of deported illegal immigrants.[6] Such semantic confusion and statistical ambiguity thus serves to facilitate and fuel the politicization of the economic and social impacts of immigration in French electoral debates.

Furthermore, an enduring discursive confusion was to be noted in the different candidates' declarations and programs. They employed the terms "foreigners" and "immigrants" interchangeably when these in fact designate very different social realities: all foreigners are not necessarily immigrants (those who are born in France), and all immigrants are not necessarily foreigners (those who have been naturalized as French). Meanwhile, all the French people are not necessarily native-born citizens, whether or not they were born in France.

Table 12.1. The French Categorization System

Immigrants	French natives	French
	French by acquisition born in France	
	French by acquisition born outside France	
	Foreigners born outside France	Foreigners
	Foreigners born in France	

Finally, even if the law on French nationality officially distinguishes between only two categories of residents (those who are French citizens by birth or naturalization, and those who do not enjoy French citizenship), the fact remains that many French citizens of foreign origin continue to be perceived as immigrants. This is notably the case of so-called second-generation immigrants, and even more so of French Muslims suspected of belonging to a community that is "foreign" to French values. To these are to be added EU citizens who, though officially designated as immigrants, are seen to be less "foreign" than other non-French residents and who have gained the right to vote in France for the European parliamentary elections.

Statistical ambivalence and semantic ambiguity: as recent debates on national identity, the prohibition of the burqa, and the situation of Roma in France have shown, these two factors encourage politicization of the questions of immigration and integration. According to the National Consultative Commission on the Rights of Man (Commission Nationale Consultative des Droits de l'Homme; CNCDH), such politicization has had two principal effects. First, "the quasi-permanent placement on the political agenda of issues related to the question of foreigners in France and of the challenges linked to their integration ... creates or entrenches the impression that the management of difference, of what is foreign, is a problem in France." Second, this perception has been accompanied by the "emergence of a political discourse" that tends to normalize xenophobic prejudice: "[T]his discourse that was heretofore restricted to the extreme right [is] today being advanced by politicians with governing responsibilities, thereby conferring upon it a certain legitimacy. ... These factors (including the linkage established by certain politicians between immigration and crime) thereby contribute to the emergence of a discourse which, if not racist, at the very least tends to justify attitudes of wariness towards the other, the different, or the foreign."[7] Accordingly, a majority of the French people consider "that there are too many immigrants in France," with 56 percent to 65 percent of people polled expressing this opinion in a number of recent surveys. This widespread negative view of "foreigners" paradoxically reinforces the belief of political actors that they must address the expectations and concerns of the French through words and actions that tend to reinforce these anti-immigrant prejudices. In this respect, it should be noted that prejudice toward immigrants is increasing. According to the CNCDH, 67 percent of the French (up 5 percent compared to 2009) believe that "many immigrants come to France exclusively in order to take advantage of welfare benefits," and 44 percent (up 8 percent) are convinced that "immigration is the principal cause of crime" in the country. Similarly, 26 percent of respondents agree with the assertion, "the children of immigrants are not really French," a 5 percent increase.[8] Whatever their legal status, Gypsies (*les gens du voyage*) are perceived by 72 percent of those polled, a 3 percent increase compared to 2009, as "a group apart," versus 48 percent for Muslims (up 4 percent), and 35 percent (up 2 percent) for Maghrebis. Islam evokes "something positive" for only 24 percent (down 3 percent) of respondents.[9]

The final factor that explains the growing attention paid by the mainstream parties to immigration and integration concerns the role played by the FN in French political life. On the right as on the left, attempting to win over the FN's electorate—or at the very least, to reclaim voters who cast their ballots in favor of the FN in order to register their disappointment with the mainstream parties—has been a recurrent temptation since the 1980s. The principal element of this strategy has been the instrumentalization of the immigration issue either to discredit and/or compete with the FN. In turn, such a strategy has fueled political controversies over the role of multiculturalism in France—in particular, over the wearing of the head scarf in schools—and led to the promulgation of laws designed to highlight the state's determination to defend French national identity, as in the case, for example, of the 1993 Pasqua reform limiting the principle of *ius soli*. The political earthquake provoked by the 4.8 million votes garnered by Jean-Marie Le Pen in the first round of the 2002 presidential election further encouraged the mainstream parties "to hunt on the FN's territory," giving the immigration issue seminal importance in French political life.[10] In response to Le Pen's accession to the second-round runoff, the mainstream right advocated three principal courses of action on immigration: distinguishing between "desirable" versus "undesirable" immigrants, "reinforcing the integration process" through the introduction of stricter criteria reflecting the "values of the republic," and hardening the struggle against illegal immigration. What is more, the ineffective strategy of trying to demonize and isolate the FN has progressively given way to the cynical one of trying to seduce the FN's electorate. Accordingly, the leaders of the mainstream parties have sought to distinguish between the illegitimate xenophobic tenor of the FN's discourse and the legitimate motivations of its voters. The notion of "protest voting" has made it possible for these parties to try to coopt the FN's discourse on the grounds of responding to the "concerns" of its electorate.

At the governmental level, the most significant manifestations of this strategy have been the laws of November and December 2003 on immigration control, foreigner residency, naturalization, and political asylum;[11] the establishment of a National Agency for the Welcome of Foreigners and Migration (ANAEM) commissioned with drafting a contract on integration on which the residency of recent immigrants is to be predicated; the law of March 2004 prohibiting ostentatious religious symbols in public schools; the July 2006 law making the signing of the contract on integration obligatory for all new arrivals as of January 1, 2007;[12] the creation in July 2006 of the ELOI register on illegal immigration that reinforces the surveillance of French citizens in regular contact with foreigners; the November 2006 law enforcing the validity of marriages; and the establishment in March 2007 of a national Observatory on *laïcité*. On the eve of the 2007 presidential and parliamentary elections, Nicolas Sarkozy, then interior minister, presented an account of his achievements by declaring, "[T]he truth is that many French people see in immigration a threat to their security, to their jobs, to their way of life, to the preservation of the values to which they are attached, to the unity and cohesion of the nation. It would be totally irresponsible to ignore this anxiety. We have a duty to formulate a response to it, through our words and our deeds."[13]

For their part, while decrying what they termed "the trend of lepenization" evinced by Sarkozy and the UMP, the opposition parties nevertheless subscribed to certain aspects of the outgoing government's immigration policies. The PCF, for example, agreed to the UMP's proposal of creating a "ministry specifically of immigration."[14] The electoral platform adopted by the Socialists in July 2006 drew on several elements of the UMP's immigration program, including the reference to "a policy of firmness with respect to illegal immigration" and the creation of "a common police force on the boundaries of Europe." For its part, the MoDem underscored in its platform "the responsibility of the state to control immigration quantitatively and in terms of its pace." Finally, the FN continued to denounce the "false promises and muscular declarations" that Nicolas Sarkozy was "declaiming for purely electoral ends," while at the same time enumerating the convergence of its objectives with those of the UMP: the reduction of the number of asylum seekers, the fight against illegal immigration, the creation of a global Ministry of Immigration, and the reaffirmation of the republican model and of French values.[15] In announcing his candidacy for the presidential election of 2007, Jean-Marie Le Pen reiterated his conviction that the French would not be duped by Nicolas Sarkozy and that they would instead "prefer the original [FN] to the copy [UMP]."

The Immigration Issue and Electoral Outcomes

At first blush, Nicolas Sarkozy's strategy, which aimed to trump the FN on the themes of immigration, integration and national identity, proved effective in helping him to win the 2007 presidential election. According to an Institut Français d'Opinion Publique (IFOP) survey conducted in July 2006, he was viewed by 37 percent of voters as the candidate most likely to combat illegal immigration, placing him substantially ahead of Jean-Marie Le Pen on this question (11 percent).[16] The electoral decline suffered by Le Pen in the first round of the 2007 elections (10.44 percent of votes cast versus 16.86 percent in 2002) appeared to politically justify the strategy pursued by Sarkozy as interior minister, first in draining electoral support for the FN, and second in reinforcing the government's popularity.

The principal immigration policies that were introduced by Sarkozy during his five-year term include the November 2007 law establishing an integration contract to which immigrant families would have to subscribe in order to be eligible for social assistance, as well as the creation of a new Ministry of Immigration, Integration, National Identity, and Codevelopment. This ministry was charged with intensifying Sarkozy's repressive immigration policies, curtailing the rights of immigrants to join their families in France, and making the conditions of naturalization more difficult. The introduction of immigration quotas was approved by a large majority of the French (74.5 percent), as well as the proposal to restrict the reuniting of families to "those persons who already master the French language" (74 percent).[17] The government and the UMP also rekindled the debate on French national identity by focusing on the centrality of *laïcité* within the country's model of integration and by adopting in October 2010 a law banning the burqa in public spaces. Finally, the security dimension of immigration policy was reinforced following a number of clashes between the police and "travelers" (Roma, or Gypsies) in the department of the Isère throughout the summer of 2010. In a speech given on July 30 in Grenoble, Sarkozy proclaimed his determination to not only dismantle illegal Roma encampments, but also to make it easier to strip convicted criminals of the French nationality (particularly in cases of violence perpetrated against agents of the state), to reinforce video surveillance in sensitive urban zones, and to suppress family assistance in cases of school truancy.[18] Thus, on the eve of the 2012 elections, Nicolas Sarkozy was widely viewed as the candidate most determined to combat illegal immigration (for 68 percent of voters polled, compared to only 29 percent for François Hollande).[19] Furthermore, a large majority of Sarkozy voters (64 percent) called for allying with the FN in the run-up to the parliamentary elections.[20]

A deeper analysis of Sarkozy's victory in 2007 and of his defeat in 2012 reveals the limitations of attempting to instrumentalize immigration policy for political ends, however. The popularity gains achieved by stigmatizing immigrants and playing on the fears and fantasies linked to immigration proved insufficient to win an electoral mandate. In 2007 Sarkozy was elected *despite* growing public disapproval of his immigration policies—60 percent of the French judging them to be ineffective in 2008—and his initiatives to integrate minorities (particularly through policies to speed integration through employment).[21] Immigration did constitute the third-most important issue for voters in the second round of the 2007 presidential election (garnering 26 percent of respondents), but reducing unemployment (32 percent) and maintaining purchasing power (33 percent) were more important factors affecting voter preferences. Even FN voters, 70 percent of whom voted for Sarkozy in the second round, rapidly withdrew their support for the government's policies in the March 2010 regional elections. Therefore, despite the centrality of the theme of immigration in the 2007 campaign, economic and social issues primarily drove voters' preferences.

In turn, the relative insignificance of immigration for the electorate explains in large part the results of the 2012 presidential elections. On the eve of the first round, an IFOP survey revealed that the preoccupations driving voter preferences could be ordered as follows: reducing the public debt (42 percent), lowering unemployment (38 percent), increasing wages and purchasing power (35 percent)—and, at lesser levels of importance, combating illegal immigration (28 percent), education (25 percent), reducing petty crime (18 percent) and alleviating poverty (18 percent). According to these metrics, though Nicolas Sarkozy was judged to be more capable than François Hollande in curbing illegal immigration, the reverse was seen to be the case when it came to reducing unemployment (with Hollande obtaining a favorability rating of 58 percent on this issue versus only 39 percent for Sarkozy).[22]

Of course, this ranking of motivations varies according to electoral affiliation. In the case of Jean-Luc Mélenchon voters, for example, the issue of purchasing power was of paramount importance (67 percent). At the other extreme, 77 percent of Marine Le Pen's electorate identified the fight against illegal immigration as their greatest concern. Having obtained over 6.4 million votes (i.e., 18 percent of the votes cast), the 2012 election saw the FN achieve its highest ever score in a presidential election. The spectacular nature of this result explains Sarkozy's attempt to woo FN voters between the first and second rounds but also, and perhaps more crucially, illustrates two important drawbacks inherent in the attempt to politicize the immigration debate.[23] On the one hand, the "lepenization" of political discourse does not contribute to weakening the FN but on the contrary ends up normalizing anti-immigrant prejudices both among the mainstream parties as well as the public at large. On the other hand, contrary to what these parties' candidates asserted, politicization of the immigration issue does not correspond to the principal preoccupations of the French. While recognizing the reality of widespread xenophobia in France, it is nevertheless important to recall that the French continue to assess the political class in terms of its economic and social accomplishments and not in terms of the number of "illegals" deported. This is true of voters of all persuasions, including the FN, for whom other issues are just as important as immigration, in particular socioeconomic issues and the rejection of globalization.[24]

Politicizing Immigration and Immigration Policy

A second paradox of this politicization of the immigration debate concerns the evolution of public policy in this area. The more attention has been paid to the issue, the less effective the measures put in place have proven due to the complexity of the immigration trends they seek to address. The problem of illegal immigration is particularly revelatory in this regard. A majority of the political parties support the idea that strengthening border controls is the only solution to reducing the number of illegal immigrants entering the country. Beyond the technical difficulty of implementing such a policy (particularly in France's overseas departments), it is necessary to point out that the majority of the foreigners who now find themselves illegally in France entered the country legally and then remained there illegally — a situation reminiscent of visa overstayers in the United States. Furthermore, all the people who are illegally working in France are not necessarily immigrants.[25]

By the same token, the majority of the political parties have also proposed measures to streamline the pool of candidates eligible for legal immigration. This convergence was translated in 2012 by Sarkozy's reprise of the theme of voluntary immigration (*l'immigration choisie*), Hollande's proposal to institute an annual parliamentary debate on the number of immigrant workers required by the labor market, and Le Pen's radical proposal to reduce the number of legal immigrants by 95 percent over the next five years. Notwithstanding that work-driven immigration remains only one subset of legal immigration (the other being composed of reunited family members), such a selective process would be very difficult to implement for at least two reasons. First, as was previously mentioned, the statistical instruments required to assess the nature of immigration flows into

France, let alone to measure the sectoral needs of the French economy, are totally lacking. Second, although the idea of holding a parliamentary debate on immigration was enshrined in laws passed in 2003 and 2006, such a debate has yet to be held. Accordingly, the 2008 Mazeaud Report that was commissioned by President Sarkozy concluded that immigration quotas would be either unfeasible or worthless. State authorities do not enjoy the discretionary power that would allow them to determine the magnitude of immigration flows according to their two principal sources: family reunification and asylum. With regard to labor-driven immigration, a quota policy would in practice be pointless. Finally, such a policy makes no sense in terms of controlling illegal immigration. Better instruments of control need to be found that rely on empirical studies and a diversity of approaches worked out in close coordination with France's European partners rather than through seeking ever-more-repressive nationally based solutions. Perhaps in this area, more than others, methodical policies that are both resolute and mindful of the complexities raised by the immigration issue must be preferred to "outwardly spectacular but ultimately illusory remedies."[26] Needless to say, as was illustrated by the Law of June 2011 and the April 2012 *lettre aux français* from Nicolas Sarkozy, the government refused the Mazeaud Report's conclusions and instead reiterated its determination to introduce immigration quotas.

Last but not least, since the end of the 2000s measures to determine how new arrivals are to be accepted in France have come to constitute the principal pillars of French integration policy rather than measures that encourage the integration of second-generation immigrants through work, and that combat racial discrimination.[27] Thus, in April 2003 the Interministerial Committee on Integration proposed fifty-five groundbreaking measures, including the Contract on Arrival and Integration (Contrat d'Accueil et d'Intégration; CAI) proposed to new immigrants—the acceptance of which was made compulsory in 2006 and extended to entire families in 2007 in order to ensure the integration of children newly arrived in France. However, even if obtaining the residency permit is conditional on the CAI, actual implementation of the law has been limited by the lack of resources granted to prefectures to ensure that adequate linguistic training is afforded new immigrants, the mastery of French having been stipulated as the principal precondition for acceding to the CAI. As a result, only 101,355 CAI were signed in 2011 (9,000 under the auspices of the family reunification provision, the remainder overwhelmingly concerning francophone immigrants).[28] Furthermore, foreigners who signed CAIs often experienced difficulty finding work and, when they did find work, most often secured jobs that failed to correspond to their qualifications, despite the law's provisions on the professional integration of foreigners. In turn, in the name of defending *laïcité* and the values of the republic, the pathway to naturalization has been rendered more difficult. As a result, naturalizations declined by 30 percent in 2011. Thus, as several immigrant-rights organizations have shown, though they were passed under the auspices of facilitating immigrants' integration into French society, such measures have in fact restricted their capacity to integrate into the latter, a conclusion that was echoed by the High Council on Integration in its 2011 annual report.

Conclusion

In short, policies to integrate immigrants and minorities into French society have been either designed with an eye to addressing the security implications of immigration or else fail to address key socioeconomic factors that are linked to integration and continue to fuel social tensions throughout the country. Policies to address the situation of youths of immigrant backgrounds, for example, such as the 2004 Diversity Charter or the granting of the "diversity" label to enterprises that employ minority workers, have plainly been inadequate in reducing hiring discrimination. As a report by the national Court des Comptes noted, "the integration process has been stalled for years."[29] Thus, it is not surprising that the gap between the stated objectives and concrete achievements of successive governments on the issue of immigration and integration continues to fuel French people's concerns regarding the (in)capacity of the political class to manage the impacts of the latter. Indeed, nearly 59 percent of the French believe that the integration of foreigners in France is "working rather badly" (compared to 14 percent who stated that it was "working very badly.") This belief is further fueling the resurgence of xenophobia among the French—50 percent declaring that "one does not feel oneself at home as before in France," thereby inciting the political parties to propose "solutions" to the "problems" posed by immigration and the growing ethnic and cultural diversity of French society.[30]

The various parties are mobilizing along the same lines in anticipation of the next electoral cycle. For the new Socialist government, the principal objective is to formally distinguish itself from the UMP's policies while pursuing the same goals of controlling immigration and defining integration in increasingly nationalized terms. Accordingly, Manuel Valls, interior minister until 2014, enumerated the following priorities to address these issues: to "control immigration inflows," "fight against illegal immigration," and create "priority security zones" in crime-ridden, heavily immigrant urban areas. For the UMP, the main strategy is to denounce the initiatives undertaken by the new government as being contrary to the French national interest. Hence, the government's announcements of a reform of the naturalization criteria, an end to family detentions, and the introduction of multi-annual residency permits have been attacked by the UMP as demonstrating "laxism and political irresponsibility ... at the risk of seeing our country readopt a policy of uncontrolled immigration."[31] Finally, the FN, fresh from reentering the National Assembly following the election of two deputies in the 2012 parliamentary elections, continues to accuse the PS and UMP of similarly practicing a policy of preference for foreigners. Thus, it hopes to consolidate and expand its electorate by continuing to evoke the "obvious link between immigration and crime."[32] This strategy has proven to be effective, as illustrated by the results of the 2014 European elections. The FN received 24.9 percent of the vote compared to 20.8 percent for the UMP and 13.9 percent for the Socialist Party.[33] We may thus reasonably suspect that immigration issues will continue at the center of the 2017 presidential campaign.

Notes

Translated from the French by Gabriel Goodliffe.
1. This dimension was particularly emphasized following the murders of three French soldiers of Arab descent and three Jewish schoolchildren and their teacher in Toulouse and Montauban by Mohamed Merah, a French Al-Qaeda sympathizer of Algerian extraction, in March 2012.
2. At a speech delivered in Toulouse on April 29, 2012, Sarkozy proclaimed, "My dear friends, in a week the French people will choose its destiny. This will be a historic choice, historic because of the historical importance of the current circumstances. ... France cannot afford to make a mistake because such a mistake would take decades to rectify. France cannot afford a mistake because she cannot waste her heritage of twenty centuries of work, twenty centuries of effort, twenty centuries of civilization. A heritage, the heritage of Christianity, the heritage of the Enlightenment, the heritage of the Revolution and the heritage of the Resistance. ... When one denies the importance of the Nation, we open the door to the law of communitarianism and the law of tribalism. If there is communitarianism and tribalism, it is because we have not sufficiently defended the idea of the Nation. ... In the five years ahead, I will therefore not accept that there is no difference between being French and not being French because I do not want France to leave History; I do not want France to leave History either as a people or as a nation. And I will not accept this now that the prospect has been raised that we might disappear as a civilization." http://discours.vie-publique.fr/notices/123000880.html.
3. Thus, on May 1, in Nevers, Hollande asked, "But why this fear that one would want to incite and why make of the foreigner, of the immigrant, the principal issue in this presidential election? Well no, the principal question is unemployment, it is the standard of living, it is the fight against inequality." Speech given in Nevers, May 1, 2012. http://discours.vie-publique.fr/notices/123000901.html.

4. It is important to note that different state agencies use separate sources of data since immigration policy is not centralized. These agencies include the Ministry of Foreign Affairs (Office of the French residing abroad and of foreigners living in France) which is also in charge of the Office for the Protection of Refugees and Stateless Persons (OFPRA); the Ministry of the Interior, with its Office of Public Liberties and Judicial Affairs and Central Office of Border Police; and the Ministry of Work and Employment, with its Office of Population and Migration. This last ministry also oversees the National Agency for the Welcome of Foreigners and Migrations that was established by the law of January 18, 2005, the Office of International Migration (OMI), and the Social Services to Assist Immigrants (SSAE).
5. Thus, in the television debate of May 2, 2012, François Hollande declared, "Nicolas Sarkozy has been responsible for immigration during the past ten years: first as Minister of the Interior, then as President of the Republic. The number of people who are entering our territory legally is of 200,000 per year. 200,000 per year. It was 150,000 under the Jospin government. Thus, you have accepted during your ten years in charge that 200,000 additional immigrants enter our country under legal auspices." Nicolas Sarkozy refuted this claim: "Well, we do not agree on the numbers. And once again, different observers will draw differing conclusions on this. Annual immigrant flows reached their historic high during the final year of Lionel Jospin's premiership, in which 215,000 residency permits were issued. 215,000—which followed the amnesty extended to 80,000 people who were here illegally. Annual immigration flows today are of 180,000 [per year]. I thus formally repudiate your numbers." According to the Institut National des Etudes Démographiques (INED), it turns out that the high of 215,000 residency permits intervened in 2003, that is one year after the departure of Lionel Jospin, and that neither the 150,000 immigrants cited by F. Hollande nor the 180,000 cited by N. Sarkozy included EU citizens.
6. A 2005 senate report on illegal immigration underscored the fact that state authorities have never provided numerical data to the INSEE, this agency having not yet been commissioned to assess immigration flows using the same methodology as that employed in other countries. (http://www.senat.fr/rap/r05-300-1/r05-300-19.html).
7. CNCDH, *Rapport d'activité de la CNCDH 2010* (Paris: La Documentation Française, 2010), 34.
8. Ibid., 72.
9. Ibid., 68.
10. A speech delivered by Nicolas Sarkozy on the subject of immigration on December 11, 2006, is particularly revealing in this regard. Recapitulating his accomplishments as minister of the Interior, Sarkozy justified the thrust of his policies by referring to the "earthquake of April 21, 2002" which, according to him, was triggered by the "deep divide that exists in the approach to the immigration issue that prevails among the elites and the dominant perspective on the question among the population at large." http://www.interieur.gouv.fr/Archives/Archives-de-Nicolas-Sarkozy-2005-2007/Interventions/11.12.2006-Deplacement-de-Nicolas-SARKOZY-a-la-prefecture-de-Seine-Saint-Denis.
11. These laws modify the status of foreigners by subordinating the issuance of residency permits to criteria of integration while strengthening the provisions to reduce illegal immigration. They also define as a crime fake or sham marriages orchestrated for the purpose of gaining the French nationality and put in place mechanisms to verify the authenticity of marriage ceremonies. Finally, they modify the procedures of administrative detention in order to facilitate the deportation of illegal immigrants.
12. Accordingly, the July 2006 law forces newly arrived immigrants to undergo a compulsory civic training course on French institutions and the values of the republic, to take French language courses, and to subject themselves to an employability assessment. It

reduces from nineteen to twelve months the period in which a legal resident can request immigration visas for his or her family. Finally, the law reinforces the enforcement mechanisms overseeing the validity of marriages.
13. Speech of December 11, 2006. http://www.interieur.gouv.fr/Archives/Archives-de-Nicolas-Sarkozy-2005-2007/Interventions/11.12.2006-Deplacement-de-Nicolas-SARKOZY-a-la-prefecture-de-Seine-Saint-Denis.
14. "Migrations et Citoyenneté," policy orientations agreed at the 33rd Congress of Le Bourget, March 20, 2006.
15. FN Program, http://www.frontnational.com/le-projet-de-marine-le-pen/.
16. IFOP survey conducted for *Le Figaro*, "Les Français et la régularisation des immigrés en situation irrégulière," July 21 2006, http://www.ifopf.com.
17. Opinionway survey for *Le Figaro*, "Sarkozy convainc mais l'opinion reste dans l'attente," November 30, 2007, http://www.lefigaro.fr/politique/2007/12/01/01002-20071201ARTFIG00129-sarkozy-convainc-mais-lopinion-reste-dans-lattente-.php.
18. It should be noted that in March 2011 the Constitutional Court invalidated the majority of the amendments that were adopted by the National Assembly and senate on the basis of the Grenoble speech.
19. IFOP survey conducted for *Le Figaro*–CEVIPOF, "Présidentielle 2012," April 24, 2012, http://www.cevipof.com/fr/2012/resultas/les-pages-cevipof-le-figaro-sur-les-analyses-du-scrutin-du-1er-tour/.
20. Opionway survey conducted for *Les Echos*, "Baromètre de la présidentielle 2012," April 24, 2012, http://www.opinion-way.com/pages/expertise-etudes.php?idTheme=1&idSubtheme=29.
21. Opinionway survey conducted for *Le Figaro*, "Le Politoscope," June 27, 2008, http://www.opinion-way.com/english/pages/expertise-etudes.php.
22. Ibid. Hollande also attained extremely favorable ratings in terms of his perceived capacity to maintain purchasing power (62 percent) and reduce social inequalities (70 percent).
23. On this score, Sarkozy affirmed that Marine Le Pen was "compatible with the Republic" while Hollande declared that he "understood the anger expressed by the Le Pen vote."
24. Underscoring this point, Nicolas Sarkozy won just over 50 percent of FN voters in the second round (compared to 14 percent for François Hollande). And only 27 percent of industrial workers who voted for Le Pen in the first round supported Sarkozy in the second.
25. See 2005 senate report on illegal immigration, http://www.senat.fr/rap/r05-300-1/r05-300-111.html.
26. Rapport Mazeaud, *Pour une politique des migrations transparente, simple et solidaire*, (Paris: La Documentation Française, 2008), 11.
27. This latter development was most spectacularly underscored by the dissolution in 2011 of the High Authority of the Struggle against Discrimination and for Equality, or HALDE, that was established by Jacques Chirac in 2005.
28. Office Français de l'Immigration et de l'Intégration, *Rapport d'activité 2011* (Paris: La Documentation Française, 2012), 135.
29. Rapport de la Cour des Comptes sur l'immigration et l'intégration, 2012. http://www.vie-publique.fr/politiques-publiques/politique-immigration/immigres-cite/.
30. CNCDH, *Rapport d'activité de la CNCDH 2010*, 72.
31. UMP website, http://www.u-m-p.org/actualites/espace-presse/politique-dimmigration-manuel-valls-persiste-et-signe-dans-lirresponsabilite-72432607.
32. FN website, http://www.frontnational.com/2012/08/emeutes-damiens-voila-ou-menent-le-laxisme-et-limmigration/.
33. http://www.results-elections2014.eu/en/country-results-fr-2014.html.

Conclusion
Assessing the Hollande Presidency One Year into Office

Riccardo Brizzi

As candidate to the French presidency, François Hollande quipped that "a five-year term is judged at the beginning and condemned at the end."[1] He had anticipated even before his election that, given the country's current situation of crisis, there would be no basking in any honeymoon with the French. Yet no-one foresaw the *lune de fiel* (a play on *lune de miel* the French term for honeymoon, with *fiel* the word for bile) which, a year after he entered the Elysée, would see the Socialist president recording the lowest popularity ratings ever garnered by a sitting president in the history of the Fifth Republic. He has earned the nickname of "Monsieur 75 percent," which first applied for his proposed tax increase on the very rich, and now refers to the record level of unpopularity he has reached after only twelve months in office. Accordingly, marking a break from his predecessors, the first anniversary of his election has come and gone without fanfare from Hollande and his entourage. In May 1982 François Mitterrand celebrated his historic victory the year before by formally accepting the PS's leadership at a banquet held by the PS in its Paris headquarters for the occasion. In May 1996 Jacques Chirac opted to return to his electoral fiefdom of the Corrèze (coincidentally also Hollande's own electoral department) where he and his wife were fêted by his former constituency's elite. For his part, Sarkozy was so embroiled in his so-called bling-bling scandals that upon the one-year anniversary of his election, he pulled out at the last minute from a banquet organized for the occasion at Paris's prestigious Salle Gaveau. And when it came time to celebrate Hollande's one-year election anniversary on May 6, 2013, radical left-wing militants and activists from the traditional Catholic right took to the streets to shout their frustration at the president as he sat closeted with his ministers in

---

Notes for this chapter begin on page 201.

the Elysée Palace. Marking a first in the history of the Fifth Republic, this episode gives some idea of the climate of anger and dejection that exists in France one year after the spring 2012 presidential and general elections. It conveys a pervasive sense of gloom with the political, economic, social, and moral order.

The "normal" president has failed to earn his compatriots' confidence, afflicted as he is by multiple crises: too much unemployment, EU austerity, same-sex marriage, and the Cahuzac affair. The man whose principal strength during eleven years at the helm of the PS had been his ability to unite the discordant voices within the party now seems to have failed in his quest to pacify the nation after the divisive five years of Sarkozy's presidency.

If one examines the difficulties that have beset France's new head of state during his first twelve months in office, a double paradox emerges. The first reflects Hollande's personality. He has proven to be the least popular president of the Fifth Republic and been violently criticized on both the left and the right and even within the governing majority itself, yet he has committed no particular errors of behavior. By the same point in time in his presidency, his predecessor had accumulated a whole series of gaffes—from celebrating his electoral victory at an exclusive Parisian brasserie, to vacationing on tycoon Vincent Bollore's yacht, through his messy public divorce from his second wife Cecilia Ciganer-Albéniz, and public wooing and then quick remarriage to former model-turned-singer Carla Bruni, to his appearing drunk during a press conference at the Heiligendamm G-8. By contrast, Hollande's personal conduct has been impeccable (notwithstanding his companion Valérie Trierweiler's own online gaffes and regal tastes). Yet this has not stopped him from becoming a focus of criticism, much of it contradictory. Some blame him for lacking initiative, others for an excessive reformism. He has been deemed to be too passive (particularly on the economy), but then unduly proactive on deeply divisive social issues (such as same-sex marriage).

The second paradox is political. Hollande's strategy—based on prioritizing budgetary austerity, economic competitiveness, and structural reform—meets with a broad consensus and is felt to be balanced by most legislators and a majority of public opinion (55 percent of the French judge his economic policy to be "neither too leftist nor too right-wing"). On this score, it is significant that some on the right voted for three of the government's signature economic bills already announced by Hollande during the campaign: the competitiveness pact, generation contracts, and labor market reforms agreed to by unions and employers in January 2013.[2]

Yet support for the president and his government has now shrunk to a rump minority within the country. Since late summer 2012 there has been a startling loss of confidence and popularity in the head of state. Whereas he enjoyed a popularity rating of 55.6 percent support immediately following the election, by the middle of May 2013—and slightly up from April because he kept his promise to legalize same-sex marriage— Hollande had lost half his credibility and fallen to an approval rating of only 29 percent.[3] Conversely, he achieved record disapproval ratings for a sitting president in the history of the Fifth Republic, his 74 percent rating in April 2013 beating Chirac's 70 percent from June 2006 and Sarkozy's 72 percent from April 2011.

What has gone wrong? There are two lines of explanation for this slump in popularity. The first is structural and is due to the Thirty Glorious Years losing all residual momentum, new competitors appearing on the international horizon, and the deepening of the systemic economic crisis that gradually eroded his and various predecessors' room to maneuver. If one compares the last five presidents' performance in office, it transpires that the first twelve months of Valéry Giscard d'Estaing, François Mitterrand, and even Jacques Chirac's seven-year mandates were more packed with symbolic acts and reforms than the respective starts to Sarkozy's and Hollande's five-year terms. Paradoxically, the first three presidents, though having less time to enact their agenda, found their stride more quickly than their successors. The latter had much less time for action, but proved unable to reform the system and showed no real desire for change. One year after his swearing in, Hollande has got one social law through—the same-sex marriage bill—though mayors are still not obliged to apply it. True, he did show decisiveness over the Mali mission, he helped achieve the employment agreement, and he has increased the number of teachers. But his credibility has been eroded by dissent from within the majority and his apparent inability to rekindle growth and address the economic and social crisis. A glance at previous presidents' popularity curves sums up the difficulties dogging this head of state's plan of action since taking office. One year after entering the Elysée Palace, Valéry Giscard d'Estaing found that 33 percent of the country was disgruntled with his performance, François Mitterrand 35 percent, Jacques Chirac 49 percent, Nicolas Sarkozy 64 percent, and François Hollande 74 percent.[4] The number of unemployed has soared from half a million to over 3 million in the space of a few decades, proving that the curve of presidential unpopularity is indexed to unemployment, purchasing power, and tax rates.

Like his predecessor, Hollande is paying for his failure to deliver results in the face of an apparently intractable crisis. By April 2013 the unemployment rate had risen for twenty-two consecutive months, bordering on the negative peak of 1993. In 2012 the nation's purchasing power diminished for the first time since 1984 as a result of increased taxation. The national debt rose by €116.9 billion (i.e., 4.4 percent of GDP) between late 2011 and late 2012, amounting to 90.2 percent of GDP, while the budget deficit in 2012 reached 4.8 percent instead of the forecast 4.5 percent. According to the BVA polling institute, twelve months into his presidency only 34 percent of interviewees deemed Hollande's policies to be fair, and only 19 percent viewed them as effective.[5]

Then there is the problem of Hollande's image and his approach to the presidential role. The idea of a normal presidency proved a winner during the electoral campaign. But though anti-Sarkozyism proved an effective strategy for gaining power, when it came to exercising office, Hollande's normalcy turned out to be an anomaly within a political system that traditionally favored the solemnity of the presidential role in which the head of state is cast as a republican monarch. The genesis and history of the Fifth Republic show that times of crisis and collective depression call for charismatic leadership and skilful authoritative dialogue with public opinion. Against this, Hollande is obsessed with needing to break with his predecessor's manic activism, but the low profile he has cultivated also perturbs the French: it comes across as a flimsy, wishy-washy leadership style. The head of state and his team have failed to distinguish the Sarkozy method from what is germane to any president's authority. At the moment, it is the president's very normality and dullness that is causing disquiet in the nation at large.

First and foremost, this is an issue of degree. If Hollande is even less popular than his already disliked predecessor, it is not—as it was for Sarkozy—due to his character flaws. IFOP data suggest Hollande is still broadly seen as *sympathique* (a nice guy) (52 percent) and honest (50 percent). What he is blamed for is a lack of what it takes to be a president. Hence the success of his old and now revived nickname Flamby, which fellow Socialist Arnaud Montebourg coined ten years ago, drawing on a well-known brand of caramel flan. Only 27 percent of interviewees think Hollande is competent, barely 20 percent think he knows where he is going, and only 14 percent think he carries any authority. The lack of authority and appearance of dithering are proving particularly disastrous at this moment of crisis because they render the political aims and actions of the government increasingly unfathomable to the electorate. It is no accident that many reforms have been approved by most of the nation: the generation contracts (77 percent), restoring the age of retirement to sixty for employees who began work at eighteen (68 percent), jobs for the future (64 percent), raising the tax on lottery winnings (64 percent), and the creation of 60,000 new jobs in public education (62 percent). But the global verdict on the president's performance on the principal political indicators is brutal: only 13 percent think he is going the right way about tackling unemployment, 16 percent think he is rebooting growth, 21 percent think his fiscal policy is appropriate.[6]

The normal president has failed to overcome the current crisis and ensuing worsening mood of French public opinion. One year since his victory, he still appears to be feeling his way into the presidential role (the famous metamorphosis from presidential candidate to sitting president), while the whole institutional edifice is paying for the lack of stable relations between the Elysée and Matignon, and his team's failure to dose the president's utterances, let alone clarify the pace and direction of reforms. Now that he has reached the one-year mark, Hollande must launch the second phase of his presidency: persuading a skeptical public that the president and his government have taken twelve months to shake off Sarkozy's legacy but are now able to lead the country down the road of change that was advertised in the electoral campaign.

Poised to begin his second year in office, Hollande has three main issues on his agenda. The first is international. In this area, Fifth Republic tradition requires that a handover, even between presidents of opposing political views, should not entail revolution but mere adjustments to course. Thus, Hollande has not gone back on Sarkozy's decision to reintegrate the NATO military command structure, but has accelerated the withdrawal of four thousand French troops from Afghanistan and normalized relations with a series of countries (Turkey, Mexico, Japan, etc.) whom Sarkozy's pronouncements and stances had irritated. Again, the most delicate issue in the first year of office—military intervention in Mali—was a personal triumph for Hollande. Operation Serval gave the lie to those who foresaw the risk of stagnation, and French public opinion appreciated the president's decisiveness, contrasting with the hesitancy and dilatoriness with which he has been charged on the home front. (Four months since the start of the mission, 64 percent of those interviewed say they are in favor of Hollande's decision to intervene.) Thus, on the foreign policy front the overall balance is positive: a prominent role in Syria despite the odd wavering of position; a successful operation in Mali, "yes" to the resolution recognizing Palestine as an observer state and to definitive withdrawal from Afghanistan. Given that the French president has shown determination and firmness in an unexpected quarter, what is now expected after his first year in office is a coherent statement of the Hollande doctrine on France's international role in the medium term, which would go beyond his speech to the UN General Assembly on September 25, 2012.

The second issue is Europe. Here, the Socialist candidate had announced he would be distancing himself from his predecessor's line. Following his election, he would strive to adjust the political equilibrium and alliances within the EU, the aim being to end the austerity spiral that the

Merkozy tandem had imposed on the continent and instead to kick-start growth. Confronted by Berlin's firmness (typified by his failure to renegotiate the Fiscal Compact) and realizing that European issues would split French public opinion and his own party, Hollande opted for a less divisive stance, gradually abandoning his initial opposition to Germany.[7] Instead, he seems to be adopting Sarkozy's European trajectory. After verifying that independence from Berlin was not a practical option, Sarkozy had worked toward cooperation across the Rhine. Likewise, as he embarks on the second year of his mandate, Hollande appears to have gone back on his silent rejection of Angela Merkel's political proposals and distanced himself from left-wingers baying for a break with the German chancellor and her austerity policies. At a press conference on May 16, 2013, Hollande unveiled Europeanist ambitions that had not been expressed on the left since the days of Delors and Mitterrand. The head of state confirmed that the second year of his presidency would hinge on implementing a broad European agenda incorporating five themes: economic governance of the eurozone, greater fiscal integration, a common energy policy, a youth inclusion plan, and an investment strategy. His proposal was supported by Chancellor Merkel (who called for achieving a Franco-German common contribution, as promised in January 2013 at the fiftieth anniversary of the Elysée Treaty) as well as French public opinion (65 percent saying they agreed with the proposal for economic governance of the eurozone). All this was satisfactory for the French president's outlook on Europe.

The final principal issue facing Hollande during the remainder of his term concerns economic and financial matters, and is undeniably the most delicate and critical. According to the INSEE, during the first quarter of 2013 France fell into recession (–0.2 percent of GDP) after a year of zero growth. This forced the country to negotiate a deferment with Brussels over restoring the deficit to below 3 percent of GDP. In 2012 it was still stuck at 4.8 percent, and the prospects for 2014 are far from rosy. This is one of the principal challenges of the five-year presidential term: how to redress the budget and reboot medium- and long-term growth by correcting the structural maladies of the French economy—high labor costs, inadequate technological development, low level of investment, and so on—in a fraught socioeconomic context. The thirty-five measures comprising the competitiveness pact—including a €20 billion tax credit for private enterprise—as well as the corporatist agreement over greater flexibility of labor, represented an important step in this direction, but not enough to pull France out of its acute unemployment crisis. (Over the past year, about nine hundred jobless registered with the National Job Center every day, bringing the overall count to more than 5 million.)

After presenting his economic stabilization plan to the European Commission in May 2013, Hollande promised not to resort to temporary expediencies and remedies, but rather to enact fundamental structural reforms to enable it to close the competitiveness gap along similar lines to Schröder's Germany almost a decade ago. The project hinges on five major reforms that would recast the French social model and that would begin to take effect during the second year of office: the reduction of family allowances (which have enabled France to set a demographic countertrend in an aging Europe); shrinking the scope of state action; and reforms to the country's pension, welfare, and occupational retraining regimes.

This ambitious scheme is now putting the president of the republic in a somewhat paradoxical position. While the PS's local and national dominance of the French political scene guarantees stability and encourages decision-making during the remainder of Hollande's term, it concentrates all power in the figure of the president. This makes it incumbent on him to discard the normal president profile, and to adopt the persona of the republican monarch dictated by the constitutional practice of the Fifth Republic and now imposed by the force of political and economic circumstances. For Hollande, this necessarily entails reducing his unpopularity, inevitably spelling disappointment for a part of his majority. The risk in that case is policy paralysis and slowing down the course of reform.[8] But should his political strategy fail and his interpretation of the presidential role remain inadequate, Hollande will not only lose all credit as head of state, but he will also plunge the country into disarray. With party in-fighting tearing apart the UMP and jeopardizing its ability to serve as a credible opposition, the country could then fall further prey to antipolitics and democratic disillusionment.

Notes

1. François Hollande, "Conférence de presse de François Hollande à l'Union nationale des chemins de fer, 25/04/2012." April 25, 2012, https://www.youtube.com/watch?v=USoUyKc5Cs0.
2. Gérard Biseau, "Président depuis un an, c'est pas la fête," *Libération,* May 5, 2013, http://www.liberation.fr/politiques/2013/05/05/president-depuis-un-an-c-est-pas-la-fete_901104.
3. IFOP poll for *le Journal du Dimanche,* "Les indices de popularité, mai 2013." May 26, 2013, http://www.ifop.com/?option=com_publication&type=poll&id=2246.
4. Béatrice Guerrey, "Un an à l'Elysée: les bilans," *Le Monde,* May 6, 2013, http://www.lemonde.fr/politique/article/2013/05/02/un-an-a-l-elysee-bilans-depuis-giscard_3170100_823448.html?xtmc=un_an_a_l_elysee_les_bilans&xtcr=83.

5. BVA poll for *l'Express*, the regional press and *France Inter*, "Observatoire de la politique nationale mai 2013," May 27, 2012, http://www.bva.fr/data/sondage/sondage_fiche/1299/fichier_barometre_bva_-_orange_-_lexpress_-_presse_regionale_-_france_inter_-_mai_2013cde81.pdf.
6. IFOP poll for *Financial/Europe 1*. "Bilan de l'action de François Hollande un an après l'élection présidentielle de 2012," April 18, 2013, http://www.ifop.com/=?option=com_publication&type=poll&id=2222.
7. Riccardo Brizzi, "Francia : l'europeismo tranquillo di Hollande," *Il Mulino* 465, no. 1 (2013):122–29.
8. Gérard Courtois, "Peut-on encore gouverner en étant aussi impopulaire?" *Le Monde*, April 30, 2013, http://www.lemonde.fr/politique/article/2013/04/30/peut-on-encore-gouverner-en-etant-aussi-impopulaire_3168724_823448.html?xtmc=peut_on_encore_gouverner_en_etant_aussi_impopulaire&xtcr=8.

Bibliography

Almeida d', F., and C. Delporte. Histoire des médias en France. De la Grande Guerre à nos jours. Paris: Flammarion, 2003.
Andolfatto, D. "Syndicalisme." In Lau, *L'Etat de la France*, 229–32.
Andolfatto, D., and F. Greffet. "Le Parti communiste français: une reconversion sous contraintes." In De Waele and Seiler, *Les partis de la gauche anticapitaliste*, 157–76.
Arzheimer, K. "Contextual Factors and the Extreme Right Vote in Western Europe, 1980–2002." *American Journal of Political Research* 48 (2009): 335–58.
Attali, J. *Verbatim, 1981–1986*. Paris: Fayard, 1993.
Azéma, J.-P. "La campagne présidentielle de François Mitterrand." In *François Mitterrand les années du changement 1981–1984*, edited by S. Berstein, P. Milza, and J-L. Bianco, 47–51. Paris: Perrin, 2001.
Baldini, G., and M. Lazar, eds. *La Francia di Sarkozy*. Bologna: Il Mulino, 2007.
Baverez, N. *La France qui tombe: un constat clinique du déclin français*. Paris: Perrin, 2003.
———. *Réveillez-vous!* Paris: Fayard, 2012.
Beaud, S., and M. Pialoux. *Retour sur la condition ouvrière. Enquête aux usines Peugeot de Sochaux-Montbéliard*. Paris: Fayard, 1999.
Belot, C., and B. Cautrès. L'Europe, invisible mais omniprésente. In *Le Nouveau Désordre électoral: les leçons du 21 avril 2002*, edited by B. Cautrès and N. Mayer, 119–41. Paris: Presses de Sciences Po, 2004.
Benoit, J.-M. "Communication oblige: Du candidat au Président." *Le Débat* 172, no. 5 (2012): 12–18.
Bergounioux, A., and G. Grunberg. *Les socialistes français et le pouvoir. L'ambition et le remords*. Paris: Hachette, 2007.
Bonnemaison, D. "De la Ligue Communiste Révolutionnaire au Nouveau Parti Anticapitaliste." In De Waele and Seiler, *Les partis de la gauche anticapitaliste*, 305–22.
Boy, D., and J. Chiche. "La gauche radicale et les Verts. Des contestations hétérogènes." In *Le vote européen 2004–2005. De l'élargissement au référendum français*, edited by P. Perrineau, 205–28. Paris: Presses de Sciences Po, 2005.
Bozo, F. *La politique étrangère de la France depuis 1945*. Paris: Flammarion, 2012.
Brizzi, R. "Francia: l'iperpresidente e la politica che non c'è." *Il Mulino* 436, no. 2 (2008): 323–35.

———. "L'iperpresidente e la 'febbre' francese." *Aspenia,* 45 (2009): 86–93.
———. *L'uomo dello schermo. De Gaulle e i media.* Bologna: Il Mulino, 2010.
———. "Francia: l'europeismo tranquillo di Hollande." *Il Mulino* 465, no. 1 (2013): 122–129.
Brouard, S., O. Costa, and T. König, eds. *The Europeanization of Domestic Legislatures: The Empirical Implications of the Delors Myth in Nine Countries.* New York: Springer, 2012.
Brouard, S., E. Grossman, and N. Sauger. *Les Français contre l'Europe: les sens du référendum du 29 mai 2005.* Paris: Presses de Sciences Po, 2007.
Buton, P. "Symbolique communiste." In *Dictionnaire du communisme,* edited by S. Courtois, 538–40. Paris: Larousse, 2007.
Campus, D. *L'antipolitica al governo. De Gaulle, Reagan, Berlusconi.* Bologna: Il Mulino, 2006.
———. "L'immagine della leadership nella presidenza francese." In *Una splendida cinquantenne: la Quinta Repubblica francese,* edited by G. Pasquino and S. Ventura, 61–90. Bologna: Il Mulino, 2010.
Cautrès, B., and N. Mayer, eds. *Le Nouveau Désordre électoral: les leçons du 21 avril 2002.* Paris: Presses de Sciences Po. 2004.
Cayrol, R. *La nouvelle communication politique.* Paris: Larousse, 1986.
———. "Election et communication." *Commentaire* 139 (2012): 845–852.
———. "Médias et sondages: le couple maudit des élections présidentielles françaises." In *Médias, opinions et présidentielles,* edited by R. Cayrol and J-M. Charon, 59–68. Bry-sur-Marne: INA Editions, 2012.
Charillon, F. *La France peut-elle encore agir sur le monde?* Paris: A. Colin, 2010.
———. *La politique étrangère de la France. De la fin de la guerre froide aux révolutions arabes.* Paris: La Documentation Française, 2011.
Choffat, T. "Lutte Ouvrière, entre continuité et renouvellement." In De Waele and Seiler, *Les partis de la gauche anticapitaliste,* 292–304.
Crépon, S. *Enquête au cœur du nouveau Front National.* Paris: Nouveau Monde Editions, 2012.
Dakhlia, J. *Politique people.* Paris: Bréal Editions, 2008.
———. *Les politiques sont-ils des people comme les autres?* Paris: Bréal Editions, 2012.
De Waele, J-M., and D-L. Seiler, eds. *Les partis de la gauche anticapitaliste en Europe.* Paris: Economica, 2012.
Dehousse, R. *La fin de l'Europe.* Paris: Flammarion, 2005.
———. "Nicolas Sarkozy l'Européen." In *Les politiques publiques sous Sarkozy,* edited by J. de Maillard and Y. Surel, 153–66. Paris: Presses de Sciences Po, 2012.
Denni, B. "Du référendum du 20 septembre 1992 sur l'Union européenne auxélections législatives de mars 1993." In *Le vote sanction. Les élections législatives des 21 et 28 mars 1993,* edited by P. Habert, C. Ysmal, and P. Perrineau, 91–109. Paris: Presses de Sciences Po, 1993.
Dolez, B., and A. Laurent. "Marche et marges de la gauche." In *Le vote de tous les refus. Les élections présidentielles et législatives de 2002,* edited by P. Perrineau and C. Ysmal, 251–73. Paris: Presses de Sciences Po, 2003.
Dunphy, R. *Contesting Capitalism? Left Parties and European integration.* Manchester, UK: Manchester University Press, 2004.

Fayette, J. "Il volontarismo politico di fronte al realismo economico." In *La Francia di Sarkozy*, edited by G. Baldini and M. Lazar, 193–206. Bologna: Il Mulino, 2007.
Garrigues, J. and S. Guillaume, eds. *Centre et centrisme en Europe aux XIXe et XXe siècles. Regards croisés*. Brussells: Peter Lang, 2006.
———. "Le centre introuvable?" In *Comprendre la Ve République*, edited by J. Garrigues, S. Guillaume, and J-F. Sirinelli, 277–94. Paris: PUF, 2010.
Gervasoni, M. *François Mitterrand una biografia politica e intellettuale*. Torino: Einaudi, 2007.
Goodliffe, G. *The Resurgence of the Radical Right in France: From Boulangisme to the Front National*. New York: Cambridge University Press, 2012.
Grunberg, G. "I paradossi dei socialisti francesi." In *La Francia di Sarkozy*, edited by G. Baldini and M. Lazar, 127–42. Bologna: Il Mulino, 2007.
Guibert, P. *La téléprésidente*. Paris: Plon, 2007.
Haegel, F. "The Transformation of the French Right: Institutional Imperatives and Organizational Changes." *French Politics* 2 (2004): 185–202.
———. "Nicolas Sarkozy a-t-il radicalisé la droite française? Changements idéologiques et étiquetage politique." *French Politics, Culture and Society* 29, no. 3 (2011): 62–77.
———. *Les droites en fusion*. Paris: Presses de Sciences Po, 2012.
Holcblat, N. "Politique macroéconomique. Une mise en perspective." In Lau, *L'Etat de la France*, 170–78.
Hollande, F. *Changer de destin*. Paris: Laffont, 2012.
Howell, C. "The Dilemmas of Post-Fordism: Socialists, Flexibility and Labour Market Deregulation in France." *Politics and Society* 20, no. 1 (1992): 71–99.
Jaffré, J. "La victoire étroite de François Hollande." In *Le vote normal: les élections présidentielle et législatives d'avril-juin 2012*, edited by P. Perrineau, 133–60. Paris: Presses de Sciences Po, 2013.
Jost, F., and D. Muzet. *Le téléprésident. Essai sur un pouvoir médiatique*. Paris: Aube, 2008.
Katz, R., and P. Mair. "Changing Models of Party Organization and Party Democracy. The Emergence of the Cartel Party." *Party Politics* 1, no. 1 (1995): 5–27.
Kirchheimer, O. "The Transformation of Western European Party System." In *Political Party and Political Development*, edited by J. La Palombara and M. Werner, 177–200. Princeton, NJ: Princeton University Press, 1966.
Kolodny, R. "Electoral Partnership: Political Consultants and Political Parties." In *Campaign Warriors. Political Consultants in Elections*, edited by J.A. Thurber, and J.N. Candice, 110–32. Washington, DC: Brookings Institution Press, 2000.
Kriegel, A. Les communistes français: essai d'ethnographie politique. Paris: Le Seuil, 1985.
Lau, E., ed. *L'Etat de la France2011–2012: Un panorama unique et complet de la France*. Paris: La Découverte, 2011.
Le Béguec, G. "Bipolarisation." In *Comprendre la Ve République*, edited by J. Garrigues, S. Guillaume, and J-F. Sirinelli, 195–208. Paris: PUF, 2010.
Le Pen, M. *Pour que vive la France*. Paris: Grancher, 2012.

Levy, J. "Redeploying the State: Liberalisation and Social Policy in France." In *Beyond Continuity: Institutional Change in Advanced Political Economies*, edited by W. Streeck and K. Thelen, 103–26. New York: Oxford University Press, 2005.

Linhart, D. "Travail: Grandes tendances." In Lau, *L'Etat de la France*, 65–69.

Maarek, P.J. "La comunicazione politica in Francia sotto la Quinta Repubblica: professionalizzazione, personalizzazione o «peopolisation»?" In *Una splendida cinquantenne: la Quinta Repubblica francese*, edited by G. Pasquino and S. Ventura, 185–218. Bologna: Il Mulino, 2010.

Maillard de, J., and Y. Surel, eds. *Les politiques publiques sous Sarkozy*. Paris: Presses de Sciences Po, 2012.

Mair, P. "The Limited Impact of Europe on National Party System." *West European Politics* 23, no. 4 (2000): 27–51.

———. "Political Opposition and the European Union." *Government and Opposition* 42, no. 1 (2007): 1–17.

Martinetti, C. *L'autunno francese*. Milan: Feltrinelli, 2007.

Mayer, N. "Comment Nicolas Sarkozy a rétréci l'électorat Le Pen." *Revue Française de Science Politique* 57, no. 3–4 (2007): 429–45.

———. "From Jean-Marie to Marine Le Pen. Electoral Change on the Far Right." *Parliamentary Affairs* 66, no. 1 (2013): 160–78.

Mazeaud, P. *(Report of commission). Pour une politique des migrations transparente, simple et solidaire*. Paris: La Documentation Française, 2008.

Meeus, C. "Nicolas Sarkozy à la reconquete de son électorat." In *SOFRES, L'Etat de l'opinion en 2012*. Paris: TNS-SOFRES, 2012.

Mitterrand, F. *Politique 2*. Paris: Fayard, 1981.

Monnier, J-M. "Politique fiscale. Une mise en perspective." In Lau, *L'Etat de la France*, 179–88.

Monnot, C., and A. Mestre. *Le système Le Pen. Enquête sur les réseaux du Front National*. Paris: Denoël, 2011.

Muxel, A. "La participation électorale. Une bonne mobilisation à la présidentielle, un décrochage aux législatives." In *Le vote normal: les élections présidentielle et législatives d'avril-juin 2012*, edited by P. Perrineau, 93–110. Paris: Presses de Sciences Po, 2013.

Nava, M. *Il francese di ferro*. Torino, Einaudi, 2007.

Office français de l'immigration et de l'intégration. *Rapport d'activité 2011*. Paris: La Documentation française, 2012.

Pace, L. *Nicolas Sarkozy. L'ultimo gollista*. Milan: Boroli, 2007.

Panebianco, A. *Political Parties: Organization and power*. Cambridge, UK: Cambridge University Press, 1988.

Pedder, S. *Le déni français. Les derniers enfants gâtés de la crise*. Paris: J-C Lattès, 2012

Perrineau, P. ed. *Le desénchantement démocratique*. Paris: Aube, 2003.

Perrineau, P., and C. Ysmal, eds. *Le vote de tous les refus: les élections présidentielle et législatives de 2002*. Paris: Presses de Sciences Po, 2003.

Petitfils, A.-S. "L'institution partisane à l'épreuve du management. Rhétorique et pratiques managériales dans le recrutement des 'nouveaux adhérents' au sein de l'Union pour un Mouvement Populaire (UMP)." *Politix* 79, no. 3 (2007): 53–76.

Peyrelevade, J. *France, état critique*. Plon, Paris: 2011.

Quagliariello, G. *La Francia da Chirac a Sarkozy.* Soveria Mannelli: Rubbettino, 2007.
Raffy, S. *Le président. François Hollande, itinéraire secret.* 2nd ed. Paris: Fayard, 2012.
Raynaud, P. *L'extrême gauche plurielle. Entre démocratie radicale et révolution.* Paris: Autrement, 2006.
Rémond, R. *Les droites en France.* Paris: Aubier-Montaigne, 1982.
Rémond, R., and C. Neuschwander. "Télévision et comportement politique." *Revue française de science politique* 13, no. 2 (1963): 325–47.
Rosanvallon, P. *La contre-démocratie: la politique à l'âge de la défiance.* Paris: Seuil, 2006.
Salmon, F. *Atlas électoral de la France, 1848–2001.* Paris: Le Seuil, 2001.
Schmidt, V. *Democracy in Europe: The EU and National Polities.* Oxford: Oxford University Press, 2006.
Sieffert, D., and M. Soudais. *Mélenchon et les médias.* Paris: Politis, 2012.
Sirinelli, J-F. "L'histoire politique à l'heure du transnational turn: l'agora, la Cité, le monde . . . et le temps." *Revue historique* 658, no. 2 (2011): 391–408.
SOFRES. *L'Etat de l'opinion en 2012.* Paris: Tns SOFRES.
Spanje van, J., and W. Brug van der. "The Party as Pariah: The Exclusion of Anti-Immigration Parties and its Effect on their Ideological Positions." *West European Politics* 30, no. 5 (2007): 1022–40.
Tiberj, V. "L'extrême gauche électorale: une résistible ascension?" In *Présidentielle 2007. Atlas électoral. Qui vote quoi, où, comment?* edited by P. Perrineau, 41–44. Paris: Presses de Sciences Po, 2007.
Vaïsse, M. *Puissance ou influence? La France dans le monde depuis 1958.* Paris: Fayard, 2009.
Valensise, M. *Sarkozy. La lezione francese.* Milan: Mondadori, 2007.
Védrine, H. *Rapport pour le président de la République sur la France et la mondialisation.* Paris: Fayard, 2007.
Verret, M. *La culture ouvrière.* Paris: L'Harmattan, 1996.

Contributors

Gilles Le Béguec is professor emeritus of the University of Paris X Nanterre–La Défense and president of the scientific council of the Fondation Charles de Gaulle and the Association Georges Pompidou.

Riccardo Brizzi teaches contemporary history and history of political communication in the Department of Political and Social Science at the University of Bologna.

Philippe Buton teaches contemporary history at the University of Reims.

Frédéric Charillon teaches at the University of the Auvergne and at the Institut d'Etudes Politiques de Paris and is director of the Institut de Recherches Stratégiques de l'Ecole Militaire.

Ariane Chebel d'Appollonia teaches public policy at the School of Public Affairs and Administration at Rutgers University.

Renaud Dehousse teaches at the Institut d'Etudes Politiques of Paris and is the director of the Centre d'Etudes Européennes de Sciences Po.

Jacques Fayette is professor emeritus of the University of Lyon III.

Marco Gervasoni teaches contemporary history at the University of Molise.

Gabriel Goodliffe teaches international relations and political economy at the Instituto Tecnológico Autónomo de México.

Gérard Grunberg is director emeritus of the Centre d'Etudes Européennes de Sciences Po.

Florence Haegel teaches at the Centre d'Etudes Européennes de Sciences Po, where she directs the masters program in Comparative Political Sociology.

Jean-François Sirinelli teaches political and cultural history at the Institut d'Etudes Politiques of Paris and is director of the Centre d'Histoire de Sciences Po.

Angela Tacea is a doctoral candidate at the Centre d'Etudes Européennes de Sciences Po.

Index

A
AAA credit rating, French loss of, 53, 119, 139, 148–49
Africa, French foreign policy and, 170, 173–74
aggiornamento strategy, Front National, 119–26
Algerian war, presidential politics and, 16, 23, 68
Atlantic Alliance, 172, 176
anti–Semitism, Front National and, 123–24
Arthuis, Jean, 172, 176
Attali, Jacques, 31, 134
Attali Commission, 134–35, 139
Aubry, Martine, 29, 31–32, 35–36, 54, 75, 77–79, 135–36
Aubry Law, 135–36
Ayrault, Jean–Marc, 7, 31, 38, 86, 142–49

B
Balladur, Edouard, 28, 34, 53, 100–101
banking policies, 136–42
Barre, Raymond, 17, 100–101, 110n1, 110n5
Bayrou, François, 3, 49, 52–54, 101–10, 110n4, 110n10, 111n13, 111n18, 140, 155
Bérégovoy, Pierre, 28, 31, 37
Besancenot, Olivier, 88, 97
Blair, Tony, 30, 177
Blum, Léon, 29–30
Bockel, Jean-Marie, 170, 178n4
Bongrand, Michel 43–44
Borloo, Jean-Louis, 102–3, 107–10, 111n16, 111n18
bouclier fiscal (tax shield), 118–19, 135
budget polices, 142, 144–49, 157–60

budgetary pact. *See* Fiscal Stability Treaty
business model, professionalization of politics and, 62–63

C
Cameron, David, 155–56
Center for France (Centre pour la France), 104–5, 107
Center for Social Democrats, 106, 109
centrist politics
  evolution in France of, 100–110
  future of, 107–10
  historical evolution of, 102–5
"Charter of the Popular Right Collective," 67–69
Chirac, Jacques, 4, 6, 18, 24, 28, 46, 51, 65, 75–76, 106, 110n1, 138, 195
  electoral campaign of, 34–35, 61
  foreign policy under, 168, 170, 172, 180n21
  presidency of, 12–13, 15–17, 22, 28, 32, 40, 52, 133, 197
Christian Democracy movement, 105–7
Christian Democratic Union (CDU) (Germany), 61–62
cohabitation, in presidential politics, 24–26, 138
Cohen, Elie, 143, 146–47, 149
communication strategies, 49–51, 55–56, 62–63, 90–93
comparative analysis of French presidential politics, 11–23
Contract on Arrival and Integration (Contrat d'Accueil et d'Intégration; CAI), 190–92
Contribution Sociale Généralisé (CSG), 137, 141, 143–45
Copé, Jean-François, 7, 64, 66, 68, 71

Index 211

Court of Auditors (Cour des Comptes), 76, 137, 142, 145
crisis management, presidential politics and, 14–16

D

De Gaulle, Charles, 6, 13, 16, 22–23, 32, 42–44, 56, 106, 168
deindustrialization, 115–19, 143, 149
Delors, Jacques, 27, 30, 32–33, 39, 76
demand-side policies, French electoral politics and, 4–5
Democratic Movement (MoDem), 2–3, 49, 102–10, 110n2, 110n10
déplanification strategies, Front National resurgence and, 115–19
Des paroles et des actes broadcasts, 48–51
différencialisme (differentialism), Front National resurgence and, 122–26
dirigisme, Sarkozy's economic policies and, 135–39
Droit, Michel, 43–44
droitisation (shift to the right), 127, 157–60
Dupont-Aignan, Nicolas, 52, 70, 140, 156, 162

E

economic integration
    Europe and, 153–56
    French electoral politics and, 5–8, 69–71
    Front National resurgence and, 116–19
economic policies
    Front National resurgence and, 112–19
    of Hollande, 32–40, 133–49, 197–201
    presidential politics and, 3–5, 16–18, 52–55, 139–42
electoral campaigns (France)
    candidate strategies in, 51–55
    communications in, 42–56
    comparison of 2007 and 2012 elections, 2–8
    economic themes in, 139–42
    Europe as issue in, 152–64
    immigration issue and, 187–92
    Mitterrandisme and, 33–40
    political and economic factors in, 1–8
    presidential campaigns of Fifth Republic, 11–26
    television and, 46–51
Epinay Conference, 28, 32–33
étatisme (statism), 122–26
Europe, 110n5
    definitions, 153–56
    Hollande presidency and role of, 152–64, 165n17, 199–200
    influence in French electoral politics of, 4–8, 69–71
    national sovereignty issues in, 156–60
    2012 French presidential election and, 152–64
European Central Bank, 121, 134, 156
European Commission, 121, 134, 139, 201
European Constitutional Treaty, 5, 29, 32, 77, 171, 176–77
European Monetary Union (EMU), 4–5, 121–26
European Union (EU), 4–5, 114–15, 121–26, 171
eurozone crisis, 136–39, 154–56
executive power, French division of, 5–6

F

Fabius, Laurent, 29, 38, 172
Facebook, Mélenchon's use of, 90–93
Fifth Republic
    candidate strategies during presidential campaigns in, 51–55
    diarchy of, 22–26
    evolution of presidency during, 11–26
    presidential polling in, 44–46
Fillon, François, 17, 30, 45–46, 71, 138–39
Fiscal Stability Treaty (Fiscal Compact), 79–80, 85, 142, 176, 200
foreign policy, 167–78, 199–201
Forza Italia, 62–63
fracture sociale (Chirac campaign issue), 22, 51
fragmentation, in French electoral politics, 2–3
France, election results of 2012 and, 1–2
French Communist Party (PCF), 8n2, 31, 88–90, 93–94, 98n3, 186
    Front National and, 116–19
    limits on resurgence of, 94–97
    Mélenchon and, 90–93
French National Assembly, 64, 76–77, 82–8, 104, 112

French national identity, 121–26, 153, 183–92
Front de Gauche (Left Front), 2, 37, 88
    Hollande and, 80–82
    Mélenchon's candidacy and, 90–94
    parliamentary elections and, 82–86
    radical left politics and, 95–97
    Web campaigns by, 49–51
Front National (FN), 2, 6, 53, 126–27, 159–60
    aggiornamento of, 119–26
    immigration politics and, 182–92, 194nn23–24
    petits indépendants and industrial workers' support for, 115–19
    resurgence of, 112–27
    UMP radicalization and resurgence of, 65–69

G

Gaddafi, Muammar (Col.), 170–71, 174
Gallois Report, 146–49
General Revision of Public Policies (Révision Générale des Politiques Publiques, RGPP), 134–35
Germany, 4, 123–24, 143, 145, 155–60, 199–200
Giscard d'Estaing, Valéry, 13–15, 24, 51, 62, 168
    centrist politics and, 101, 108–9, 110n1
    election of, 39–40, 100
    presidential policies of, 17, 22, 34–35, 38, 52, 197
globalization, 15, 114–15, 119–26
Greens (Europe Ecology), 2–3, 8n2, 34, 80, 82–86

H

Herriot, Edouard, 102–3
historiography, of French presidential politics, 11–26
Hollande, François, 1, 3, 55–56, 106–7
    budget preparations of, 144–49
    campaign strategies of, 52–55
    economic policies under, 3–5, 32–40, 140–49
    electoral campaign of, 33–40, 48–51, 80–82
    European integration and, 152–64, 165n17, 199–200
    foreign policy under, 167–78, 199–201
    Gallois Report and, 146–49
    immigration politics and, 182–91, 192n3
    leadership style of, 5–7
    Mitterrandisme and, 27–40, 86–87
    parliamentary elections and, 82–86
    political career of, 13–14, 75–78
    post-election assessment of, 195–201
    presidency of, 38–40
    Socialist Party and, 29–31, 74–75
Holocaust, 123–24
"hyperpresidency" of Sarkozy, 5–6, 44–46, 167

I

ideology, 16–18, 67–69, 115
immigration, 121–27, 181–92, 193nn11–12
impôt de solidarité sur la fortune (ISF wealth tax), 119, 135
industrial workers, Front National resurgence and, 115–19
institutionalization in presidential politics, 63–64, 91–93
Internet, 46–51, 62–63, 90–93
Islamic immigrants, 169
    Front National resurgence and criticism of, 123–26
    immigration politics and, 182–92
    party radicalization and debate over, 66–69, 72n16
    presidential politics and, 36–37, 192n1
Israel, French foreign policy and, 169–70, 173

J

Jaurès, Jean, 29–30
Jospin, Lionel, 4–5, 18, 24, 27–31, 34–36, 74, 76, 85, 135–36, 138
Jouyet, Jean-Pierre, 168, 178n4
Juppé, Alain, 46, 70–71, 72n16, 138, 169, 172–73

K

Kouchner, Bernard, 168–69, 174, 178n4, 179n12, 180n22

L

labor market, 115–19, 135–36

La Droite Populaire, 64, 67–68
Lagarde, Jean-Christophe, 110n7, 111n18
Laguiller, Arlette, 88, 91, 97
laïcité (secularity), 124–25, 186–92
la préférence nationale (national preference), 123–26
leadership styles, 5–6, 16–18
Lecanuet, Jean, 43–44, 100–101, 105–6, 110n3, 110n5
Le Pen, Jean-Marie, 6, 15, 31, 34, 39–40, 61, 124, 186–92
Le Pen, Marine, 2–3, 6, 34, 52–53, 66, 81, 112–27, 140, 153, 156, 162–64, 188–89
Libya, French foreign policy in, 170–71, 175
Ligue Communiste Révolutionnaire (Revolutionary Communist League), 88, 93, 95, 97
Lutte Ouvrière (Workers' Struggle), 80, 88, 95, 97

M

Maastricht Treaty (1992), 5, 29, 69
Marchais, Georges, 34, 37, 91
marketization of presidential politics, 62–63
Mauroy, Pierre, 31, 46, 76
media coverage, 89–90, 141–42, 193n5
    of French politics and government, 148–49
    history in electoral politics of, 42–44
    "hyperpresidency" and, 44–46
    Mélenchon's use of, 90–93
    presidential politics and role of, 42–56
    2012 presidential campaign, 46–51
Mélenchon, Jean-Luc, 2–3, 6, 29, 34, 37, 49, 52
    economic policies of, 139–42
    electoral campaign of, 88–89, 105
    European integration and, 156–60, 162
    French Trotskyism and, 94–97
    Front de Gauche and, 90–93
    Hollande and, 76, 80–82
    immigration issue and, 188–89
    posters in campaign of, 90–94
Merah, Mohamed, 36–37, 192n1
Merkel, Angela, 4–5, 155–56, 175, 200
"Merkozy" policy coalition, 158, 164, 177, 200

middle-class voters, Front National resurgence and, 112–27
Middle East, French foreign policy and, 169–74, 176–78, 179n12
military intervention, French foreign policy and, 173–74
Mitterrand, François, 2, 6, 20, 24, 28, 43–44, 46, 51, 56, 98n3, 101, 108, 138, 150n21, 168, 195
    Hollande presidency and legacy of, 27–40, 75–76, 85–87
    presidency of, 13, 15, 17, 22, 133, 197
    Socialist Party and, 27–31, 74
monetary sovereignty, Front National resurgence and issue of, 122–26
Montebourg, Arnaud, 36, 140, 142–43, 198
Monti, Mario, 134, 148
Morin, Hervé, 101, 103–4, 111n18
Moscovici, Pierre, 142–43, 148–49
Mouvement Républicain Populaire, 106, 111n14

N

National Consultative Commission on the Rights of Man (Commission Nationale Consultative des Droits de l'Homme; CNCDH), 184–92
national greatness *(grandeur)* ideology, 16–17
national sovereignty, presidential politics and issues of, 156–64
nation-state, 21–22, 122–26
NATO, French foreign policy and, 171–74, 179n10, 199
New Center (Nouveau Centre), 101, 103–5, 108, 110n7, 111n16
normalization strategy, Front National resurgence and, 114–15
Nouveau Parti Anticapitaliste (New Anticapitalist Party, NPA), 49, 80, 93, 95

O

Obama, Barack, 36, 172
open primary. *See* primary system
Operation Cast Lead, 169–70
opinion polls. *See* public opinion
Organisation Communiste Internationaliste, 94–95
overtime tax exemption, 135–36, 143

P

parliamentary elections, 25, 41n16
    centrist politicians and, 108–10
    Hollande's presidential victory and, 33–40, 48–51, 80–82
    radical left vote and, 95–97
    Socialist supremacy and, 82–86
Paroles de candidat broadcasts, 48–51
Parti de Gauche, 88, 91, 93, 96, 159–60
Partido Popular (Spain), 61–62
Parti Radical de Gauche (PRG), 106, 111n15
Parti Radical Valoisien, 104–5, 107–8, 111n12
party politics, French electoral history and, 4–8
PCF. *See* French Communist Party (PCF)
pension system, 19–22, 119, 137–38, 141–42
peopleisation (celebrity seeking), Sarkozy presidency and, 45–46
personalization of politics
    French presidential campaigns and, 6, 52–55
    Hollande's post-election unpopularity and, 196–201
    radical left vote and, 91–93
petits indépendants, Front National resurgence and, 113, 115–19
Poher, Alain, 101, 110n3, 110n5
political broadcasts, 2012 presidential campaign, 48–51
political voluntarism, presidential politics and, 18–22
Pompidou, George, 13, 16–18, 22–24, 36, 101, 168
population demographics, 19–22, 183–92
populist ideology, Front National adoption of, 122–26
postindustrial economic policies, Front National resurgence and, 116–19
Poutou, Philippe, 49, 52, 162
presidential politics
    candidate strategies and, 51–55
    centrism in, 100–110
    comparisons of French presidents and, 12–16
    economic policies and, 139–42
    European influence in French elections and, 152–64
    exogenous factors in, 22–26
    foreign policy and, 167–78
    Front National resurgence and, 112–27
    history in Fifth Republic of, 11–26
    immigration and, 181–92
    media coverage and, 42–56
    post-election assessment of Hollande and, 195–201
primary system, 6, 78–80, 87n3
prime minister-presidential relations, 5–6, 22–26, 45–46, 85–86
professionalization of politics, UMP restructuring and, 62–63, 72n8
progressive values, Front National embrace of, 124–26
protectionist ideology, Front National resurgence and, 122–26
PSA Peugeot Citroën case, 143–44
public opinion, 43–47
    on Hollande, 55–56, 149, 195–201
    immigration politics and, 188–92
    toward Europe, 158–64
public spending, Sarkozy's economic policies and growth of, 134–39

Q

quinquennat (five-year term), 1, 7, 12–13
quota systems, immigration politics and, 187–92

R

radicalization, of UMP, 65–69
radical left, 88–97, 156–60
Radical Party (Parti Radical), 97n1, 108, 110n3, 156–60
Rassemblement pour la République (Rally for the Republic, RPR), 61–62, 69–71, 75
Reims Conference of 2008, 35, 75–77
Republic, Environmental, and Social Alliance (l'Alliance Républicaine, Ecologique et Sociale, ARES), 103–5, 110n3, 111nn16–17
retirement age, increase in, 138–39, 143
right-wing candidates, 66–71, 127
Rocard, Michel, 24, 27–28, 31, 33, 35, 39, 137
Roma ethnic minority, immigration politics and, 187–92
Royal, Ségolène, 52, 92, 106, 179n16
    Hollande and, 78–80
    media coverage of, 49–51
    presidential campaign of, 29–31, 33, 36

Index 215

S

Sarkozy, Nicolas, 1, 3–4, 20, 29, 63–64, 92, 106, 145, 195
    campaign strategies of, 51–55
    centrist politics and, 101–6, 110n10
    economic crisis and policies of, 136–39
    economic policies under, 133–39
    electoral campaign of, 33–34, 36–40
    European integration and, 153–56, 157–64
    foreign policy under, 167–78, 180n18
    Front National resurgence and, 112–14, 118–19
    historical analysis of administration of, 12–16
    Hollande's campaign against, 78–82
    ideological ambivalence, 18–22
    immigration politics and, 182–92, 192n2, 193n10
    leadership style of, 5–7, 16, 32
    media coverage and "hyper-presidency" of, 44–46
    president-prime minister relations under, 22–26
    strategic and cultural radicalization strategies of, 65–69
    2012 presidential campaign and, 48–51
    Union for a Popular Movement and, 61–71
Sayda, Abdel Basset, 175–76
Schengen Accords, 126, 158, 181
single European market, French electoral politics and, 4–8
Socialist Party (PS) (France), 1–2, 6, 8n2, 93–95, 105
    campaign of 2012 of, 74–87
    economic policies and, 140–42
    foreign and, 174–78
    Front National and, 116–19
    Hollande and, 34–40, 74–87
    immigration politics and, 182–92
    Mitterrand's legacy in, 28–31
    parliamentary elections and, 82–86
    presidential politics and, 24–25, 27–40
social media
    in 2012 presidential campaign, 49–51
    Mélenchon's use of, 90–93
    2012 presidential campaign and use of, 49–51
social security reforms, 137, 141, 143, 147–49
sociocultural issues
    European integration and, 162–64
    Fifth Republic presidencies and, 20–22
    Front National resurgence and, 112, 115, 119–26
    petits indépendants and, 115–19
    UMP radicalization and, 65–69
Stability and Growth Pact, 4, 134
state intervention, Sarkozy's economic policies and, 133–39
stratégie de l'ouverture (strategy of openness), 65–69
Strauss-Kahn, Dominique, 6, 29, 31, 54, 75, 78
supply-side policies, 4–5, 119–26
Syrian National Council, 175–76

T

tax policies, 135–37, 140–44
télécratie (TV-cracy), in de Gaulle government, 42–44
television
    Mélenchon's use of, 90–93
    presidential elections and, 42–44
    2012 presidential campaign coverage, 46–51
Thirty Glorious Years era, 14–16, 197
time parameter in presidential administrations, 12–16
Travail, Emploi, Pouvoir d'Achat (work, employment and purchasing power; TEPA) Act, 135–36
Trierweiler, Valérie, 50, 196
Trotskyist candidates
    French Communist Party and, 94–97
    geographic vote structure for, 96–97, 99n14
    presidential politics and, 34, 80, 88
    radical left vote and, 89–91, 93–97
TVA sociale (social VAT), 118–19
2012 French presidential election
    centrist politics and, 102–5
    economic issues in, 133–49
    Europe and, 152–64
    immigration and, 181–92

media coverage of, 46–51
Twitter, 50–51, 90–93

U

unemployment, 3, 115–19, 134–35, 149
Union des Démocrates et des Indépendants (Union of democrats and independents, UDI), 108–10, 111n17
Union for a Popular Movement (UMP), 2–3, 6–7, 52–53, 62–64, 71n4, 75, 82
    centrist politics and, 109–10, 110n10, 111n16
    Europeanization of French right and, 69–71
    immigration politics and, 182–92
    parliamentary elections and, 82–86
    post-Sarkozy changes in, 61–71, 126–27
    Sarkozy foreign policy and, 175–78
    strategic and cultural radicalization of, 65–69, 105
Union for the Mediterranean (Union pour la Méditerranée, UPM), 172–73, 179n11
union movement, 116–19, 149
Union pour la Démocrátie Française (Union for French Democracy, UDF), 2–3, 100–101, 105–10, 110n1

V

Valls, Manuel, 7, 36
value-added tax policies, 118–19, 136–39, 143–45, 147–49
Védrine, Hubert, 169, 172, 176
Venezuelan political model, French politics and, 95–97
voluntarism, Sarkozy's embrace of, 133–34, 189–92
vote de rupture (radical left vote), 89–90
voter information sources, 2012 presidential campaign, 48–51

W

wage deindexation, Front National resurgence and, 116–19
Web-based interaction. *See* Internet
working-class voters, Front National resurgence and, 115–19